Basic
Chinese

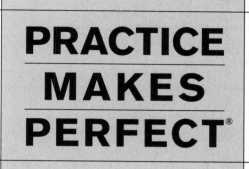

PRACTICE MAKES PERFECT®

Basic Chinese

Xiaozhou Wu, Feng-hsi Liu, Rongrong Liao

Mc
Graw
Hill
Education

New York   Chicago   San Francisco   Athens   London   Madrid
Mexico City   Milan   New Delhi   Singapore   Sydney   Toronto

1 2 3 4 5 6 7 8 9 10 11 12 13 14 15 16 17 18 RHR/RHR 1 0 9 8 7 6 5 4 3

ISBN   978-0-07-178426-9
MHID   0-07-178426-8

e-ISBN   978-0-07-178427-6
e-MHID   0-07-178427-6

Library of Congress Control Number 2013934655

McGraw-Hill Education products are available at special quantity discounts to use as premiums and sales promotions or for use in corporate training programs. To contact a representative, please visit the Contact Us pages at www.mhprofessional.com.

This book is printed on acid-free paper.

Contents

Preface

Practice Makes Perfect: Basic Chinese is an effective companion text to whatever book(s) you may be using in your first- or second-year Chinese class. This highly useful workbook is well suited for high school and college students of Chinese.

This book is not meant to introduce concepts or to be the primary teaching tool. Rather, its purpose is to reinforce what has been presented already, whether by a teacher's instruction or in a formal textbook. Very basic grammar is presented, typically in tables, as preparation for the material covered in the exercises.

The easiest way to know what to expect from *Practice Makes Perfect: Basic Chinese* is to scan the Contents. There you will find the grammatical concepts and vocabulary topics covered.

Grammatical concepts are emphasized more than vocabulary, as every student needs to master these one at a time and to relative completion. Vocabulary, on the other hand, is an ongoing process, frequently dictated by the student's particular interests and needs.

Also presented, in the early chapters, is crucial everyday vocabulary that helps the beginning student express himself or herself more clearly and authentically, even early in the process of learning to speak, write, and read Chinese.

This book provides:

- Reinforcement for concepts already presented in another format or setting
- An emphasis on broad, basic concepts—not grammatical minutiae
- Texts presented in the simplified version of Chinese characters with the pinyin transliteration to facilitate easy reading for the beginning student
- Examples that illustrate grammar points with English translations
- Useful vocabulary lists for a variety of topics closely related to the grammar items
- About 150 entertaining exercises (true/false, fill in the blanks, translation, answer the questions, etc.) dealing with the basic structure of the Chinese language
- Six sets of unit review exercises—called "单元复习 *dānyuán fùxí*"—each of which tests the information gleaned from the previous five lessons in a comprehensive way
- Answers to all exercises

- Two glossaries—English-Chinese and Chinese (Pinyin)–English—that draw together vocabulary from throughout the book

Chinese is a beautiful language that you can appreciate and enjoy more fully by mastering the fundamentals of its structure. This workbook will help you achieve your goals in a user-friendly, student-driven fashion.

祝您马到成功 *Zhù nín mǎ dào chénggōng!* (Wish you win instant success!)

PRACTICE
MAKES
PERFECT®

Basic
Chinese

Grammar

Vocabulary

Do you know?

Pronouns •
Simple sentence structure •
Nations and nationalities

Pronouns

	SINGULAR			PLURAL		
FIRST PERSON	我	*wǒ*	I; me	我们	*wǒmen*	we; us
SECOND PERSON	你	*nǐ*	you (*sing.*)	你们	*nǐmen*	you (*pl.*)
THIRD PERSON	他	*tā*	he; him	他们	*tāmen*	they; them
	她	*tā*	she; her	她们	*tāmen*	they; them (*fem.*)

生词　SHĒNGCÍ (VOCABULARY)

Nations and nationalities

In Chinese, to form a word about nationality, simply add the word 人 ***rén*** after the name of the country. For example, 中国人 ***Zhōngguórén***, *a Chinese person/Chinese people*.

人	*rén*	person; people
中国	*Zhōngguó*	China
德国	*Déguó*	Germany
俄国	*Éguó*	Russia
美国	*Měiguó*	USA
日本	*Rìběn*	Japan
英国	*Yīngguó*	Great Britain
印度	*Yìndù*	India
法国	*Fǎguó*	France

Match each English word with its Chinese translation.

1. _____ we
2. _____ USA
3. _____ they
4. _____ Russia
5. _____ he
6. _____ China
7. _____ I
8. _____ Great Britain
9. _____ you (*sing.*)
10. _____ Japan

a. 俄国 *Éguó*
b. 英国 *Yīngguó*
c. 我们 *wǒmen*
d. 他 *tā*
e. 中国 *Zhōngguó*
f. 我 *wǒ*
g. 美国 *Měiguó*
h. 日本 *Rìběn*
i. 他们 *tāmen*
j. 你 *nǐ*

生词 **SHĒNGCÍ (VOCABULARY)**

Everyday words

是	*shì*	am; is; are
不	*bù*	no; not

Simple sentences

Basic simple sentences have the following structure: **Subject + Predicate**. There is no conjugation of verbs or declension of nouns.

SUBJECT	+	PREDICATE	
我	是	美国人。	I am American.
Wǒ	*shì*	*Měiguórén.*	
他	不是	美国人。	He is not American.
Tā	*bú shì*	*Měiguórén.*	

Match the following famous people with their nationalities.

1. _____ Beethoven
2. _____ Tchaikovsky
3. _____ Yao Ming
4. _____ Ichiro Suzuki
5. _____ Steve Jobs
6. _____ Napoleon
7. _____ Shakespeare
8. _____ Gandhi

a. 中国人 *Zhōngguórén*
b. 美国人 *Měiguórén*
c. 日本人 *Rìběnrén*
d. 印度人 *Yìndùrén*
e. 法国人 *Fǎguórén*
f. 德国人 *Déguórén*
g. 俄国人 *Éguórén*
h. 英国人 *Yīngguórén*

翻译成英文 Fānyì chéng Yīngwén *Translate into English.*

1. 他是日本人。*Tā shì Rìběn rén.*

_____

2. 他们不是法国人。*Tāmen bú shì Fǎguórén.*

_____

3. 我们是中国人。*Wǒmen shì Zhōngguórén.*

_____

4. 你不是英国人。*Nǐ bú shì Yīngguórén.*

_____

5. 他是美国人。*Tā shì Měiguórén.*

_____

6. 你们不是俄国人。*Nǐmen bú shì Éguórén.*

_____

7. 我是印度人。*Wǒ shì Yìndùrén.*

_____

8. 她们不是德国人。*Tāmen bú shì Déguórén.*

_____

翻译成中文 **Fānyì chéng Zhōngwén**   *Translate into Chinese and pinyin.*

1. I am American.

   _____

2. They are not Russians.

   _____

3. We are not Japanese.

   _____

4. You (*sing.*) are French.

   _____

5. He is Chinese.

   _____

6. You (*pl.*) are not British.

   _____

7. They are Germans.

   _____

8. She is not Indian.

   _____

你知道吗? *Nǐ zhīdao ma?* Do you know?

国籍 *guójí* Nationalities

- Gary Lock (骆家辉 *Luò Jiāhuī*) 是美国人，不是中国人。
- Yao Ming (姚明 *Yáo Míng*) 是中国人，不是美国人。
- Joe Tanaka 不是日本人，他是美国人。

The verb 有 *yǒu* (I)
to have • Family

·2·

The verb 有 *yǒu* (I)

有	*yǒu*	to have
没有	*méiyǒu*	to not have

STATEMENT	他有儿子	*Tā yǒu érzi.*	He has sons.
NEGATION	他没有儿子	*Tā méiyǒu érzi.*	He has no sons.

生词 SHĒNGCÍ (VOCABULARY)

Family members

爸爸	*bàba*	father; dad	爷爷	*yéye*	grandfather (paternal)
妈妈	*māma*	mother; mom	奶奶	*nǎinai*	grandmother (paternal)
哥哥	*gēge*	older brother	先生	*xiānsheng*	husband
姐姐	*jiějie*	older sister	太太	*tàitai*	wife, Mrs.; madam
弟弟	*dìdi*	younger brother	儿子	*érzi*	son
妹妹	*mèimei*	younger sister	女儿	*nǚ'ér*	daughter

EXERCISE
2·1

Match each Chinese word with its English translation.

1. _____ 奶奶 *nǎinai*   a. son

2. _____ 先生 *xiānsheng*   b. wife

3. _____ 儿子 *érzi*   c. daughter

4. _____ 太太 *tàitai*   d. grandfather

5. _____ 女儿 *nǚ'ér*   e. husband

6. _____ 爷爷 *yéye*   f. grandmother

7. _____ 哥哥 *gēge*   g. younger brother

8. _____ 妹妹 *mèimei*   h. father

9. _____ 姐姐 *jiějie*   i. older brother

10. _____ 弟弟 *dìdi*   j. mother

11. _____ 爸爸 *bàba*   k. older sister

12. _____ 妈妈 *māma*   l. younger sister

EXERCISE
2·2

Follow the examples provided and negate the following statements.

EXAMPLES

你是哥哥。 → 你**不是**哥哥。
Nǐ shì gēge. *Nǐ **bú shì** gēge.*

你有哥哥。 → 你**没有**哥哥。
Nǐ yǒu gēge. *Nǐ **méi yǒu** gēge.*

1. 他是爷爷。 *Tā shì yéye.*

    _____

2. 你是姐姐。 *Nǐ shì jiějie.*

    _____

3. 她是妹妹。 *Tā shì mèimei.*

    _____

4. 他是哥哥。 *Tā shì gēge.*

    _____

5. 你是妈妈。 *Nǐ shì māma.*

    _____

6. 我有先生。 *Wǒ yǒu xiānsheng.*

    _____

7. 他们有儿子。 *Tāmen yǒu érzi.*

    _____

8. 她们有奶奶。 *Tāmen yǒu nǎinai.*

    _____

9. 我们有弟弟。 *Wǒmen yǒu dìdi.*

    _____

10. 我有太太。 *Wǒ yǒu tàitai.*

    _____

11. 他们有女儿。*Tāmen yǒu nǚ'ér*

_____

12. 她有爸爸。*Tā yǒu bàba.*

_____

翻译成中文 **Fānyì chéng Zhōngwén** *Translate into Chinese and pinyin.*

1. You have older brothers.

_____

2. You (*pl.*) don't have younger sisters.

_____

3. They have sons.

_____

4. We don't have a daughter.

_____

5. She has a husband.

_____

6. He has no wife.

_____

7. Grandma has an older brother.

_____

8. You have no grandfather.

_____

9. Mom has younger brothers.

_____

10. They have no grandmother.

_____

11. She doesn't have any younger brothers.

_____

12. Dad has older sisters.

_____

13. He has no father.

_____

14. Grandpa has younger sisters.

_____

15. I have no mother.

_____

你知道吗? *Nǐ zhīdao ma? Do you know?*

家人 *jiārén Family*

- Barack Obama 的 (*de*,'s) 妈妈是美国人, 可是 (*kěshì*, but) 他的爸爸, 爷爷和 (*hé*, and) 奶奶不是美国人。
- Steve Jobs 有妹妹, 可是没有姐姐, 哥哥和弟弟。
- George W. Bush 有太太和女儿, 可是没有儿子。
- Julia Roberts 有先生, 儿子和女儿。
- Brad Pitt 有弟弟和妹妹, 可是没有哥哥和姐姐。

NOTE   The word 的 *de* is a particle, which marks possession. Here, **Obama 的妈妈 Obama *de māma*** means *Obama's mother*. See Lesson 14 for further explanation.

Questions with 吗 *ma* • Fruits

Questions with 吗 *ma*

吗   *ma*   question particle

To make a 吗 *ma* question, attach 吗 *ma* to the end of a statement.

STATEMENT	他有哥哥。	*Tā yǒu gēge.*	He has brothers.
QUESTION WITH 吗	他有哥哥吗?	*Tā yǒu gēge ma?*	Does he have brothers?
ANSWER	有, 他有哥哥。	*Yǒu, tā yǒu gēge.*	Yes, he has brothers.
	没有, 他没有哥哥。	*Méi yǒu, tā méi yǒu gēge.*	No, he has no brothers.
STATEMENT	他吃苹果。	*Tā chī píngguǒ.*	He eats apples.
QUESTION WITH 吗	他吃苹果吗?	*Tā chī píngguǒ ma?*	Does he eat apples?
ANSWER	吃, 他吃苹果。	*Chī, tā chī píngguǒ.*	Yes, he eats apples.
	不, 他不吃苹果。	*Bù, tā bù chī píngguǒ.*	No, he doesn't eat apples.

生词 SHĒNGCÍ (VOCABULARY)

Fruits

香蕉	*xiāngjiāo*	banana		葡萄	*pútao*	grape
苹果	*píngguǒ*	apple		梨	*lí*	pear
桔子	*júzi*	orange		西瓜	*xīguā*	watermelon
柠檬	*níngméng*	lemon		草莓	*cǎoméi*	strawberry
菠萝	*bōluó*	pineapple		桃子	*táozi*	peach
香瓜	*xiāngguā*	honeydew		柚子	*yòuzi*	grapefruit

Everyday word

吃	*chī*	to eat

EXERCISE

3·1

Match each Chinese word with its English translation.

1. _____ 香蕉 *xiāngjiāo*   a. grape

2. _____ 桔子 *júzi*   b. apple

3. _____ 苹果 *píngguǒ*   c. peach

4. _____ 葡萄 *pútao*   d. banana

5. _____ 桃子 *táozi*   e. pear

6. _____ 梨 *lí*   f. orange

7. _____ 菠萝 *bōluó*   g. strawberry

8. _____ 草莓 *cǎoméi*   h. lemon

9. _____ 西瓜 *xīguā*   i. grapefruit

10. _____ 柠檬 *níngméng*   j. pineapple

11. _____ 香瓜 *xiāngguā*   k. watermelon

12. _____ 柚子 *yòuzi*   l. honeydew

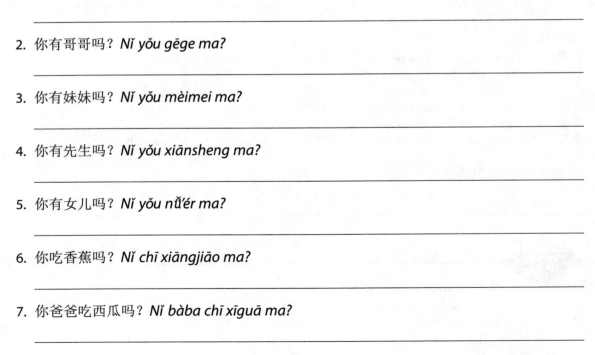

EXERCISE
3·2

Follow the examples given and answer the following questions. Answers may vary.

EXAMPLES

你有爷爷吗？   有，我有爷爷。/   没有，我没有爷爷。
Nǐ yǒu yéye ma?   *Yǒu, wǒ yǒu yéye.*   *Méiyǒu, wǒ méiyǒu yéye.*
你吃苹果吗？   吃，我吃苹果。/   不，我不吃苹果。
Nǐ chī píngguǒ ma? *Chī, wǒ chī píngguǒ.* *Bù, wǒ bù chī píngguǒ.*

1. 你有妈妈吗？*Nǐ yǒu māma ma?*

_____

2. 你有哥哥吗？*Nǐ yǒu gēge ma?*

_____

3. 你有妹妹吗？*Nǐ yǒu mèimei ma?*

_____

4. 你有先生吗？*Nǐ yǒu xiānsheng ma?*

_____

5. 你有女儿吗？*Nǐ yǒu nǚ'ér ma?*

_____

6. 你吃香蕉吗？*Nǐ chī xiāngjiāo ma?*

_____

7. 你爸爸吃西瓜吗？*Nǐ bàba chī xīguā ma?*

_____

8. 你爷爷吃柠檬吗？ *Nǐ yéye chī níngméng ma?*

_____

9. 你先生吃柚子吗？ *Nǐ xiānsheng chī yòuzi ma?*

_____

10. 你儿子吃桔子吗？ *Nǐ érzi chī júzi ma?*

_____

NOTE   Here the phrase "你爸爸 *nǐ bàba*" means "your father." A personal pronoun can be used directly to modify a noun that denotes a family member or a close relationship. See Lesson 14 for further explanation.

生词   SHĒNGCÍ (VOCABULARY)

Everyday word
喜欢   *xǐhuan*   to like

EXERCISE
3·3

As in the given examples, change the following statements into questions with 吗.

EXAMPLES   你爸爸吃苹果。   你爸爸吃苹果**吗**？
Nǐ bàba chī píngguǒ.   *Nǐ bàba chī píngguǒ **ma**?*
他妹妹喜欢吃香蕉。   他妹妹喜欢吃香蕉**吗**？
Tā mèimei xǐhuan chī xiāngjiāo.   *Tā mèimei xǐhuan chī xiāngjiāo **ma**?*

1. 我弟弟吃菠萝。 *Wǒ dìdi chī bōluó.*

_____

2. 你姐姐吃香蕉。 *Nǐ jiějie chī xiāngjiāo.*

_____

3. 她妹妹吃西瓜。 *Tā mèimei chī xīguā.*

_____

4. 他哥哥吃苹果。 *Tā gēge chī píngguǒ.*

_____

5. 我先生吃香瓜。 *Wǒ xiānsheng chī xiāngguā.*

6. 他们儿子吃梨。*Tāmen érzi chī lí.*

_____

7. 我们爷爷喜欢柠檬。*Wǒmen yéye xǐhuan níngméng.*

_____

8. 她们奶奶喜欢草莓。*Tāmen nǎinai xǐhuan cǎoméi.*

_____

9. 我太太喜欢吃桃子。*Wǒ tàitài xǐhuan chī táozi.*

_____

10. 你妈妈喜欢吃桔子。 *Nǐ māma xǐhuan chī júzi.*

_____

11. 他们女儿喜欢吃柚子。*Tāmen nǚ'ér xǐhuan chī yòuzi.*

_____

12. 你们爸爸喜欢吃葡萄。*Nǐmen bàba xǐhuan chī pútao.*

_____

EXERCISE 3·4

翻译成中文 Fānyì chéng Zhōngwén   *Translate into Chinese and pinyin.*

1. I like eating bananas.

_____

2. Do you eat pears?

_____

3. My father does not like eating lemons.

_____

4. Does his mother like eating strawberries?

_____

5. Her older brother doesn't eat grapes.

_____

6. Does your younger sister like oranges?

_____

7. Your grandmother likes watermelons.

_____

8. Does her husband eat grapefruit?

   _____

9. Their mother likes eating honeydew.

   _____

10. Does his grandfather like peaches?

    _____

11. Our son doesn't like eating apples.

    _____

12. Does his wife eat pineapples?

    _____

你知道吗? *Nǐ zhīdao ma?* Do you know?

水果 *shuǐguǒ* Fruit

美国人喜欢吃香蕉, 苹果, 桔子, 葡萄和 (*hé*, and) 草莓。每 (*měi*, per) 年 (*nián*, year) 美国人平均 (*píngjūn*, on average) 每人吃:

- 33 磅 (*sānshísān bàng*, pound) 香蕉。
- 18 磅 (*shíbā bàng*) 苹果。
- 12.3 磅 (*shí'èr diǎn sān bàng*) 桔子。
- 7.5 磅 (*qī diǎn wǔ bàng*) 葡萄。
- 3.4 磅 (*sān diǎn sì bàng*) 草莓。

Adverbs 也 yě and 都 dōu • Food

Adverbs 也 yě and 都 dōu

也	*yě*	also, too
都	*dōu*	both, all

The adverb always precedes the verb in Chinese.

SUBJECT + 也/都 + VERB + OBJECT

Statement

他们也吃法国餐。	*Tāmen yě chī Fǎguócān.*	They also eat French food.
他们都吃法国餐。	*Tāmen dōu chī Fǎguócān.*	They all eat French food.

Negation

他们不吃法国餐。	*Tāmen bù chī Fǎguócān.*	They don't eat French food.
他们也不吃法国餐。	*Tāmen yě bù chī Fǎguócān.*	They don't eat French food, either.
他们都不吃法国餐。	*Tāmen dōu bù chī Fǎguócān.*	None of them eats French food.

生词 SHĒNGCÍ (VOCABULARY)

Food

米饭	*mǐfàn*	(cooked) rice	馒头	*mántou*	steamed bread
面条	*miàntiáo*	noodles	米粉	*mǐfěn*	rice noodles
饺子	*jiǎozi*	dumpling	包子	*bāozi*	steamed stuffed bun
烧饼	*shāobing*	sesame cake	面包	*miànbāo*	bread
披萨饼	*pīsàbǐng*	pizza	三明治	*sānmíngzhì*	sandwich
奶酪	*nǎilào*	cheese	汉堡包	*hànbǎobāo*	hamburger
餐	*cān*	food; meal	意大利	*Yìdàlì*	Italy

16

EXERCISE 4·1

Match each Chinese word with its English translation.

1. _____ 面包 *miànbāo*	a. steamed bread
2. _____ 米粉 *mǐfěn*	b. dumpling
3. _____ 三明治 *sānmíngzhì*	c. bread
4. _____ 饺子 *jiǎozi*	d. cheese
5. _____ 馒头 *mántou*	e. rice noodles
6. _____ 奶酪 *nǎilào*	f. sandwich
7. _____ 米饭 *mǐfàn*	g. steamed stuffed bun
8. _____ 披萨饼 *pīsàbǐng*	h. sesame cake
9. _____ 面条 *miàntiáo*	i. hamburger
10. _____ 包子 *bāozi*	j. noodles
11. _____ 烧饼 *shāobing*	k. pizza
12. _____ 汉堡包 *hànbǎobāo*	l. rice

生词 SHĒNGCÍ (VOCABULARY)

Everyday word

和　　*hé*　　**and**

EXERCISE 4·2

Insert 也 **yě** *into the first four sentences and* 都 **dōu** *into the last four sentences where appropriate.*

EXAMPLE　我喜欢吃面包。　　*Wǒ xǐhuan chī miànbāo.*

　　　　　我**也**喜欢吃面包。　　*Wǒ **yě** xǐhuan chī miànbāo.*

1. 他儿子喜欢吃饺子和包子。*Tā érzi xǐhuan chī jiǎozi hé bāozi.*

_____

2. 我女儿喜欢吃三明治。*Wǒ nǚ'ér xǐhuan chī sānmíngzhì.*

_____

3. 她先生喜欢吃馒头和烧饼。*Tā xiānsheng xǐhuan chī mántou hé shāobing.*

_____

4. 他太太喜欢吃米饭和米粉。 *Tā tàitai xǐhuan chī mǐfàn hé mǐfěn.*

_____

5. 我爸爸和妈妈喜欢吃汉堡包。 *Wǒ bàba hé māma xǐhuan chī hànbǎobāo.*

_____

6. 爷爷和奶奶喜欢吃面条。 *Yéye hé nǎinai xǐhuan chī miàntiáo.*

_____

7. 他姐姐和妹妹喜欢吃意大利餐。 *Tā jiějie hé mèimei xǐhuan chī Yìdàlì cān.*

_____

8. 她哥哥和弟弟喜欢吃奶酪披萨饼。 *Tā gēge hé dìdi xǐhuan chī nǎilào pīsàbǐng.*

_____

生词　SHĒNGCÍ (VOCABULARY)

Everyday words

| 买 | *mǎi* | to buy |
| 做 | *zuò* | to make; to do |

EXERCISE 4·3

*First, fill in the blanks with 也 **yě**, 都 **dōu**, 也不 **yě bù**, or 都不 **dōu bù**, according to the English words or phrases in the parentheses, and then translate the sentences into English.*

1. 他哥哥和姐姐 _____ 喜欢吃米粉。 (*both*)

   Tā gēge hé jiějie _____ xǐhuan chī mǐfěn.

   _____

2. 她爷爷 _____ 喜欢买奶酪披萨饼。 (*also*)

   Tā yéye _____ xǐhuan mǎi nǎilào pīsàbǐng.

   _____

3. 他弟弟和妹妹 _____ 喜欢吃面条。 (*none*)

   Tā dìdi hé mèimei _____ xǐhuan chī miàntiáo.

   _____

4. 她们 _____ 喜欢做馒头和烧饼。 (*not...either*)

   Tāmen _____ xǐhuan zuò mántou hé shāobing.

   _____

5. 你先生和我太太 ＿＿＿＿＿＿＿＿＿＿ 喜欢吃米饭。(*both*)

   Nǐ xiānsheng hé wǒ tàitai ＿＿＿＿＿＿＿＿＿＿ *xǐhuan chī mǐfàn.*

   ＿＿＿＿＿＿＿＿＿＿＿＿＿＿＿＿＿＿＿＿＿＿＿＿＿＿＿＿＿＿＿＿

6. 我们奶奶 ＿＿＿＿＿＿＿＿＿＿ 喜欢做饺子和包子。(*also*)

   Wǒmen nǎinai ＿＿＿＿＿＿＿＿＿＿ *xǐhuan zuò jiǎozi hé bāozi.*

   ＿＿＿＿＿＿＿＿＿＿＿＿＿＿＿＿＿＿＿＿＿＿＿＿＿＿＿＿＿＿＿＿

7. 我爸爸和妈妈 ＿＿＿＿＿＿＿＿＿＿ 喜欢买面包。(*not…either*)

   Wǒ bàba hé māma ＿＿＿＿＿＿＿＿＿＿ *xǐhuan mǎi miànbāo.*

   ＿＿＿＿＿＿＿＿＿＿＿＿＿＿＿＿＿＿＿＿＿＿＿＿＿＿＿＿＿＿＿＿

8. 他们 ＿＿＿＿＿＿＿＿＿＿ 喜欢做三明治和汉堡包。(*all*)

   Tāmen ＿＿＿＿＿＿＿＿＿＿ *xǐhuan zuò sānmíngzhì hé hànbǎobāo.*

   ＿＿＿＿＿＿＿＿＿＿＿＿＿＿＿＿＿＿＿＿＿＿＿＿＿＿＿＿＿＿＿＿

EXERCISE

4·4

翻译成中文 **Fānyì chéng Zhōngwén** *Translate into Chinese and pinyin.*

1. My husband also likes eating rice.

   ＿＿＿＿＿＿＿＿＿＿＿＿＿＿＿＿＿＿＿＿＿＿＿＿＿＿＿＿＿＿＿＿

2. My wife doesn't like Italian pizza, either.

   ＿＿＿＿＿＿＿＿＿＿＿＿＿＿＿＿＿＿＿＿＿＿＿＿＿＿＿＿＿＿＿＿

3. Do all of you like to make dumplings?

   ＿＿＿＿＿＿＿＿＿＿＿＿＿＿＿＿＿＿＿＿＿＿＿＿＿＿＿＿＿＿＿＿

4. None of my daughters buys hamburgers.

   ＿＿＿＿＿＿＿＿＿＿＿＿＿＿＿＿＿＿＿＿＿＿＿＿＿＿＿＿＿＿＿＿

5. All of you like eating French cheese.

   ＿＿＿＿＿＿＿＿＿＿＿＿＿＿＿＿＿＿＿＿＿＿＿＿＿＿＿＿＿＿＿＿

6. My son does not like making rice noodles, either.

   ＿＿＿＿＿＿＿＿＿＿＿＿＿＿＿＿＿＿＿＿＿＿＿＿＿＿＿＿＿＿＿＿

7. Her brothers also like to buy stuffed buns.

   ＿＿＿＿＿＿＿＿＿＿＿＿＿＿＿＿＿＿＿＿＿＿＿＿＿＿＿＿＿＿＿＿

8. All of us like eating sesame cakes.

   ＿＿＿＿＿＿＿＿＿＿＿＿＿＿＿＿＿＿＿＿＿＿＿＿＿＿＿＿＿＿＿＿

9. Do Japanese also like making noodles?

_____

10. All of the Germans like hamburgers.

_____

11. Do Indians also make sandwiches?

_____

12. Do Russians also buy steamed bread?

_____

你知道吗? *Nǐ zhīdao ma?* *Do you know?*

食物 *shíwù* Food

美国人喜欢吃面包和奶酪，也喜欢吃三明治，披萨饼和汉堡包。每 (*měi*, per) 年 (*nián*, year) 美国人平均 (*píngjūn*, on average) 每人吃:

- 53 磅 (*wǔshísān bàng*, pound) 面包。
- 31 磅 (*sānshíyī bàng*) 奶酪。
- 23 磅 (*èrshísān bàng*) 披萨饼。
- 193 个 (*yì bǎi jiǔshísān ge*, a classifier) 三明治。
- 150 个 (*yì bǎi wǔshí ge*) 汉堡包。

Sentences with a verbal predicate • Time words and daily activities

·5·

Sentences with a verbal predicate

In a simple sentence with a verbal predicate, the verb functions as the main part of the predicate, and an adverb usually precedes the verb in the sentence.

SUBJECT	+ PREDICATE					
	ADVERB(S) +		VERB + OBJECT			
他们 *Tāmen*	晚上 *wǎnshang*		看 *kàn*	电视。 *diànshì.*		They watch TV in the evening.
他们 *Tāmen*	晚上 *wǎnshang*	常 *cháng*	看 *kàn*	电视 *diànshì*	吗? *ma?*	Do they often watch TV in the evening?
他们 *Tāmen*	晚上 *wǎnshang*	不常 *bù cháng*	看 *kàn*	电视。 *diànshì.*		They don't often watch TV in the evening.

NOTE The time phrase indicating when an event takes place (晚上) occurs before the verb.

生词 SHĒNGCÍ (VOCABULARY)

Time, meals, and daily activities

早上	*zǎoshang*	**morning**
中午	*zhōngwǔ*	**noon**
下午	*xiàwǔ*	**afternoon**
晚上	*wǎnshang*	**evening**
白天	*báitiān*	**daytime**
今天	*jīntiān*	**today**
明天	*míngtiān*	**tomorrow**
常	*cháng*	**often**
早饭	*zǎofàn*	**breakfast**

晚饭	*wǎnfàn*	**supper; dinner**
午饭	*wǔfàn*	**lunch**
上班	*shàngbān*	**to go to work**
上学	*shàngxué*	**to go to school**
上网	*shàngwǎng*	**to go online**
运动	*yùndòng*	**to work out**
看	*kàn*	**to watch; to look**
电视	*diànshì*	**television; TV**
睡觉	*shuìjiào*	**to sleep**

EXERCISE 5·1

Match each Chinese word with its English translation.

1. _____	今天 *jīntiān*	a.	to sleep
2. _____	明天 *míngtiān*	b.	dinner
3. _____	早上 *zǎoshang*	c.	today
4. _____	中午 *zhōngwǔ*	d.	to go online
5. _____	看 *kàn*	e.	to work out
6. _____	上网 *shàngwǎng*	f.	noon
7. _____	运动 *yùndòng*	g.	to watch
8. _____	睡觉 *shuìjiào*	h.	morning
9. _____	晚饭 *wǎnfàn*	i.	tomorrow
10. _____	晚上 *wǎnshang*	j.	often
11. _____	白天 *báitiān*	k.	afternoon
12. _____	早饭 *zǎofàn*	l.	to go to work
13. _____	常 *cháng*	m.	television
14. _____	上学 *shàngxué*	n.	evening
15. _____	午饭 *wǔfàn*	o.	daytime
16. _____	上班 *shàngbān*	p.	breakfast
17. _____	下午 *xiàwǔ*	q.	lunch
18. _____	电视 *diànshì*	r.	to go to school

Match each Chinese sentence with its English equivalent.

1. _____ 他妈妈早上吃早饭。

   Tā māma zǎoshang chī zǎofàn.

   a. Her father works in the evening.

2. _____ 他弟弟白天睡觉。

   Tā dìdi báitiān shuìjiào.

   b. None of my brothers eats lunch.

3. _____ 她爸爸晚上上班。

   Tā bàba wǎnshang shàngbān.

   c. His wife doesn't work tomorrow.

4. _____ 他奶奶常看电视。

   Tā nǎinai cháng kàn diànshì.

   d. His mother eats breakfast in the morning.

5. _____ 我爷爷下午运动。

   Wǒ yéye xiàwǔ yùndòng.

   e. I won't go to school today.

6. _____ 我哥哥和弟弟都不吃午饭。

   Wǒ gēge hé dìdi dōu bù chī wǔfàn.

   f. Her husband does not go online often.

7. _____ 他姐姐和妹妹今天上学。

   Tā jiějie hé mèimei jīntiān shàngxué.

   g. His grandmother often watches TV.

8. _____ 她先生不常上网。

   Tā xiānsheng bù cháng shàngwǎng.

   h. His younger brother sleeps during the day.

9. _____ 他太太明天不上班。

   Tā tàitai míngtiān bú shàngbān.

   i. My grandfather works out in the afternoon.

10. _____ 我今天不上学。

   Wǒ jīntiān bú shàngxué.

   j. His sisters go to school today.

EXERCISE

5·3

Answer the following questions in Chinese and pinyin according to real situations. Answers may vary.

1. 你常看电视吗？ *Nǐ cháng kàn diànshì ma?*

_____

2. 你喜欢晚上运动吗？ *Nǐ xǐhuan wǎnshang yùndòng ma?*

_____

3. 我晚上常上网，你也常上网吗？ *Wǒ wǎnshang cháng shàngwǎng, nǐ yě cháng shàngwǎng ma?*

_____

4. 我们今天不上班，你今天也不上班吗？ *Wǒmen jīntiān bú shàngbān, nǐ jīntiān yě bú shàngbān ma?*

_____

5. 你爷爷喜欢白天睡觉吗？ *Nǐ yéye xǐhuan báitiān shuìjiào ma?*

_____

6. 我妹妹明天不上学，你也不上学吗？ *Wǒ mèimei míngtiān bú shàngxué, nǐ yě bú shàngxué ma?*

_____

EXERCISE 5·4

翻译成中文 Fānyì chéng Zhōngwén   *Translate into Chinese and pinyin.*

1. My older brother often does not eat breakfast.

_____

2. Her father and mother both work in the evening.

_____

3. Does his wife go online in the evening?

_____

4. Our grandmother often works out in the afternoon.

_____

5. All of my sisters will go to school tomorrow.

_____

6. Does your husband often sleep during the day?

_____

7. His grandfather watches TV in the morning.

_____

8. Do you often eat Italian bread and French cheese for dinner?

_____

9. None of my sons or daughters goes online often.

_____

10. Chinese people often watch TV in the evening.

    _____

11. Americans often work out in the morning.

    _____

12. My younger sister works during the day, (and) my older sister works in the evening.

    _____

你知道吗? *Nǐ zhīdao ma?* Do you know?

食物 *shíwù* Food

中国人喜欢吃，他们发明了 (*fāmíng le*, invented)

- 饺子
- 包子
- 馒头
- 面条
- 米粉
- 豆腐 (*dòufu*, tofu)

欧洲人 (*Ōuzhōurén*, Europeans) 也喜欢吃。英国人发明了三明治，德国人发明了汉堡包，意大利人发明了披萨饼。

Lessons 1–5

Place an X in the appropriate column.

你是 _____ 吗？

Nǐ shì _____ ma?

	是	不是			是	不是
	shì	**bú shì**			**shì**	**bú shì**
1. 英国人	_____	_____		6. 美国人	_____	_____
Yīngguórén				*Měiguórén*		
2. 日本人	_____	_____		7. 法国人	_____	_____
Rìběnrén				*Fǎguórén*		
3. 印度人	_____	_____		8. 中国人	_____	_____
Yìndùrén				*Zhōngguórén*		
4. 俄国人	_____	_____		9. 德国人	_____	_____
Éguórén				*Déguórén*		
5. 意大利人	_____	_____				
Yìdàlìrén						

你有 _____ 吗？

Nǐ yǒu _____ ma?

	有	没有			有	没有
	yǒu	**méi yǒu**			**yǒu**	**méi yǒu**
10. 奶奶	_____	_____		11. 爷爷	_____	_____
nǎinai				*yéye*		

12. 妈妈 _____ _____ 17. 妹妹 _____ _____
   māma   *mèimei*

13. 爸爸 _____ _____ 18. 弟弟 _____ _____
   bàba   *dìdi*

14. 太太 _____ _____ 19. 哥哥 _____ _____
   tàitai   *gēge*

15. 先生 _____ _____ 20. 女儿 _____ _____
   xiānsheng   *nǚ'ér*

16. 姐姐 _____ _____ 21. 儿子 _____ _____
   jiějie   *érzi*

你喜欢吃 _____ 吗？

Nǐ xǐhuan chī _____ ma?

	喜欢吃 *xǐhuan chī*	不喜欢吃 *bù xǐhuan chī*		喜欢吃 *xǐhuan chī*	不喜欢吃 *bù xǐhuan chī*
22. 香瓜 *xiāngguā*	_____	_____	30. 汉堡包 *hànbǎobāo*	_____	_____
23. 菠萝 *bōluó*	_____	_____	31. 面条 *miàntiáo*	_____	_____
24. 草莓 *cǎoméi*	_____	_____	32. 披萨饼 *pīsàbǐng*	_____	_____
25. 桔子 *júzi*	_____	_____	33. 面包 *miànbāo*	_____	_____
26. 苹果 *píngguǒ*	_____	_____	34. 饺子 *jiǎozi*	_____	_____
27. 葡萄 *pútao*	_____	_____	35. 中国餐 *Zhōngguó cān*	_____	_____
28. 馒头 *mántou*	_____	_____	36. 美国餐 *Měiguó cān*	_____	_____
29. 奶酪 *nǎilào*	_____	_____	37. 印度餐 *Yìndù cān*	_____	_____

Complete the sentences with the appropriate adverbs 不 **bù**, 也 **yě**, 都 **dōu**, 常 **cháng**, 也不 **yě bù**, 都不 **dōu bù**. (Note: Some of the adverbs can be used more than once.)

1. 他爷爷和奶奶 _____ 是英国人。(both)

   Tā yéye hé nǎinai _____ shì Yīngguó rén.

2. 他妈妈 _____ 有哥哥。(also)

   Tā māma, _____ yǒu gēge.

3. 我爸爸今天早上 _____ 吃早饭。(not)

   Wǒ bàba jīntiān zǎoshang _____ chī zǎofàn.

4. 她先生白天 _____ 睡觉吗？(often)

   Tā xiānsheng báitiān _____ shuìjiào ma?

5. 哥哥, 姐姐, 弟弟和妹妹 _____ 喜欢吃香蕉。(none)

   Gēge, jiějie, dìdi hé mèimei _____ xǐhuan chī xiāngjiāo.

6. 他太太 _____ 喜欢吃美国奶酪。(not … either)

   Tā tàitai _____ xǐhuan chī Měiguó nǎilào.

7. 我儿子和女儿 _____ 喜欢做德国汉堡包。(all)

   Wǒ érzi hé nǚ'ér _____ xǐhuan zuò Déguó hànbǎobāo.

Select the appropriate option   *When do you do the following daily activities?*
Answers may vary.

	上班 shàngbān	上学 shàngxué	上网 shàngwǎng	运动 yùndòng	睡觉 shuìjiào	看电视 kàn diànshì
1. 上午 shàngwǔ	_____	_____	_____	_____	_____	_____
2. 中午 zhōngwǔ	_____	_____	_____	_____	_____	_____
3. 下午 xiàwǔ	_____	_____	_____	_____	_____	_____

4. 白天 ___ ___ ___ ___ ___

   báitiān

5. 晚上 ___ ___ ___ ___ ___

   wǎnshang

EXERCISE
R1·4

翻译成中文 **Fānyì chéng Zhōngwén**   *Translate into Chinese and pinyin.*

1. I am not British; I am American.

   _____

2. She is Chinese, (and) her husband is also Chinese.

   _____

3. She doesn't have an older brother, (and) she doesn't have an older sister, either.

   _____

4. Do you have a grandfather and grandmother?

   _____

5. Do all of his sons and daughters like eating Chinese rice noodles?

   _____

6. Her father and mother often buy steamed bread and sesame cakes for breakfast.

   _____

7. Chinese people often eat rice and noodles for supper.

   _____

8. Do Germans make hamburgers for lunch?

   _____

9. I sleep during the day (and) work in the evening.

   _____

10. My wife often goes online at noon (and) works out in the afternoon.

    _____

11. None of his daughters likes watching TV.

    _____

12. Her mother rarely eats honeydew or watermelon.

    _____

True or False? *After reading the following Chinese dialogue, mark the English statements either **true** or **false**.*

Anna is chatting with her new roommate, Lily, at the student dormitory about Lily's family members.

A: Lily, 我知道 (*zhīdao*, to know) 你是美国人。你爸爸, 妈妈也是美国人吗?

    Lily, wǒ zhīdao nǐ shì Měiguórén. Nǐ bàba, māma yě shì Měiguórén ma?

L: 是, 我爸爸, 妈妈也都是美国人。

    Shì, wǒ bàba, māma yě dōu shì Měiguórén.

A: 你爷爷, 奶奶也都是美国人吗?

    Nǐ yéye, nǎinai yě dōu shì Měiguórén ma?

L: 不, 我爷爷是英国人, 可是 (*kěshì*, but) 我奶奶是法国人。

    Bù, wǒ yéye shì Yīngguórén, kěshì wǒ nǎinai shì Fǎguórén.

A: 你有哥哥和弟弟吗? *Nǐ yǒu gēge hé dìdi ma?*

L: 我有哥哥, 没有弟弟。 *Wǒ yǒu gēge, méiyǒu dìdi.*

A: 你有姐姐和妹妹吗? *Nǐ yǒu jiějie hé mèimei ma?*

L: 没有。 *Méi yǒu.*

They also discuss Lily's likes and dislikes.

A: Lily, 你喜欢吃水果吗? *Lily, nǐ xǐhuan chī shuǐguǒ ma?*

L: 喜欢, 我喜欢吃苹果, 菠萝和香蕉, 可是不喜欢吃桔子, 柠檬和柚子。

    Xǐhuan, wǒ xǐhuan chī píngguǒ, bōluó hé xiāngjiāo, kěshì bù xǐhuan chī júzi, níngméng hé yòuzi.

A: 你喜欢吃汉堡包和三明治吗? *Nǐ xǐhuan chī hànbǎobāo hé sānmíngzhì ma?*

L: 我喜欢吃三明治, 不喜欢吃汉堡包。

    Wǒ xǐhuan chī sānmíngzhì, bù xǐhuan chī hànbǎobāo.

A: 你喜欢运动吗? *Nǐ xǐhuan yùndòng ma?*

L: 喜欢, 我每天 (*měitiān*, every day) 早上都运动。

    Xǐhuan, wǒ měitiān zǎoshang dōu yùndòng.

A: 你也喜欢看电视吗? *Nǐ yě xǐhuan kàn diànshì ma?*

L: 不, 我不喜欢, 可是我喜欢上网。 *Bù, wǒ bù xǐhuan, kěshì wǒ xǐhuan shàngwǎng.*

1. _____ Lily and her parents are American.

2. _____ Her paternal grandparents are both American, too.

3. _____ She has an older brother but does not have a younger brother.

4. _____ She has sisters.

5. _____ She likes eating all kinds of fruits.

6. _____ She likes eating hamburgers but does not like eating sandwiches.

7. _____ She does not like sports at all.

8. _____ She likes getting online but does not like watching TV.

Grammar

Vocabulary

Do you know?

Questions with an interrogative pronoun • Beverages

Questions with an interrogative pronoun

To form this type of question, simply replace the element you want to ask a question about with an interrogative pronoun. The question particle 吗 *ma* is not used.

Statement		
他喝苹果汁。	*Tā hē píngguǒzhī.*	He drinks apple juice.
Questions		
他喝什么?	*Tā hē **shénme**?*	What does he drink?
他喝什么汁?	*Tā hē **shénme** zhī?*	What juice does he drink?
谁喝苹果汁?	***Shéi** hē píngguǒzhī?*	Who drinks apple juice?

生词　SHĒNGCÍ (VOCABULARY)

Interrogative pronouns

什么	*shénme*	what
哪	*nǎ*	which
谁	*shéi/shuí*	who; whom

Beverages

饮料	*yǐnliào*	beverages
咖啡	*kāfēi*	coffee
茶	*chá*	tea
可乐	*kělè*	coke
豆浆	*dòujiāng*	soybean milk
牛奶	*niúnǎi*	milk
啤酒	*píjiǔ*	beer
果汁	*guǒzhī*	fruit juice
汁	*zhī*	juice
矿泉水	*kuàngquánshuǐ*	mineral water
水	*shuǐ*	water
葡萄酒	*pútao jiǔ*	grape wine
酒	*jiǔ*	liquor, wine
喝	*hē*	to drink

Choose the appropriate column. Answers may vary.

你喜欢喝什么饮料?   喜欢喝   不喜欢喝

Nǐ xǐhuan hē shénme yǐnliào?   *xǐhuan hē*   *bù xǐhuan hē*

1. 茶 *chá* _____ _____

2. 水 *shuǐ* _____ _____

3. 酒 *jiǔ* _____ _____

4. 果汁 *guǒzhī* _____ _____

5. 牛奶 *niúnǎi* _____ _____

6. 咖啡 *kāfēi* _____ _____

7. 豆浆 *dòujiāng* _____ _____

8. 可乐 *kělè* _____ _____

9. 啤酒 *píjiǔ* _____ _____

10. 葡萄酒 *pútaojiǔ* _____ _____

11. 桔子汁 *júzi zhī* _____ _____

12. 苹果汁 *píngguǒzhī* _____ _____

13. 葡萄汁 *pútaozhī* _____ _____

14. 菠萝汁 *bōluózhī* _____ _____

15. 矿泉水 *kuàngquánshuǐ* _____ _____

Follow the examples given and turn each of the following statements into a question by replacing the element in bold with an appropriate interrogative pronoun.

EXAMPLES   他常喝美国可乐。 *Tā cháng hē Měiguó kělè.*

他常喝**什么**? *Tā cháng hē **shénme**?*

他常喝**什么**可乐? *Tā cháng hē **shénme** kělè?*

谁常喝可乐? ***Shéi** cháng hē kělè?*

1. 你妈妈今天喝**咖啡**。 *Nǐ māma jīntiān hē **kāfēi**.*

_____

2. **爸爸**明天喝中国茶。 ***Bàba** míngtiān hē Zhōngguó chá.*

_____

3. 她先生中午喝**葡萄**酒。*Tā xiānsheng zhōngwǔ hē **pútao** jiǔ.*

_____

4. 他太太晚上喝**啤**酒。*Tā tàitai wǎnshang hē **píj**iǔ.*

_____

5. **他们儿子**早上喝豆浆。***Tāmen érzi** zǎoshang hē dòujiāng.*

_____

6. 我女儿上午喝**牛奶**。*Wǒ nǚ'ér shàngwǔ hē **niúnǎi**.*

_____

7. 她哥哥下午常喝**葡萄**酒。*Tā gēge xiàwǔ cháng hē **pútao** jiǔ.*

_____

8. **她姐姐**常喝饮料。***Tā jiějie** cháng hē yǐnliào.*

_____

9. 爷爷也喜欢喝**矿泉水**。*Yéye yě xǐhuan hē **kuàngquánshuǐ**.*

_____

10. **我奶奶**不喝菠萝汁。***Wǒ nǎinai** bù hē bōluó zhī.*

_____

11. 他姐姐和妹妹都喜欢喝**可乐**。*Tā jiějie hé mèimei dōu xǐhuan hē **kělè**.*

_____

12. 她弟弟都不喝**苹果**汁。*Tā dìdi dōu bù hē **píngguǒ** zhī.*

_____

EXERCISE
6·3

Answer the following questions with the words given according to the best of your knowledge. Answers may vary. (Note: You may name more than one country's people for each question.)

美国人 *Měiguórén*, 中国人 *Zhōngguórén*, 法国人 *Fǎguórén*, 德国人 *Déguóren*,
英国人 *Yīngguórén*, 日本人 *Rìběnrén*, 意大利人 *Yìdàlìrén*, 俄国人 *Éguórén*

1. 哪国人 (which nationality) 喜欢喝啤酒？*Nǎ guó rén xǐhuan hē píjiǔ?*

_____

2. 哪国人喜欢喝茶？*Nǎ guó rén xǐhuan hē chá?*

_____

3. 哪国人喜欢喝可乐？ *Nǎ guó rén xǐhuan hē kělè?*

_____

4. 哪国人喜欢喝牛奶？ *Nǎ guó rén xǐhuan hē niúnǎi?*

_____

5. 哪国人喜欢喝豆浆？ *Nǎ guó rén xǐhuan hē dòujiāng?*

_____

6. 哪国人喜欢喝葡萄酒？ *Nǎ guó rén xǐhuan hē pútao jiǔ?*

_____

7. 哪国人喜欢喝咖啡？ *Nǎ guó rén xǐhuan hē kāfēi?*

_____

生词　SHĒNGCÍ (VOCABULARY)

Everyday word

| 家里人 | *jiālǐrén* | **family members** |

EXERCISE
6·4

Answer the following questions according to real situations. Answers may vary.

1. 早饭你常吃什么，喝什么？ *Zǎofàn nǐ cháng chī shénme, hē shénme?*

_____

2. 午饭你常吃什么，喝什么？ *Wǔfàn nǐ cháng chī shénme, hē shénme?*

_____

3. 晚饭你常吃什么，喝什么？ *Wǎnfàn nǐ cháng chī shénme, hē shénme?*

_____

4. 你家里人，谁喜欢喝咖啡？ *Nǐ jiālǐrén, shéi xǐhuan hē kāfēi?*

_____

5. 你家里人，谁喜欢葡萄酒？ *Nǐ jiālǐrén, shéi xǐhuan hē pútao jiǔ?*

_____

6. 你家里人，谁喜欢喝可乐？ *Nǐ jiālǐrén, shéi xǐhuan hē kělè?*

_____

7. 你家里人，谁喜欢喝茶？ *Nǐ jiālǐrén, shéi xǐhuan hē chá?*

_____

8. 你家里人，谁喜欢喝矿泉水？ *Nǐ jiālǐrén, shéi xǐhuan hē kuàngquánshuǐ?*

_____

9. 你家里人，谁喜欢喝果汁？ *Nǐ jiālǐrén, shéi xǐhuan hē guǒzhī?*

_____

10. 你家里人，谁喜欢喝豆浆？ *Nǐ jiālǐrén, shéi xǐhuan hē dòujiāng?*

_____

11. 你家里人，谁喜欢喝牛奶？ *Nǐ jiālǐrén, shéi xǐhuan hē niúnǎi?*

_____

12. 你家里人，谁喜欢喝啤酒？ *Nǐ jiālǐrén, shéi xǐhuan hē píjiǔ?*

_____

EXERCISE 6·5

翻译成中文 Fānyì chéng Zhōngwén *Translate into Chinese and pinyin.*

1. Sir (先生 *xiānsheng*), what do you drink?

_____

2. Mom, what fruit juice do you like to drink?

_____

3. What (kind of) beverage does his older brother often drink in the afternoon?

_____

4. Among your family members, who does not like drinking milk?

_____

5. What does your father like to eat and drink for supper?

_____

6. Which country's people like drinking coffee during the day?

_____

7. Among your family members, who likes German beer?

_____

8. Which country's people like drinking grape wine for lunch?

_____

9. What liquor does your grandmother like drinking in the evening?

_____

10. What do Chinese people often drink for breakfast?

_____

你知道吗？ *Nǐ zhīdao ma?* Do you know?

饮料 *yǐnliào* Beverages

美国人很 (*hěn*, very much) 喜欢喝咖啡, 可乐, 牛奶, 啤酒和桔子汁等 (*děng*, etc.) 饮料。
每(*měi*, per) 年(*nián*, year) 美国人平均 (*píngjūn*, on average) 每人喝:

- 1000 (*yī qiān*) 杯 (*bēi*, cup) 咖啡。
- 600 (*liù bǎi*) 罐 (*guàn*, can) 可乐。
- 25 (*èrshíwǔ*) 加仑 (*jiālún*, gallon) 牛奶。
- 20 (*èrshí*) 加仑啤酒。
- 5 (*wǔ*) 加仑桔子汁。

Numbers 1–100 • Arithmetic expressions

Numbers 1–100

The cardinal numbers from 0 to 100 are shown in the following table.

零 *líng* 0	一 *yī* 1	二 *èr* 2	三 *sān* 3	四 *sì* 4	五 *wǔ* 5	六 *liù* 6	七 *qī* 7	八 *bā* 8	九 *jiǔ* 9
(一)十 *(yī)shí* 10	十一 *shíyī* 11	十二 *shí'èr* 12	十三 *shísān* 13	十四 *shísì* 14	十五 *shíwǔ* 15	十六 *shíliù* 16	十七 *shíqī* 17	十八 *shíbā* 18	十九 *shíjiǔ* 19
二十 *èrshí* 20	二十一 *èrshíyī* 21	二十二 *èrshí'èr* 22	二十三 23	二十四 24	二十五 25	二十六 26	二十七 27	二十八 28	二十九 29
三十 *sānshí* 30	三十一 31	三十二 32	三十三 33	三十四 34	三十五 35	三十六 36	三十七 37	三十八 38	三十九 39
四十 *sìshí* 40	四十一 41	四十二 42	四十三 43	四十四 44	四十五 45	四十六 46	四十七 47	四十八 48	四十九 49
五十 *wǔshí* 50	五十一 51	五十二 52	五十三 53	五十四 54	五十五 55	五十六 56	五十七 57	五十八 58	五十九 59
六十 *liùshí* 60	六十一 61	六十二 62	六十三 63	六十四 64	六十五 65	六十六 66	六十七 67	六十八 68	六十九 69
七十 *qīshí* 70	七十一 71	七十二 72	七十三 73	七十四 74	七十五 75	七十六 76	七十七 77	七十八 78	七十九 79
八十 *bāshí* 80	八十一 81	八十二 82	八十三 83	八十四 84	八十五 85	八十六 86	八十七 87	八十八 88	八十九 89
九十 *jiǔshí* 90	九十一 91	九十二 92	九十三 93	九十四 94	九十五 95	九十六 96	九十七 97	九十八 98	九十九 99
一百 *yībǎi* 100									

For 200, one can either say 二百 **èr bǎi** or 两百 **liǎng bǎi**.

Numbers and arithmetic expressions

零	*líng*	zero
一	*yī*	one
二	*èr*	two
三	*sān*	three
四	*sì*	four
五	*wǔ*	five
六	*liù*	six
七	*qī*	seven
八	*bā*	eight
九	*jiǔ*	nine
十	*shí*	ten
百	*bǎi*	hundred
加	*jiā*	to add; plus
减	*jiǎn*	to subtract; minus
乘	*chéng*	to multiply; times
等于	*děngyú*	equal
几	*jǐ*	how many; how much
多少	*duōshao*	how many; how much

NOTE   Idiomatically, the word 几 *jǐ* refers to a number less than ten, while the word 多少 *duōshao* refers to any number.

EXERCISE 7·1

Answer the following questions according to the example given.

EXAMPLE   一加二等于几？ *Yī jiā èr děngyú jǐ?*

一加二等于三。 *Yī jiā èr děngyú sān.*

1. 六加二等于几？ *Liù jiā èr děngyú jǐ?*

_____

2. 四加十等于多少？ *Sì jiā shí děngyú duōshao?*

_____

3. 九加一等于多少？ *Jiǔ jiā yi děngyú duōshao?*

_____

4. 二加七等于几？ *Èr jiā qī děngyú jǐ?*

_____

5. 八十六加四等于多少？ *Bāshíliù jiā sì děngyú duōshao?*

_____

6. 二十加三十五等于多少？ *Èrshí jiā sānshíwǔ děngyú duōshao?*

_____

EXERCISE 7·2

Answer the following questions according to the example given.

EXAMPLE   二十减一等于多少？ *Èrshí jiǎn yī děngyú duōshao?*
二十减一等于十九。 *Èrshí jiǎn yī děngyú shíjiǔ.*

1. 八减六等于几？ *Bā jiǎn liù děngyú jǐ?*

_____

2. 十减三等于多少？ *Shí jiǎn sān děngyú duōshao?*

_____

3. 七减二等于几？ *Qī jiǎn èr děngyú jǐ?*

_____

4. 九减五等于多少？ *Jiǔ jiǎn wǔ děngyú duōshao?*

_____

5. 三十四减二十一等于多少？ *Sānshísì jiǎn èrshíyī děngyú duōshao?*

_____

6. 九十八减十八等于多少？ *Jiǔshíbā jiǎn shíbā děngyú duōshao?*

_____

EXERCISE 7·3

Answer the following questions according to the example given.

EXAMPLE   一乘二等于几？ *Yī chéng èr děngyú jǐ?*
一乘二等于二。 *Yī chéng èr děngyú èr.*

1. 二乘四等于几？ *Èr chéng sì děngyú jǐ?*

_____

2. 三乘三等于几？ *Sān chéng sān děngyú jǐ?*

_____

3. 七乘一等于几？ *Qī chéng yī děngyú jǐ?*

_____

4. 五乘二等于多少？ *Wǔ chéng èr děngyú duōshao?*

_____

5. 六乘九等于多少？ *Liù chéng jiǔ děngyú duōshao?*

_____

6. 四十乘七等于多少？ *Sìshí chéng qī děngyú duōshao?*

_____

EXERCISE

7·4

翻译成中文 **Fānyì chéng Zhōngwén** *Translate into Chinese and pinyin.*

1. What does 3 plus 4 equal?

_____

2. 15 plus 27 equals 42.

_____

3. 70 plus 20 equals 90.

_____

4. 60 plus 40 equals 100.

_____

5. 9 minus 8 equals 1.

_____

6. What does 36 minus 4 equal?

_____

7. 10 minus 1 equals 9.

_____

8. 31 minus 23 equals 8.

_____

9. What does 2 times 4 equal?

_____

10. 10 times 4 equals 40.

_____

11. 9 times 8 equals 72.

_____

12. What does 20 times 3 equal?

_____

你知道吗? *Nǐ zhīdao ma? Do you know?*

人口 **rénkǒu** *Population numbers*

2011 年 (*nián*, year):

- 中国有 (*yǒu*, to have) 十三亿 (*yì*, hundred million) 人口 (*rénkǒu*, population)。
- 印度有十一亿人口。
- 美国有三点 (*diǎn*, point) 一亿人口。
- 俄国有一点四亿人口。
- 日本有一点三亿人口。

Sentences with a nominal predicate • Expressing age • Telling time

SUBJECT +	PREDICATE	
	(NOMINAL PHRASE)	
他爸爸 *Tā bàba*	四十六岁。 *sìshíliù suì.*	His father is 46 years old.
现在 *Xiànzài*	两点钟。 *liǎng diǎn zhōng.*	It's two o'clock now.

Expressing age

When asking about age, different questions are used for children, teenagers, adults, and elderly people. For elderly people especially, we use a polite form.

For young kids
你几岁? *Nǐ jǐ suì?*   How old are you?
我六岁。*Wǒ liù suì.*   I'm 6 years old.

For teenagers or adults
你/您多大? *Nǐ / nín duōdà?*   How old are you?
我十八岁。*Wǒ shíbā suì.*   I'm 18 years old.

For elderly people
您多大岁数? *Nín duōdà suìshu?*   How old are you?
我八十六岁。*Wǒ bāshíliù suì.*   I'm 86 years old.

NOTE   In the expressions for elderly people, the word 岁 *suì* is used in the answer, and **not** the word 岁数 *suìshu*.

生词	SHĒNGCÍ (VOCABULARY)				

Asking about age

请问	*qǐngwèn*	**May I ask?**	岁数	*suìshu*	**age; years**
今年	*jīnnián*	**this year**	姑娘	*gūniang*	**girl**
您	*nín*	**you (*polite*)**	朋友	*péngyou*	**friend**
多大	*duōdà*	**how old**	老	*lǎo*	**old**
岁	*suì*	**year (of age)**	小	*xiǎo*	**little; small; young**

What to use? Match the words on the left column with those on the right.

1. _____ For a 75-year-old lady

   a. 小朋友，你今年几岁？

     Xiǎo péngyou, nǐ jīnnián jǐ suì?

2. _____ For a 36-year-old gentleman

   b. 请问，小姐，你今年多大？

     Qǐngwèn, xiǎojie, nǐ jīnnián duōdà?

3. _____ For a 7-year-old girl

   c. 请问，老先生，您今年多大岁数？

     Qǐngwèn, lǎo xiānsheng, nín jīnnián duōdà suìshu?

4. _____ For a 28-year-old woman

   d. 小姑娘，你今年几岁？

     Xiǎo gūniang, nǐ jīnnián jǐ suì?

5. _____ For a 5-year-old boy

   e. 请问，先生，您今年多大？

     Qǐngwèn, xiānsheng, nín jīnnián duōdà?

6. _____ For an 86-year-old man

   f. 请问，老太太，您今年多大岁数？

     Qǐngwèn, lǎo tàitai, nín jīnjián duōdà suìshu?

Answer the following questions as appropriate for you. Answers may vary.

1. 您今年多大？ *Nín jīnnián duōdà?*

_____

2. 您爷爷和奶奶今年多大岁数？ *Nín yéye hé nǎinai jīnnián duōdà suìshu?*

_____

3. 您爸爸和妈妈今年多大？ *Nín bàba hé māma jīnnián duōdà?*

_____

4. 您先生/太太今年多大？ *Nín xiānsheng/tàitai jīnnián duōdà?*

_____

5. 您哥哥/弟弟今年多大？ *Nín gēge/dìdi jīnnián duōdà?*

_____

6. 您姐姐/妹妹今年多大？ *Nín jiějie/mèimei jīnnián duōdà?*

_____

7. 您儿子/女儿今年几岁？ *Nín érzi/nǚ'ér jīnnián jǐ suì?*

_____

Telling time

现在几点钟?	*Xiànzài jǐ diǎn zhōng?*	What time is it now?
现在三点十分。	*Xiànzài sān diǎn shí fēn.*	It is 10 past 3.

1:00	一点钟 *yì diǎn zhōng*
2:00	两点钟 *liǎng diǎn zhōng*
2:05	两点零五分 *liǎng diǎn líng wǔ fēn*
2:15	两点十五分 *liǎng diǎn shíwǔ fēn* = 两点一刻 *liǎng diǎn yí kè*
2:20	两点二十分 *liǎng diǎn èrshí fēn*
2:30	两点三十分 *liǎng diǎn sānshí fēn* = 两点半 *liǎng diǎn bàn*
2:45	两点四十五分 *liǎng diǎn sìshíwǔ fēn* = 两点三刻 *liǎng diǎn sān kè*
2:55	两点五十五分 *liǎng diǎn wǔshíwǔ fēn*
8:15 a.m.	早上/上午八点一刻 *zǎoshang /shàngwǔ bā diǎn yí kè*
12:00 p.m.	中午十二点钟 *zhōngwǔ shí'èr diǎn zhōng*
2:30 p.m.	下午两点半 *xiàwǔ liǎng diǎn bàn*
8:45 p.m.	晚上八点三刻 *wǎnshang bā diǎn sān kè*
12:00 a.m.	半夜十二点钟 *bànyè shí'èr diǎn zhōng*

NOTE   To express the hour, the word 钟 *zhōng* (time) is optional.

生词　SHĒNGCÍ (VOCABULARY)

Time expressions

现在	*xiànzài*	now; nowadays
钟	*zhōng*	time; clock; bell
点	*diǎn*	o'clock
两	*liǎng*	two (usually goes with a measure word)
分	*fēn*	minute
刻	*kè*	a quarter
半	*bàn*	half
半夜	*bànyè*	midnight

EXERCISE
8·3

Match the expressions of time with their Chinese counterparts.

1. _____ 2:20 p.m.

2. _____ 1:30 p.m.

3. _____ 5:05 p.m.

4. _____ 12:00 p.m.

5. _____ 7:25 a.m.

6. _____ 11:02 a.m.

7. _____ 2:15 p.m.

a. 下午五点零五分 *xiàwǔ wǔ diǎn líng wǔ fēn*

b. 下午两点二十分 *xiàwǔ liǎng diǎn èrshí fēn*

c. 中午十二点钟 *zhōngwǔ shí'èr diǎn zhōng*

d. 上午七点二十五分 *shàngwǔ qī diǎn èrshíwǔ fēn*

e. 上午十一点零二分 *shàngwǔ shíyī diǎn líng èr fēn*

f. 下午一点半　*xiàwǔ yī diǎn bàn*

g. 早上六点三刻 *zǎoshang liù diǎn sān kè*

8. _____ 10:35 a.m.   h. 下午三点半 xiàwǔ sān diǎn bàn

9. _____ 6:45 a.m.   i. 晚上九点十分 wǎnshang jiǔ diǎn shí fēn

10. _____ 3:30 p.m.   j. 半夜十二点钟 bànyè shí'èr diǎn zhōng

11. _____ 9:10 p.m.   k. 上午十点三十五分 shàngwǔ shí diǎn sānshíwǔ fēn

12. _____ 12:00 a.m.   l. 下午两点一刻 xiàwǔ liǎng diǎn yí kè

EXERCISE
8·4

Answer the question according to the picture of the clock given.

EXAMPLE   现在几点?   *Xiànzài jǐ diǎn?*

               现在两点。   *Xiànzài liǎng diǎn.*

1. _____

2. _____

3. _____

4. _____

5. _____

6. _____

7. _____

8. _____

翻译成中文 **Fānyì chéng Zhōngwén**   *Translate into Chinese and pinyin.*

1. I'm 20 years old.

_____

2. How old will your grandfather be this year?

_____

3. Hello little girl! How old will you be this year?

_____

4. My younger sister will be 18 years old this year.

_____

5. It is 9 o'clock now.

_____

6. It is midnight now.

_____

7 It is 8:15 now.

_____

8. What time is it now?

_____

你知道吗? *Nǐ zhīdao ma? Do you know?*

这些 (zhèxiē) 名人 (míngrén) 几岁/ 多大 / 多大岁数? *How old are these famous people?*

- Mark Zuckerberg 是 1984 年生的。他今年多大?
- 姚明 (Yáo Míng) 是 1980 年生的。他今年多大?
- 她几岁? When Tatum O'Neal, the youngest Oscar winner, won the Oscar for "Paper Moon", 她才 (*cái*, only) 十岁!
- 他已经 (*yǐjīng*, already) 多大岁数了? According to the legend, when Laozi (老子 *Lǎozǐ*, which literally means "old son") was born, 他已经八十一岁了!

Years, months, dates, days of the week • Expressing dates

·9·

Years, months, dates, days of the week

年 *nián* years

To express years, 年 is always placed after the numbers.

二零二五年	*èrlíng'èrwǔ nián*	the year 2025
一七七六年	*yīqīqīliù nián*	the year 1776
一九九四年	*yījiǔjiǔsì nián*	the year 1994

Question:	那是哪一年? *Nà shì nǎ yī nián?*	What year was that?
Answer:	那是二零零八年。 *Nà shì èrlínglíngbā nián.*	That was 2008.

月 *yuè* months

Months in Chinese do not have names as they do in English (e. g., January) and some other languages. Rather, January is simply "first month," February is "second month," and so forth.

一月 *Yīyuè*	January (first month)
二月 *Èryuè*	February
十二月 Shí'èryuè	December

Question:	现在 (是) 几月? *Xiànzài (shì) jǐ yuè?*	What month is it now?
Answer:	现在二月。 *Xiànzài Èryuè.*	It is now February.

日/号 *rì/hào* dates

Dates are expressed by a number, from 1 to 31, followed by the word 日 *rì* or 号 *hào*. In spoken Chinese 号 *hào* is used more often. It is less formal than 日 *rì*,

一日 / 一号 *yī rì / yī hào*	the 1st
二日 / 二号 *èr rì / èr hào*	the 2nd
三十日 / 三十号 *sānshí rì / sānshí hào*	the 30th
三十一日 / 三十一号 *sānshíyī rì / sānshí yī hào*	the 31st

Question:	今天几号? *Jīntiān jǐ hào?*	What is the date today?
Answer:	今天十六号。 *Jīntiān shíliù hào.*	Today is the 16th.

星期 *xīngqī* days of the week

Days of the week, except for Sunday, are expressed by 星期 *Xīngqī* "week," followed by numbers from *"one"* to *"six."*

星期一 *Xīngqīyī*	Monday
星期二 *Xīngqī'èr*	Tuesday
星期三 *Xīngqīsān*	Wednesday
星期四 *Xīngqīsì*	Thursday
星期五 *Xīngqīwǔ*	Friday
星期六 *Xīngqīliù*	Saturday
星期日 / 星期天 *Xīngqīrì / Xīngqītiān*	Sunday

Question: 今天星期几? *Jīntiān Xīngqī jǐ?* What day is it today?
Answer: 今天星期四。*Jīntiān Xīngqīsì.* Today is Thursday.

月, 日, 星期 *yuè, rì, xīngqī* months, dates, days of the week

The Chinese word order for expressing the date and days of the week is the opposite of its English counterpart.

Question: 今天几月几号, 星期几? *Jīntiān jǐ yuè jǐ hào, Xīngqī jǐ?* What is the date, and what day is it today?

Answer: 今天二月十六号, 星期四。 *Jīntiān Èryuè shíliù hào, Xīngqīsì.* Today is Thursday, February 16.

生词 SHĒNGCÍ (VOCABULARY)

More time expressions

年	*nián*	**year**	号	*hào*	**date (*informal*)**
去年	*qùnián*	**last year**	星期	*xīngqī*	**week**
明年	*míngnián*	**next year**	这个	*zhège*	**this (one)**
月	*yuè*	**month**	上个	*shàngge*	**last**
昨天	*zuótiān*	**yesterday**	下个	*xiàge*	**next**
日	*rì*	**date**			

Expressions of day, year, month, and week for immediate past, present, and immediate future

PAST	NOW	FUTURE
昨天 *zuótiān* yesterday	**今天** **jīntiān** **today**	明天 *míngtiān* tomorrow
去年 *qùnián* last year	**今年** **jīnnián** **this year**	明年 *míngnián* next year
上个月 *shàngge yuè* last month	**这个月** **zhège yuè** **this month**	下个月 *xiàge yuè* next month
上个星期 *shàngge xīngqī* last week	**这个星期** **zhège xīngqī** **this week**	下个星期 *xiàge xīngqī* next week

Give the Chinese and pinyin translations for the words in the following table. An example has been provided for you.

yesterday	今天 jīntiān today	tomorrow
last year	this year	next year
last month	this month	next month
last week	this week	next week

Answer the following questions according to real situations. Answers may vary.

1. 去年是哪一年？今年是哪一年？明年是哪一年？ *Qùnián shì nǎ yì nián? Jīnnián shì nǎ yì nián? Míngnián shì nǎ yì nián?*

_____

2. 昨天几号？今天几号？明天几号？ *Zuótiān jǐ hào? Jīntiān jǐ hào? Míngtiān jǐ hào?*

_____

3. 昨天星期几？今天星期几？明天星期几？ *Zuótiān Xīngqī jǐ? Jīntiān Xīngqī jǐ? Míngtiān Xīngqī jǐ?*

_____

4. 这个月五号星期几？ *Zhège yuè wǔ hào Xīngqī jǐ?*

_____

5. 上个星期六几月几号？ *Shàngge Xīngqīliù jǐ yuè jǐ hào?*

_____

6. 下个月二十日星期几？ *Xiàge yuè èrshí rì Xīngqī jǐ?*

_____

7. 下个星期五几月几日？ *Xiàge Xīngqīwǔ jǐ yuè jǐ rì?*

_____

8. 今天几月几号？ *Jīntiān jǐ yuè jǐ hào?*

_____

Everyday words

的	*de*	structural particle
生日	*shēngri*	birthday

NOTE   The particle 的 *de* is used to indicate possession or ownership. The phrase 你的 *nǐ de* and 你爷爷的 *nǐ yéye de* mean *your* and *your grandfather's* respectively. Please see Lesson 14 for a further explanation.

EXERCISE
9·3

Answer the following questions according to real situations. Answers may vary.

1. 你的生日几月几号？ *Nǐ de shēngri jǐ yuè jǐ hào?*

_____

2. 你爷爷的生日几月几号？ *Nǐ yéye de shēngri jǐ yuè jǐ hào?*

_____

3. 你妈妈的生日几月几号？ *Nǐ māma de shēngri jǐ yuè jǐ hào?*

_____

4. 你朋友的生日几月几号？ *Nǐ péngyou de shēngri jǐ yuè jǐ hào?*

_____

5. 你有哥哥吗？他的生日几月几号？ *Nǐ yǒu gēge ma? Tā de shēngri jǐ yuè jǐ hào?*

_____

6. 你有弟弟吗？他的生日几月几号？ *Nǐ yǒu dìdi ma? Tā de shēngri jǐ yuè jǐ hào?*

_____

7. 你有姐姐吗？她的生日几月几号？ *Nǐ yǒu jiějie ma? Tā de shēngri jǐ yuè jǐ hào?*

_____

8. 你有妹妹吗？她的生日几月几号？ *Nǐ yǒu mèimei ma? Tā de shēngri jǐ yuè jǐ hào?*

_____

9. 你有儿子吗？他的生日几月几号？ *Nǐ yǒu érzi ma? Tā de shēngri jǐ yuè jǐ hào?*

_____

10. 你有女儿吗？她的生日几月几号？ *Nǐ yǒu nǚ'ér ma? Tā de shēngri jǐ yuè jǐ hào?*

_____

EXERCISE

9·4

翻译成中文 **Fānyì chéng Zhōngwén**   *Translate into Chinese and pinyin.*

1. What is the date today?

   _____

2. What day of the week is today?

   _____

3. Yesterday was Sunday, February 12.

   _____

4. Today is Monday, February 13.

   _____

5. Tomorrow will be Tuesday, February 14.

   _____

6. What is the date of your mother's birthday?

   _____

7. What year is it now?

   _____

EXERCISE

9·5

Answer the question according to the calendar pictures given.

EXAMPLE   今天四月二十六号。*Jīntiān Sìyuè èrshíliù hào.*

今天几月几号? *Jīntiān jǐ yuè jǐ hào?*

1. _____

2. _____

3. _____

4. **JUNE 27** _____

5. **APRIL 1** _____

6. **MARCH 22** _____

7. **JANUARY 12** _____

8. **JULY 17** _____

你知道吗? *Nǐ zhīdao ma?* Do you know?

一些(yìxiē)名人(míngrén)的生日 *Birthdays of some famous people*

- George Washington 的生日是一七三二年二月二十二日。
- Sun Yat-sen (孙中山 *Sūn Zhōngshān*) 的生日是一八六六年十一月十二日。
- William Shakespeare 的生日是一五六四年四月二十三日。
- Princess Diana 的生日是一九六一年七月一日。
- Mark Twain 的生日是一八三五年十一月三十日。

Numeral measure words • Demonstratives with a numeral measure word • Clothing • Verbs for *put on/wear*

10

Numeral measure words

When a numeral modifies a noun, it needs to occur together with a measure word, which goes before the noun. A numeral cannot directly modify a noun. Each noun has a specific measure word and should be learned together with its measure word.

Numeral word	+ measure word	+ noun	
一 *yī*	个 *gè*	美国人 *Měiguórén*	an American
两 *liǎng*	件 *jiàn*	衬衫 *chènshān*	2 shirts
十二 *shí'èr*	条 *tiáo*	裤子 *kùzi*	12 pairs of pants
二十二 *èrshí'èr*	双 *shuāng*	袜子 *wàzi*	22 pairs of socks

NOTE The numeral word 两 *liǎng* is usually used together with a measure word, but the numeral word 二 *èr* is not used in this way. In English, pants are plural and counted by *pair*, but in Chinese the whole piece counts as one, and it takes 条 *tiáo* as the measure word.

生词 *SHĒNGCÍ* (VOCABULARY)

Commonly used measure words

Indicating individuals

个	*gè*	most frequently used, for general use, e.g., week, person, country
件	*jiàn*	for upper body clothing, e.g., jackets, shirts
条	*tiáo*	for long and thin objects, e.g., pants, skirts
顶	*dǐng*	for things with a top, e.g., hats, caps

Indicating pairs

双	*shuāng*	for shoes and socks
副	*fù*	for gloves or mittens

Indicating one of a pair

只	*zhī*	for shoes, socks, gloves, mittens

NOTE   The measure word 个 *ge* is usually pronounced in the neutral tone in spoken Chinese.

Clothing

The word in the bracket is the measure word that goes with the noun. For shoes, socks, gloves, and mittens, the measure word on the left indicates a pair, while the one on the right indicates one of a pair.

[件]衬衫	*[jiàn] chènshān*	shirt; blouse
[件]上衣	*[jiàn] shàngyī*	jacket
[件]大衣	*[jiàn] dàyī*	topcoat; overcoat
[件]毛衣	*[jiàn] máoyī*	sweater
[条]裤子	*[tiáo] kùzi*	trousers; pants
[双/只]皮鞋	*[shuāng/zhī] píxié*	leather shoe
[双/只]袜子	*[shuāng/zhī] wàzi*	sock
[顶]帽子	*[dǐng] màozi*	hat; cap
[副/只]手套	*[fù/zhī] shǒutào*	glove; mitten
[条]领带	*[tiáo] lǐngdài*	tie
[件]衣服	*[jiàn] yīfu*	clothes
[条]裙子	*[tiáo] qúnzi*	skirt
[件] T-恤衫	*[jiàn]tīxùshān*	T-shirt

EXERCISE
10·1

Match each Chinese phrase with its English translation.

1. _____ 三件上衣
   sān jiàn shàngyī

2. _____ 两条裙子
   liǎng tiáo qúnzi

3. _____ 九条裤子
   jiǔ tiáo kùzi

4. _____ 五只袜子
   wǔ zhī wàzi

5. _____ 一百顶帽子
   yì bǎi dǐng màozi

6. _____ 十二件衬衫
   shí'èr jiàn chènshān

a. five socks

b. one hundred hats

c. three jackets

d. twelve shirts

e. two skirts

f. nine pairs of pants

g. seven sweaters

h. ten overcoats

i. one T-shirt

j. eight pairs of gloves

k. six pairs of leather shoes

l. four ties

7. _____ 六双皮鞋

   liù shuāng píxié

8. _____ 七件毛衣

   qī jiàn máoyī

9. _____ 八副手套

   bā fù shǒutào

10. _____ 四条领带

    sì tiáo lǐngdài

11. _____ 十件大衣

    shí jiàn dàyī

12. _____ 一件 T-恤衫

    yí jiàn tīxùshān

Demonstratives with a numeral measure word

生词 *SHĒNGCÍ* (VOCABULARY)

Everyday words

这	*zhè*	**this; these**
那	*nà*	**that; those**

Demonstratives with a numeral and a measure word

Demonstrative + numeral word + measure word + noun

这	(一)	顶	帽子	this hat
这		顶	帽子	
zhè	*(yī)*	*dǐng*	*màozi*	
那	两	件	衬衫	those two shirts
nà	*liǎng*	*jiàn*	*chènshān*	
这	五	条	裤子	these five pairs of pants
zhè	*wǔ*	*tiáo*	*kùzi*	
那	三	双	袜子	those three pairs of socks
nà	*sān*	*shuāng*	*wàzi*	

NOTE   If the numeral after the demonstrative is *one*, its presence is optional.

Match the numeral measure words with the appropriate nouns.

1. _____ 这十副 *zhè shí fù*   these ten pairs   a. 皮鞋 *píxié*   leather shoes

2. _____ 一个   *yí ge* one   b. 帽子 *màozi*   hats

3. _____ 那一双 *nà yì shuāng* that pair   c. 手套 *shǒutào*   gloves

4. _____ 十二顶 *shí'èr dǐng*   twelve   d. 裙子 *qúnzi*   skirts

5. _____ 这一只 *zhè yì zhī*   this   e. 中国人 *Zhōngguórén* Chinese people

6. _____ 三十二条 *sānshí'èr tiáo* thirty-two   f. 哥哥 *gēge*   older brother

7. _____ 那两件 *nà liǎng jiàn* those two   g. 袜子 *wàzi*   sock

8. _____ 两百个 *liǎng bǎi ge*   two hundred   h. 毛衣 *máoyī*   sweaters

Answer the following questions. Answers may vary.

1. 你有哥哥, 弟弟吗？有几个哥哥, 几个弟弟？ *Nǐ yǒu gēge, dìdi ma? Yǒu jǐ ge gēge, jǐ ge dìdi?*

   _____

2. 你有姐姐, 妹妹吗？有几个姐姐, 几个妹妹？ *Nǐ yǒu jiějie, mèimei ma? Yǒu jǐ ge jiějie, jǐ ge mèimei?*

   _____

3. 你有儿子, 女儿吗？有几个儿子, 几个女儿？ *Nǐ yǒu érzi, nǚ'er ma? Yǒu jǐ ge érzi, jǐ ge nǚ'er?*

   _____

4. 你有帽子吗？有几顶帽子？ *Nǐ yǒu màozi ma? Yǒu jǐ dǐng màozi?*

   _____

5. 你有手套吗？有几副手套？ *Nǐ yǒu shǒutào ma? Yǒu jǐ fù shǒutào?*

   _____

6. 你有领带吗？有多少条领带？ *Nǐ yǒu lǐngdài ma? Yǒu duōshao tiáo lǐngdài?*

   _____

7. 你有几件毛衣？几件衬衫？几件 T-恤衫？ *Nǐ yǒu jǐ jiàn máoyī? Jǐ jiàn chènshān? Jǐ jiàn tīxùshān?*

   _____

8. 你有几双皮鞋？多少双袜子？ *Nǐ yǒu jǐ shuāng píxié? Duōshao shuāng wàzi?*

_____

9. 你有几条裤子？几条裙子？ *Nǐ yǒu jǐ tiáo kùzi? Jǐ tiáo qúnzi?*

_____

10. 你有几件上衣？几件大衣？ *Nǐ yǒu jǐ jiàn shàngyī? Jǐ jiàn dàyī?*

_____

Verbs for *put on/wear*

生词 SHĒNGCÍ (VOCABULARY)		

Everyday words

| 穿 | *chuān* | **to put on; to wear (clothing, shoes, socks)** |
| 戴 | *dài* | **to put on; to wear (hat, tie, gloves)** |

There are two verbs that mean *wear* in Chinese.

穿 CHUĀN		TO PUT ON; TO WEAR (CLOTHING, SHOES, SOCKS)	
衣服 *yīfu*	clothes	**衬衫** *chènshān*	shirt; blouse
T-恤衫 *tīxùshān*	T-shirt	**裤子** *kùzi*	trousers; pants
裙子 *qúnzi*	skirt	**毛衣** *máoyī*	sweater
大衣 *dàyī*	overcoat	**上衣** *shàngyī*	outer upper garment
皮鞋 *píxié*	leather shoe	**袜子** *wàzi*	sock

戴 DÀI		TO PUT ON; TO WEAR (HAT, TIE, GLOVES)
帽子 *màozi*	hat; cap	**领带** *lǐngdài* tie
手套 *shǒutào*	glove; mitten	

EXERCISE 10·4

Answer the following questions according to real situations. Answers may vary.

1. 你这个星期穿T-恤衫吗？ *Nǐ zhège xīngqī chuān tīxùshān ma?*

_____

2. 你这个月穿毛衣吗？ *Nǐ zhè ge yuè chuān máoyī ma?*

_____

3. 你今天穿皮鞋吗？ *Nǐ jīntiān chuān píxié ma?*

_____

4. 你喜欢戴帽子吗？ *Nǐ xǐhuan dài màozi ma?*

_____

5. 你喜欢戴领带吗？ *Nǐ xǐhuan dài lǐngdài ma?*

_____

6. 你星期六和星期天喜欢穿什么衣服？ *Nǐ Xīngqīliù hé Xīngqītiān xǐhuan chuān shénme yīfu?*

_____

7. 你白天穿什么衣服？ *Nǐ báitiān chuān shénme yīfu?*

_____

8. 你晚上穿什么衣服？ *Nǐ wǎnshang chuān shénme yīfu?*

_____

9. 你爸爸喜欢穿什么衣服？ *Nǐ bàba xǐhuan chuān shénme yīfu?*

_____

10. 你朋友喜欢穿什么衣服？ *Nǐ péngyou xǐhuan chuān shénme yīfu?*

_____

EXERCISE 10·5

翻译成中文 **Fānyì chéng Zhōngwén** *Translate into Chinese and pinyin.*

1. My older sister has two skirts and three sweaters.

_____

2. How many Indian jackets do they have now? —They have fifty Indian jackets.

_____

3. My son is wearing a French shirt and a pair of Italian leather shoes today.

_____

4. How many overcoats will you buy today? —I will buy two hundred overcoats.

_____

5. Her friend has two Chinese ties.

_____

6. I don't like that pair of Japanese socks.

_____

7. His father wears an English hat today.

_____

8. Which T-shirt does that American like? —He likes this German T-shirt.

_____

9. How many socks will your mother make next week?

_____

你知道吗? Nǐ zhīdao ma? Do you know?

衣服 yīfu Clothing

- Mary Quant 发明了(fāmíngle, invented) 迷你裙 (mínǐqún, miniskirt)。
- Jacob Davis 和 Levi Strauss 发明了牛仔裤 (niúzǎikù, blue jeans)。
- 孙中山 (Sūn Zhōngshān, Sun Yat-sen) 发明了中山装 (zhōngshānzhuāng, the Mao suit)。
- 中国人发明了唐装 (tángzhuāng, the Tang-style jacket)。
- 中国人也发明了旗袍 (qípáo, cheongsam)。

Lessons 6–10

Select the option in the appropriate column.
Answers may vary.

你现在常喝什么饮料? *Nǐ xiànzài cháng hē shénme yǐnliào?*	常喝 *cháng hē*	不常喝 *bù cháng hē*
1. 水 *shuǐ*	_____	_____
2. 茶 *chá*	_____	_____
3. 牛奶 *niúnǎi*	_____	_____
4. 果汁 *guǒzhī*	_____	_____
5. 可乐 *kělè*	_____	_____
6. 啤酒 *píjiǔ*	_____	_____
7. 豆浆 *dòujiāng*	_____	_____
8. 桔子汁 *júzi zhī*	_____	_____
9. 矿泉水 *kuàngquánshuǐ*	_____	_____
10. 葡萄汁 *pútao zhī*	_____	_____

*Following the example given, turn each of the following statements into a question by replacing the element in **bold** with an appropriate interrogative pronoun.*

什么 **shénme**	谁 **shéi**	哪 **nǎ**	几 **jǐ**
多少 **duōshao**	几岁 **jǐ suì**	多大 **duōdà**	多大岁数 **duōdà suìshu**
几点 **jǐ diǎn**	几号 **jǐ hào**	几月 **jǐ yuè**	星期几 **Xīngqī jǐ**
哪一年 **nǎ yì nián**	几件 **jǐ jiàn**	几条 **jǐ tiáo**	多少双 **duōshao shuāng**

EXAMPLE   他常喝**桔子汁**。   *Tā cháng hē **júzi zhī**.*

他常喝**什么**?   *Tā cháng hē **shénme**?*

1. 他爸爸喜欢喝**果汁**。 *Tā bàba xǐhuan hē **guǒzhī**.*

_____

2. **她爷爷**早上常喝牛奶。 ***Tā yéye** zǎoshang cháng hē niúnǎi.*

_____

3. 你妈妈喜欢喝**意大利**咖啡。 *Nǐ māma xǐhuan hē **Yìdàlì** kāfēi.*

_____

4. **法**国人中午喜欢喝葡萄酒。 ***Fǎ**guórén zhōngwǔ xǐhuan hē pútao jiǔ.*

_____

5. 四加三等于**七**。 *Sì jiā sān děngyú **qī**.*

_____

6. 五乘九等于**四十五**。 *Wǔ chéng jiǔ děngyú **sìshíwǔ**.*

_____

7. 他奶奶今年**八十六岁**。 *Tā nǎinai jīnnián **bāshíliù suì**.*

_____

8. 她儿子去年**两岁**。 *Tā érzi qùnián **liǎng suì**.*

_____

9. 他朋友明年**二十二岁**。 *Tā péngyou míngnián **èrshí'èr suì**.*

_____

10. 明天**二月十九号，星期天**。 *Míngtiān **Èryuè shíjiǔ hào, Xīngqītiān**.*

_____

11. 现在晚上**七点半**。 *Xiànzài wǎnshang **qī diǎn bàn**.*

_____

12. 他太太有一百双袜子。*Tā tàitai yǒu **yì bǎi** shuāng wàzi.*

_____

13. 他们有九件衬衫。*Tāmen yǒu **jiǔ jiàn** chènshān.*

_____

14. 你女儿有五条裙子。*Nǐ nǚ'ér yǒu **wǔ tiáo** qúnzi.*

_____

EXERCISE R2·3

First, complete the sentences with the appropriate measure words (个 **gè,** 件 **jiàn,** 条 **tiáo,** 双 **shuāng,** 只 **zhī,** 顶 **dǐng,** 副 **fù**), and then translate into English. (Note: A measure word can be used more than once.)

1. 他妹妹有十二 _____ 裙子和三十二 _____ 裤子。

   Tā mèimei yǒu shí'èr _____ qúnzi hé sānshí'èr _____ kùzi.

   _____

2. 那 _____ 中国人喜欢这 _____ 衬衫和这 _____
   帽子吗？

   Nà _____ Zhōngguórén xǐhuan zhè _____ chènshān hé zhè

   _____ màozi ma?

   _____

3. 他太太买这两 _____ 上衣, 那三 _____ 皮鞋和那六
   _____ 袜子。

   Tā tàitai mǎi zhè liǎng _____ shàngyī, nà sān _____ píxié hé nà

   liù _____ wàzi.

   _____

4. 我弟弟今天穿一 _____ 毛衣和一 _____ 大衣。

   Wǒ dìdi jīntiān chuān yī _____ máoyī hé yī _____ dàyī.

   _____

5. 你朋友明天戴那一 _____ 领带和那一 _____ 手套吗？

   Nǐ péngyou míngtiān dài nà yī _____ lǐngdài hé nà yī _____

   shǒutào ma?

   _____

Answer the following questions. Answers may vary.

1. 你喜欢喝什么饮料？ *Nǐ xǐhuan hē shénme yǐnliào?*

_____

2. 你早上常吃什么？ *Nǐ zǎoshang cháng chī shénme?*

_____

3. 哪国人喜欢喝豆浆？ *Nǎ guó rén xǐhuan hē dòujiāng?*

_____

4. 你家里人，谁喜欢喝茶？ *Nǐ jiāli rén, shéi xǐhuan hē chá?*

_____

5. 十五减七等于几？ *Shíwǔ jiǎn qī děngyú jǐ?*

_____

6. 八乘九十等于多少？ *Bā chéng jiǔshí děngyú duōshao?*

_____

7. 请问，现在几点钟？ *Qǐngwèn, xiànzài jǐ diǎn zhōng?*

_____

8. 你明天几点上班？ *Nǐ míngtiān jǐ diǎn shàngbān?*

_____

9. 请问，你今年多大？ *Qǐngwèn, nǐ jīnnián duōdà?*

_____

10. 你有爷爷和奶奶吗？他们多大岁数？ *Nǐ yǒu yéye hé nǎinai ma? Tāmen duōdà suìshu?*

_____

11. 你的生日是哪一年？几月几号？ *Nǐ de shēngri shì nǎ yì nián? Jǐ yuè jǐ hào?*

_____

12. 上个星期天几月几号？ *Shàng ge Xīngqītiān jǐ yuè jǐ hào?*

_____

13. 你有弟弟吗？有几个弟弟？ *Nǐ yǒu dìdi ma? Yǒu jǐ ge dìdi?*

_____

14. 你有几件衬衫？ *Nǐ yǒu jǐ jiàn chènshān?*

_____

15. 你明天穿什么？ *Nǐ míngtiān chuān shénme?*

_____

翻译成中文 Fānyì chéng Zhōngwén   *Translate into Chinese and pinyin.*

1. (Among) your family members, who likes drinking coffee?—My father likes drinking coffee.

   _____

   _____

2. What did you eat and drink today?—I ate a hamburger (and) drank a pop.

   _____

   _____

3. What is your nationality?—I am Chinese.

   _____

   _____

4. What does 5 plus 4 equal?—5 plus 4 equals 9.

   _____

   _____

5. What is 400 minus 300?—400 minus 300 equals 100.

   _____

   _____

6. How old was your grandmother last year?—She was 92 years old last year.

   _____

   _____

7. How old will your friend be this year?—He will be 25 years old this year.

   _____

   _____

8. How old will your daughter be next year?—She'll be 5 years old next year.

   _____

   _____

9. What time is it now?—It's half past two now.

   _____

   _____

10. What's the date today? (And) what day is it?—Today is Thursday, February 23.

   _____

   _____

11. What did she wear yesterday?—She wore a T-shirt.

_____

_____

12. What will you wear tomorrow?—I'll wear the French shirt.

_____

_____

True or False? *After reading the following Chinese dialogue, mark the English statements either **true** or **false**.*

Before attending class, David chats with his friend Peter on campus.

D: Peter, 你有几双皮鞋？ Peter, *nǐ yǒu jǐ shuāng píxié?*

P: 我只(*zhǐ*, only) 有一双。 *Wǒ zhǐ yǒu yì shuāng.*

D: 你不喜欢穿皮鞋吗？ *Nǐ bù xǐhuan chuān píxié ma?*

P: 不喜欢。 *Bù xǐhuan.*

D: 你喜欢穿毛衣吗？ *Nǐ xǐhuan chuān máoyī ma?*

P: 喜欢。 *Xǐhuan.*

D: 你有几件毛衣？ *Nǐ yǒu jǐ jiàn máoyī?*

P: 我有三件。 David，你也喜欢穿毛衣吗？ *Wǒ yǒu sān jiàn. David, nǐ yě xǐhuan chuān máoyī ma?*

D: 不喜欢，可是我喜欢戴帽子。 *Bù xǐhuan, kěshì wǒ xǐhuan dài màozi.*

P: 你有几顶帽子？ *Nǐ yǒu jǐ dǐng màozi?*

D: 我有五顶。 *Wǒ yǒu wǔ dǐng.*

P: 对了 *(duìle, that's right)，David，今天几月几号？星期几？ *Duìle*, David, *jīntiān jǐ yuè jǐ hào? Xīngqī jǐ?*

D: 今天六月十八号, 星期五。 *Jīntiān Liùyuè shí bā hào, Xīngqīwǔ.*

P: 明天是我的生日。 *Míngtiān shì wǒ de shēngri.*

D: 是吗？生日快乐 (*kuàilè*, happy)! *Shì ma? Shēngri kuàilè!*

P: 谢谢 (*xièxie*, to thank)！ *Xièxie!*

D: 你今年多大了**？ *Nǐ jīnnián duōdà le?*

See Lesson 28 for further explanation.
*The phrase "对了 *duìle*" is used to change the topic of a conversation.
**Here, the particle "了 *le*" is used to indicate a new situation or changed circumstances.

P: 我今年二十一岁了。 *Wǒ jīnnián èrshíyī suì le.*

D: 好！明天晚上我请 (*qǐng*, to invite) 你吃饺子, 喝啤酒。 *Hǎo! Míngtiān wǎnshang wǒ qǐng nǐ shī jiǎozi, hē píjiǔ.*

D: 谢谢你，David！…… 现在几点了？ *Xièxie nǐ, David! … Xiànzài jǐ diǎn le?*

P: 现在两点二十五分了。 *Xiànzài liǎng diǎn èrshíwǔ fēn le.*

D: 我两点半上课。再见 (*zàijiàn*, goodbye)！ *Wǒ liǎng diǎn bàn shàngkè. Zàijiàn!*

P: 我两点半也上课。再见！ *Wǒ liǎng diǎn bàn yě shàngkè. Zàijiàn!*

1. _____ Peter likes wearing both leather shoes and sweaters.

2. _____ Peter has three pairs of leather shoes and one sweater now.

3. _____ David also likes wearing sweaters.

4. _____ David has five caps or hats.

5. _____ Tomorrow will be Friday, June 18.

6. _____ Peter's birthday will be on Saturday.

7. _____ Peter was 20 years old last year.

8. _____ Peter will treat David to dumplings and beer on his birthday.

9. _____ Both of them will attend class at 2:30 p.m.

Grammar

Vocabulary

Do you know?

Sentences with an adjectival predicate • Elliptical questions with 呢 *ne* • Greetings and descriptions

11

Sentences with an adjectival predicate

In a sentence with an adjectival predicate, the adjective functions as the main part of the predicate. No verb is needed.

SUBJECT	+	PREDICATE		
		(ADVERB[S] + ADJECTIVE)		
他	很	忙。		He is very busy.
Tā	*hěn*	*máng.*		
他	很	忙	吗?	Is he very busy?
Tā	*hěn*	*máng*	*ma?*	
他	不	忙。		He is not busy.
Tā	*bù*	*máng.*		

Elliptical questions with 呢 *ne*

An elliptical question is a question expressed without a predicate. The meaning of this kind of question depends on the context. If there is no context, the particle 呢 *ne* indicates whereabouts, meaning *where*.

Noun/personal pronoun + 呢 *ne*?

Without any context: 他　呢?　　　Where is he?
　　　　　　　　　　Tā　ne?

With a context: 我很忙。　　你呢?　　I'm very busy. What about you?
　　　　　　　Wǒ hěn máng.　Nǐ ne?

73

Greetings and descriptive adjectives

很	hěn	very
忙	máng	busy
呢	ne	particle
好	hǎo	good; fine; well
早	zǎo	morning; early
怎么样	zěnmeyàng	how; how is it going?
有点儿	yǒudiǎnr	a little bit
累	lèi	tired
太	tài	too
身体	shēntǐ	health; body
最近	zuìjìn	recently; these days
还	hái	still; yet
胖	pàng	fat (people)
瘦	shòu	thin
贵	guì	expensive
便宜	piányi	inexpensive
大	dà	big; large
长	cháng	long
短	duǎn	short (length)
漂亮	piàoliang	pretty
难看	nánkàn	ugly
高	gāo	tall; high
矮	ǎi	short (height)

EXERCISE

11·1

Match each Chinese sentence with its English equivalents.

1. _____ 你妈妈最近好吗？

   Nǐ māma zuìjìn hǎo ma?

2. _____ 您早！

   Nín zǎo!

3. _____ 您好吗？

   Nín hǎo ma?

4. _____ 您爸爸身体怎么样？

   Nín bàba shēntǐ zěnmeyàng?

5. _____ 还好。你呢？

   Hái hǎo. Nǐ ne?

6. _____ 我很好。你呢？

   Wǒ hěn hǎo. Nǐ ne?

a. How are you?

b. Have you been busy recently?

c. How has your mother been recently?

d. I'm not too well, (and I'm) a little bit tired.

e. I'm very well, and you?

f. Good morning!

g. I'm still OK. And you?

h. I'm not busy, and you?

i. How is your father's health?

j. How have you been doing recently?

7. _____ 我不太好，有点儿累。

   Wǒ bú tài hǎo, yǒu diǎnr lèi.

8. _____ 你最近怎么样？

   Nǐ zuìjìn zěnmeyàng?

9. _____ 你最近忙吗？

   Nǐ zuìjìn máng ma?

10. _____ 我不忙，你呢？

    Wo bù máng, nǐ ne?

Answer the following questions according to real situations. Answers may vary.

1. 您好吗？ *Nín hǎo ma?*

   _____

2. 您忙吗？ *Nín máng ma?*

   _____

3. 你最近怎么样？ *Nǐ zuìjìn zěnmeyàng?*

   _____

4. 您早！ *Nín zǎo!*

   _____

5. 你最近很累吗？ *Nǐ zuìjìn hěn lèi ma?*

   _____

6. 你妈妈最近身体好吗？ *Nǐ māma zuìjìn shēntǐ hǎo ma?*

   _____

7. 你爸爸最近身体怎么样？ *Nǐ bàba zuìjìn shēntǐ zěnmeyàng?*

   _____

8. 你朋友最近很忙吗？ *Nǐ péngyou zuìjìn hěn máng ma?*

   _____

Following the example given, answer the questions with the appropriate antonyms.

EXAMPLE   你爸爸很高吗？   不，我爸爸很矮。

1. 你妈妈很矮吗？ *Nǐ māma hěn ǎi ma?*

_____

2. 你家很大吗？ *Nǐ jiā hěn dà ma?*

_____

3. 你爸爸很瘦吗？ *Nǐ bàba hěn shòu ma?*

_____

4. 美国水果很贵吗？ *Měiguó shuǐguǒ hěn guì ma?*

_____

5. 现在白天很长吗？ *Xiànzài báitiān hěn cháng ma?*

_____

6. 你朋友很难看吗？ *Nǐ péngyou hěn nánkàn ma?*

_____

Answer the following questions with the particle 呢 **ne**. *Answers may vary.*

1. 我爸爸身体很好。你爸爸呢？ *Wǒ bàba shēn hěn hǎo. Nǐ bàba ne?*

_____

2. 我是美国人。你呢？ *Wǒ shì Měiguórén. Nǐ ne?*

_____

3. 我有一个哥哥和一个妹妹。你呢？ *Wǒ yǒu yí gè gēge hé yí gè mèimei. Nǐ ne?*

_____

4. 我喜欢吃水果。你呢？ *Wǒ xǐhuan chī shuǐguǒ. Nǐ ne?*

_____

5. 意大利人喜欢喝咖啡。中国人呢？ *Yìdàlìrén xǐhuan hē kāfēi. Zhōngguórén ne?*

_____

6. 英国人喜欢吃三明治。德国人呢？ *Yīngguórén xǐhuan chī sānmíngzhì. Déguórén ne?*

_____

7. 我今年十八岁。你呢？ *Wǒ jīnnián shíbā suì. Nǐ ne?*

_____

8. 我的生日是六月八日。你的生日呢？ *Wǒ de shēngri shì Liùyuè bā rì. Nǐ de shēngri ne?*

_____

9. 我喜欢穿蓝裤子和白衬衫。你呢？ *Wǒ xǐhuan chuān lán kùzi hé bái chènshān. Nǐ ne?*

_____

10. 我家里有六把椅子。你家里呢？ *Wǒ jiālǐ yǒu liù bǎ yǐzi. Nǐ jiālǐ ne?*

_____

生词 **SHĒNGCÍ (VOCABULARY)**

Everyday word

可是   *kěshì*   **but; however**

翻译成中文 Fānyì chéng Zhōngwén   *Translate into Chinese and pinyin.*

1. How has your husband been doing recently?—He is doing OK.

_____

2. How have you guys been doing recently?—We're all doing very well.

_____

3. Good morning! How are you?—Not too well. I'm a bit tired today.

_____

4. How has your grandfather's health been recently?—His health is not too good.

_____

5. Are you busy?—I'm very busy. And you?

_____

6. My grandmother is very well. What about your grandmother?

_____

7. His father is very fat, but his mother is very thin.

_____

8. Is that hat too big?—No, that hat is too small!

_____

9. This shirt is very expensive, but that shirt is very cheap.

_____

10. My older brother is very short, but my younger brother is very tall.

_____

11. This short tie is very ugly.

_____

12. This long skirt is very pretty.

_____

你知道吗? *Nǐ zhīdao ma?* *Do you know?*

实体描述 *shítǐ miáoshù Physical descriptions*

◆ 邓小平 (*Dèng Xiǎopíng*, Deng Xiaoping) 很矮，拿破仑 (*Nápòlùn*, Napoleon)也很矮。

◆ 姚明 (*Yáo Míng*, Yao Ming) 很高，可是 Jeremy Lin 不很高。

◆ Audrey Hepburn 很漂亮，James Dean 也很漂亮。

◆ 三十年以前，中国的房子很便宜，可是现在很贵！

◆ Manuel Uribe Garza (who once weighed 1320 lbs) 二十岁以前不很胖，可是后来 (*hòulái*, later on)他很胖！

Affirmative-negative questions • Moods and tastes

Affirmative-negative questions

Subj. +	Adj. +	不 +		Adj. ?		
你	忙	不		忙? = 你忙吗?		Are you
Nǐ	*máng*	*bu máng?*				busy?

Subj. +	V +	不/没 +		V +	Obj. ?		
他们	是	不		是	中国人? = 他们是中国人吗?	Are they
Tāmen	*shì*	*bu*		*shì*	*Zhōngguórén?*	Chinese?
她	吃	不		吃	饺子? = 她吃饺子吗?	Does she eat
Tā	*chī*	*bu*		*chī*	*jiǎojzi?*	dumplings?
你	有	没		有	姐姐? = 你有姐姐吗?	Do you have
Nǐ	*yǒu*	*méi*		*yǒu*	*jiějie?*	any older sisters?

生词　SHĒNGCÍ (VOCABULARY)

Moods and tastes

高兴	*gāoxìng*	delighted
难过	*nánguò*	sad
紧张	*jǐnzhāng*	nervous
生气	*shēngqì*	angry
着急	*zháojí*	anxious
激动	*jīdòng*	excited
满意	*mǎnyì*	satisfied
快乐	*kuàilè*	happy
失望	*shīwàng*	disappointed
烦恼	*fánnǎo*	worried
甜	*tián*	sweet
酸	*suān*	sour
苦	*kǔ*	bitter
辣	*là*	hot; spicy
咸	*xián*	salty

Turn the following 吗 **ma** *questions into affirmative-negative questions according to the example given.*

EXAMPLE   你有爷爷吗？   *Nǐ yǒu yéye ma?*

你有没有爷爷？   *Nǐ yǒu méiyǒu yéye?*

1. 你有弟弟和哥哥吗？ *Nǐ yǒu dìdi hé gēge ma?*

_____

2. 他有姐姐和妹妹吗？ *Tā yǒu jiějie hé mèimei ma?*

_____

3. 你弟弟高吗？ *Nǐ dìdi gāo ma?*

_____

4. 你儿子今天穿毛衣吗？ *Nǐ érzi jīntiān chuān máoyī ma?*

_____

5. 你是美国人吗？ *Nǐ shì Měiguórén ma?*

_____

6. 你爷爷最近忙吗？ *Nǐ yéye zuìjìn máng ma?*

_____

7. 你爸爸看电视吗？ *Nǐ bàba kàn diànshì ma?*

_____

8. 你今天累吗？ *Nǐ jīntiān lèi ma?*

_____

9. 你朋友喝茶吗？ *Nǐ péngyou hē chá ma?*

_____

10. 你奶奶吃披萨饼吗？ *Nǐ nǎinai chī pīsàbǐng ma?*

_____

Turn the following affirmative-negative questions into 吗 **ma** questions according to the example given.

EXAMPLE   你爸爸现在紧张不紧张？ *Nǐ bàba xiànzài jǐnzhāng bu jǐnzhāng?*

你爸爸现在紧张吗？ *Nǐ bàba xiànzài jǐnzhāng ma?*

1. 你奶奶今天高兴不高兴？ *Nǐ nǎinai jīntiān gāoxìng bu gāoxìng?*

_____

2. 她朋友昨天难过不难过？ *Tā péngyou zuótiān nánguò bu nánguò?*

_____

3. 英国人现在紧张不紧张？ *Yīngguórén xiànzài jǐnzhāng bu jǐnzhāng?*

_____

4. 他妈妈上个星期一着急不着急？ *Tā māma shàng ge Xīngqīyī zháojí bu zháojí?*

_____

5. 你哥哥昨天激动不激动？ *Nǐ gēge zuótiān jīdòng bu jīdòng?*

_____

6. 他儿子现在烦恼不烦恼？ *Tā érzi xiànzài fánnǎo bu fánnǎo?*

_____

7. 你太太今年快乐不快乐？ *Nǐ tàitai jīnnián kuàilè bu kuàilè?*

_____

8. 她先生最近满意不满意？ *Tā xiānsheng zuìjìn mǎnyì bu mǎnyì?*

_____

9. 你爷爷失望不失望？ *Nǐ yéye shīwàng bu shīwàng?*

_____

10. 她姐姐生气不生气？ *Tā jiějie shēngqì bu shēngqì?*

_____

生词　SHĒNGCÍ (VOCABULARY)

Everyday words

杯	*bēi*	glass; cup
菜	*cài*	dish (of Chinese food)
些	*xiē*	some; more than one
这些	*zhè xiē*	these
那些	*nà xiē*	those

EXERCISE
12·3

Change the following statements into affirmative-negative questions according to the example given.

EXAMPLE   这个苹果很甜。   这个苹果甜不甜？

Zhè ge píngguǒ hěn tián.   *Zhè ge píngguǒ tián bu tián?*

1. 那杯果汁很酸。 *Nà bēi guǒzhī hěn suān.*

_____

2. 这些西瓜很甜。 *Zhè xiē xīguā hěn tián.*

_____

3. 那些柠檬很酸。 *Nà xiē níngméng hěn suān.*

_____

4. 这个菜很辣。 *Zhè ge cài hěn là.*

_____

5. 那杯咖啡很苦。 *Nà bēi kāfēi hěn kǔ.*

_____

6. 这些饺子很咸。 *Zhè xiē jiǎozi hěn xián.*

_____

7. 这杯葡萄酒很甜。 *Zhè bēi pútáo jiǔ hěn tián.*

_____

EXERCISE
12·4

翻译成中文 **Fānyì chéng Zhōngwén**   *Translate into Chinese and pinyin using affirmative-negative questions.*

1. Is his wife satisfied now?

_____

2. Are these oranges sweet?

_____

3. Is their daughter happy now?

_____

4. Was that Chinese guy sad yesterday?

_____

5. Is this wine bitter?

_____

6. Are you Russian?

_____

7. Are you busy this week?

_____

8. Do you eat hamburgers?

_____

9. Do you have any Chinese friends?

_____

10. Do you guys drink coffee?

_____

你知道吗? *Nǐ zhīdao ma?* Do you know?

中国人喜欢吃什么菜? *Zhōngguórén xǐhuan chī shénme cài?* What food do Chinese like to eat?

◆ 北方人 (*běifāngrén*, northerner) 喜欢吃咸的东西 (*dōngxi*, stuff)。

◆ 南方人 (*nánfāngrén*, southerner) 喜欢吃甜的东西。

◆ 四川人 (*Sìchuānrén*, Sichuan people) 和湖南人 (*Húnánrén*, Hunan people) 喜欢吃辣的东西。

◆ 山西人 (*Shānxīrén*, Shanxi people) 喜欢吃酸的东西。

Alternative questions • Occupations

Alternative questions

When forming a question involving two or more choices, the word 还是 *háishì* "or" is used.

QUESTION: **CHOICE A** + 还是 + **CHOICE B?**

他是老师还是学生? *Tā shì lǎoshī háishì xuésheng?*	Is he a teacher or a student?

ANSWER: **CHOICE A OR CHOICE B.**

他是老师。 *Tā shì lǎoshī.*	He is a teacher.

or

他是学生。 *Tā shì xuésheng.*	He is a student.

生词　SHĒNGCÍ (VOCABULARY)

Making a choice

还是	*háishì*	**or**

Occupations

老师	*lǎoshī*	**teacher**		商人	*shāngrén*	**businessperson**
学生	*xuésheng*	**student**		军人	*jūnrén*	**soldier**
医生	*yīshēng*	**doctor**		警察	*jǐngchá*	**police officer**
护士	*hùshi*	**nurse**		服务员	*fúwùy uán*	**waiter**
工人	*gōngrén*	**worker**		演员	*yǎnyuán*	**actor**
农民	*nóngmín*	**farmer**		运动员	*yùndòngyuán*	**athlete**
职员	*zhíyuán*	**clerk**		工程师	*gōngchéngshī*	**engineer**
作家	*zuòjiā*	**writer**		音乐家	*yīnyuèjiā*	**musician**
律师	*lùshī*	**lawyer; attorney**		音乐	*yīnyuè*	**music**
经理	*jīnglǐ*	**manager**				

EXERCISE
13·1

Match each English word with its Chinese equivalents.

1. _____ manager   a. 警察

2. _____ musician   b. 医生

3. _____ lawyer   c. 工程师

4. _____ doctor   d. 演员

5. _____ writer   e. 经理

6. _____ engineer   f. 律师

7. _____ police officer   g. 作家

8. _____ actor   h. 音乐家

9. _____ businessperson   i. 工人

10. _____ clerk   j. 运动员

11. _____ worker   k. 服务员

12. _____ nurse   l. 商人

13. _____ soldier   m. 农民

14. _____ waiter   n. 护士

15. _____ athlete   o. 军人

16. _____ farmer   p. 职员

EXERCISE
13·2

Answer the following questions according to real situations.

1. 你是老师还是学生？ *Nǐ shì lǎoshī háishì xuésheng?*

_____

2. Meryl Streep 是演员还是服务员？ Meryl Streep *shì yǎnyuán háishì fúwùyuán?*

_____

3. Steve Jobs 是工程师还是职员？ Steve Jobs *shì gōngchéngshī háishì zhíyuán?*

_____

4. Warren Buffett 是商人还是工人？ Warren Buffett *shì shāngrén háishì gōngrén?*

_____

5. Dr. Zhivago 是医生还是护士？ Dr. Zhivago *shì yīshēng háishì hùshi?*

_____

6. Colin Powell 是军人还是经理？ Colin Powell *shì jūnrén háishì jīnglǐ?*

_____

7. Yao Ming 是农民还是运动员？ Yao Ming *shì nóngmín háishì yùndòngyuán?*

_____

8. Beethoven 是律师还是音乐家？ Beethoven *shì lǜshī háishì yīnyuèjiā?*

_____

9. Mark Twain 是作家还是警察？ Mark Twain *shì zuòjiā háishì jǐngchá?*

_____

生词　*SHĒNGCÍ* (VOCABULARY)

Everyday words

| 想 | *xiǎng* | **to want** |
| 当 | *dāng* | **to become; to act as** |

EXERCISE

13·3

If you were given only two choices for your future career, which one would you pick?
Complete the sentences. Answers may vary.

我想当 _____。

Wǒ xiǎng dāng _____.

1. 你想当	老师	还是	律师？	_____
Nǐ xiǎng dāng	*lǎoshī*	*háishì*	*lǜshī?*	
2. 你想当	作家	还是	音乐家？	_____
Nǐ xiǎng dāng	*zuòjiā*	*háishì*	*yīnyuèjiā?*	
3. 你想当	职员	还是	服务员？	_____
Nǐ xiǎng dāng	*zhíyuán*	*háishì*	*fúwùyuán?*	
4. 你想当	护士	还是	医生？	_____
Nǐ xiǎng dāng	*hùshi*	*háishì*	*yīshēng?*	
5. 你想当	商人	还是	军人？	_____
Nǐ xiǎng dāng	*shāngrén*	*háishì*	*jūnrén?*	

6. 你想当	警察	还是	经理？	_____
Nǐ xiǎng dāng	jǐngchá	háishì	jīnglǐ?	_____
7. 你想当	演员	还是	运动员？	_____
Nǐ xiǎng dāng	yǎnyuán	háishì	yùndòngyuán?	_____
8. 你想当	农民	还是	工人？	_____
Nǐ xiǎng dāng	nóngmín	háishì	gōngrén?	_____
9. 你想当	工程师	还是	老师？	_____
Nǐ xiǎng dāng	gōngchéngshī	háishì	lǎoshī?	_____

**EXERCISE
13·4**

Answer the following questions according to whether the subject belongs to one of the two choices. Answers may vary.

	他/她是 tā shì ...	都不是 dōu bú shì
1. 你爸爸是作家还是工程师？	_____	_____
Nǐ bàba shì zuòjiā háishì gōngchéngshī?		
2. 你妈妈是老师还是护士？	_____	_____
Nǐ māma shì lǎoshī háishì hùshi?		
3. 你爷爷是警察还是军人？	_____	_____
Nǐ yéye shì jǐngchá háishì jūnrén?		
4. 你奶奶是音乐家还是经理？	_____	_____
Nǐ nǎinai shì yīnyuèjiā háishì jīnglǐ?		
5. 你朋友是农民还是医生？	_____	_____
Nǐ péngyou shì nóngmín háishì yīshēng?		
6. 你哥哥是演员还是运动员？	_____	_____
Nǐ gēge shì yǎnyuán háishì yùndòngyuán?		

翻译成中文 **Fānyì chéng Zhōngwén** *Translate into Chinese and pinyin.*

1. Are you a doctor or nurse?

   _____

2. Is Tom Hanks an actor or athlete?

   _____

3. Is your father an engineer or a manager?

   _____

4. Do you want to become a blue-collar worker or businessperson?

   _____

5. Is his wife a lawyer or musician?

   _____

6. Does his son want to become a police officer or solider?

   _____

7. Is your husband a writer or teacher?

   _____

8. Does your daughter want to become a clerk or farmer?

   _____

9. Is your mother a manager or server?

   _____

你知道吗? *Nǐ zhīdao ma?* Do you know?

职业 *zhíyè* Occupations

- 中国有很多 (*duō*, many) 老师。二零零六年，中国已经 (*yǐjīng*, already) 有 13,018,600 个老师!
- 在 (*zài*, in) 美国，只有 (*zhǐ yǒu*, only) 1% 的人口 (*rénkǒu*, population) 是农民!
- 美国的律师太多了! 二零零六年，美国已经有 1,116, 967 个律师!
- 中国有很多学生。一九九七年，中国总共 (*zǒnggòng*, totally) 有 217,920,000 个学生。
- 美国护士不很多。二零一零年，美国只 (*zhǐ*, only) 有 2,655,020 个护士。

Attributives •
Demonstratives and noun
phrases • The school

Attributives

As a rule, an attributive always precedes the modified noun, and the particle
的 *de* is usually used. When a personal pronoun is used as an attributive to modify a **bare** noun that indicates kinship or close relationship, 的 *de* is optional.

ATTRIBUTIVE(S) + 的 DE + THE MODIFIED NOUN

漂亮	的	女儿	*piàoliang de nǚ'ér*	pretty daughter
我	（的）	爸爸	*wǒ (de) bàba*	my father
你们	的	咖啡	*nǐmen de kāfēi*	your coffee
老师	的	朋友	*lǎoshī de péngyou*	teacher's friend
便宜	的	衣服	*piányi de yīfu*	inexpensive clothing
今天	的	晚饭	*jīntiān de wǎnfàn*	today's dinner

生词　SHĒNGCÍ (VOCABULARY)

The school

学校	*xuéxiào*	**school**
办公室	*bàngōngshì*	**office**
教授	*jiàoshòu*	**professor**
图书馆	*túshūguǎn*	**library**
食堂	*shítáng*	**cafeteria**
体育场	*tǐyùchǎng*	**stadium**
体育馆	*tǐyùguǎn*	**gymnasium**
宿舍	*sùshè*	**dormitory**
中文	*Zhōngwén*	**Chinese (language)**
教室	*jiàoshì*	**classroom**
书	*shū*	**book**
书店	*shūdiàn*	**bookstore**
礼堂	*lǐtáng*	**auditorium**
电脑室	*diànnǎoshì*	**computer room**
实验室	*shíyànshì*	**laboratory**
阅览室	*yuèlǎnshì*	**reading room**
楼	*lóu*	**building**
教学楼	*jiàoxué lóu*	**teaching building***

*A building containing only classrooms—no instructor or administrative offices.

Everyday words

的	*de*	structural particle
新	*xīn*	new

EXERCISE
14·1

Match each Chinese phrase with its English equivalent.

1. _____ 教授的办公室 *jiàoshòu de bàngōngshì*　　a. students' classroom

2. _____ 学校的图书馆 *xuéxiào de túshūguǎn*　　b. professor's office

3. _____ 学生的教室 *xuésheng de jiàoshì*　　c. new gymnasium

4. _____ 新的体育馆 *xīn de tǐyùguǎn*　　d. school's library

5. _____ 老师的宿舍 *lǎoshī de sùshè*　　e. our teacher

6. _____ 学校的书店 *xuéxiào de shūdiàn*　　f. pretty reading room

7. _____ 很大的体育场 *hěn dà de tǐyùchǎng*　　g. very small computer room

8. _____ 我们的老师 *wǒmen de lǎoshī*　　h. teachers' dormitory

9. _____ 很小的电脑室 *hěn xiǎo de diànnǎoshì*　　i. school's bookstore

10. _____ 漂亮的阅览室 *piàoliang de yuèlǎnshì*　　j. very large stadium

EXERCISE
14·2

According to the example given, insert 的 **de** *into the following phrases when necessary.*

EXAMPLE　　爸爸办公室 *bàba bàngōngshì*　　爸爸**的**办公室 *bàba **de** bàngōngshì*

1. 很小教室 *hěn xiǎo jiàoshì*

_____

2. 漂亮图书馆 *piàoliang túshūguǎn*

_____

3. 我们老师 *wǒmen lǎoshī*

_____

4. 很新体育馆 *hěn xīn tǐyùguǎn*

_____

5. 便宜食堂 *piányi shítáng*

_____

6. 学生实验室 xuésheng shíyànshì

   _____

7. 他们学校礼堂 tāmen xuéxiào lǐtáng

   _____

8. 我朋友书店 wǒ péngyou shūdiàn

   _____

9. 学校电脑室 xuéxiào diànnǎoshì

   _____

10. 很新阅览室 hěn xīn yuèlǎnshì

   _____

生词　SHĒNGCÍ (VOCABULARY)

Everyday word

去　　*qù*　　**to go**

EXERCISE

14·3

Answer the following questions according to real situations. Answers may vary.

1. 你们学校的图书馆漂亮不漂亮？ *Nǐmen xuéxiào de túshūguǎn piàoliang bu piàoliang?*

   _____

2. 你喜欢你们学校的食堂吗？ *Nǐ xǐhuan nǐmen xuéxiào de shítáng ma?*

   _____

3. 你常去学校的体育馆运动吗？ *Nǐ cháng qù xuéxiào de tǐyùguǎn yùndòng ma?*

   _____

4. 你喜欢不喜欢你们的中文教授？ *Nǐ xǐhuan bu xǐhuan nǐmen de Zhōngwén jiàoshòu?*

   _____

5. 你常去教授的办公室吗？ *Nǐ cháng qù jiàoshòu de bàngōngshì ma?*

   _____

6. 你们的宿舍很小吗？ *Nǐmen de sùshè hěn xiǎo ma?*

   _____

7. 你们教学楼的教室新不新？ *Nǐmen jiàoxué lóu de jiàoshì xīn bu xīn?*

   _____

8. 你常去阅览室看书吗？ *Nǐ cháng qù yuèlǎnshì kàn shū ma?*

_____

9. 你们学校的礼堂漂亮吗？ *Nǐmen xuéxiào de lǐtáng piàoliang ma?*

_____

10. 你常去学校的书店买书吗？ *Nǐ cháng qù xuéxiào de shūdiàn mǎi shū ma?*

_____

11. 你们学校的实验室大不大？ *Nǐmen xuéxiào de shíyànshì dà bu dà?*

_____

12. 你常去电脑室上网吗？ *Nǐ cháng qù diànnǎoshì shàng wǎng ma?*

_____

Demonstratives and noun phrases

When a noun phrase is modified by a demonstrative, it is usually preceded by a measure word.

DEMONSTRATIVE + MEASURE WORD + NOUN PHRASE			
那 *nà*	个 *ge*	漂亮的图书馆 *piàoliang de túshūguǎn*	That beautiful library
这 *zhè*	件 *jiàn*	便宜的上衣 *piányi de shàngyī*	This inexpensive jacket

EXERCISE

14·4

翻译成中文 **Fānyì chéng Zhōngwén** *Translate into Chinese and pinyin.*

1. Is that new classroom very large?

_____

2. All the students like that beautiful cafeteria.

_____

3. I often go to my father's office to read (books).

_____

4. The students don't like that very small stadium.

_____

5. Our classroom is very large, but our reading room is very small.

_____

6. Are the books at the bookstore very cheap?

_____

7. The auditorium of their school is very tall.

_____

8. My mother likes our dormitory.

_____

9. My friend often goes to the school's gymnasium to work out.

_____

你知道吗? *Nǐ zhīdao ma?* Do you know?

中国的大学 *Zhōngguó de dàxué* Chinese universities

中国有很多很好的大学 (*dàxué*, university)。中国最 (*zuì*, most) 好的大学是:

- 北京 (*Běijīng*, Peking) 大学
- 清华 (*Qīnghuá*, Tsinghua) 大学
- 南京 (*Nánjīng*, Nanking) 大学
- 复旦 (*Fùdàn*, Fudan) 大学
- 浙江 (*Zhèjiāng*, Zhejiang) 大学

The 的 *de* phrase • Questions with 吧 *ba* • Colors and more clothing

The 的 *de* phrase

In a noun phrase of the form "modifier + 的 *de* + modified noun," the modified noun could be omitted if the meaning is clear from the context. The remaining phrase is called the 的 phrase, and it functions the same as the full noun phrase.

ATTRIBUTIVE + 的 DE		(=	ATTRIBUTIVE + 的 DE + MODIFIED NOUN)	
(noun)	老师的	=	老师的衬衫　这件衬衫是**老师的**。 *Zhè jiàn chènshān shì lǎoshī de.*	This shirt is the teacher's.
(pronoun)	我的	=	我的衬衫　这件衬衫是**我的**。 *Zhè jiàn chènshān shì wǎ de.*	This shirt is mine.
(adjective)	蓝的	=	蓝的衬衫　这件衬衫是**蓝的**。 *Zhè jiàn chènshān shì lán de.*	This shirt is a blue one.
(subj.+ verb)	他买的	=	他买的衬衫　这件衬衫是**他买的**。 *Zhè jiàn chènshān shì tā mǎi de.*	This shirt is the one he bought.

生词　SHĒNGCÍ (VOCABULARY)

Colors and more clothing

The words in the bracket are measure words that go with the noun when the latter occurs with a demonstrative pronoun or a numeral, e.g., *this belt* is 这条皮带 *zhè tiáo pídài*.

颜色/色	*yánsè/sè*	color
白	*bái*	white
黑	*hēi*	black; dark
红	*hóng*	red
绿	*lǜ*	green
黄	*huáng*	yellow
蓝	*lán*	blue

灰	huī	gray
紫	zǐ	purple
粉红	fěnhóng	pink
桔黄	júhuáng	orange
[条]皮带	[tiáo]pídài	leather belt
[双/只]球鞋	[shuāng/zhī]qiúxié	tennis shoes
[件]西装	[jiàn]xīzhuāng	suit
[条]围巾	[tiáo]wéijīn	scarf
[件]内衣	[jiàn]nèiyī	underwear
[双/只]拖鞋	[shuāng/zhī]tuōxié	slippers
[件]睡衣	[jiàn]shuìyī	pajamas
[件]雨衣	[jiàn]yǔyī	raincoat
[条]短裤	[tiáo]duǎnkù	shorts

EXERCISE 15·1

Match each Chinese color to its English noun.

1. _____ 红 *hóng*   a. sky

2. _____ 紫 *zǐ*   b. blood

3. _____ 蓝 *lán*   c. cotton

4. _____ 绿 *lǜ*   d. violet

5. _____ 白 *bái*   e. grass

6. _____ 黄 *huáng*   f. orange

7. _____ 粉红 *fěnhóng*   g. banana

8. _____ 黑 *hēi*   h. greyhound

9. _____ 桔黄 *júhuáng*   i. cherry blossoms

10. _____ 灰 *huī*   j. coal

EXERCISE 15·2

Match each Chinese phrase with its English equivalent.

1. _____ 这条蓝短裤是我哥哥的。   a. That suit is what his father wears.

   Zhè tiáo lán duǎnkù shì wǒ gēge de.   b. These two pairs of tennis shoes are white.

2. _____ 那条黑皮带是我的。   c. This pair of blue shorts is my older brother's.

   Nà tiáo hēi pídài shì wǒ de.   d. All my underwear is pink.

3. _____ 这两双球鞋是白的。

    Zhè liǎng shuāng qiúxié shì bái de.

4. _____ 那件西装是他爸爸穿的。

    Nà jiàn xīzhuāng shì tā bàba chuān de.

5. _____ 那条红围巾是她戴的。

    Nà tiáo hóng wéijīn shì tā dài de.

6. _____ 我的内衣都是粉红色的。

    Wǒ de nèiyī dōu shì fěnhóngsè de.

7. _____ 那双新拖鞋是黄的。

    Nà shuāng xīn tuōxié shì huáng de.

8. _____ 这件桔黄色的雨衣是你的吗？

    Zhè jiàn júhuángsè de yǔyī shì nǐ de ma?

9. _____ 那件紫色的睡衣是她买的。

    Nà jiàn zǔsè de shuìyī shì tā mǎi de.

10. _____ 我弟弟喜欢穿绿色的。

    Wǒ dìdi xǐhuan chuān lǜsè de.

e. The purple pajamas is what she bought.

f. That black leather belt is mine.

g. That red scarf is what she wears.

h. My younger brother likes to wear green clothes.

i. That pair of new slippers is yellow.

j. Is this orange raincoat yours?

Questions with 吧 *ba*

The modal particle 吧 *ba* is used at the end of a question to indicate supposition or uncertainty.

Question:	你喜欢绿衬衫吧？ *Nǐ xǐhuan lǜ chènshān ba?*	You like green shirts, right?
Answers:	对，我喜欢绿衬衫。*Duì, wǒ xǐhuan lǜ chènshān.*	Yes, I like green shirts.
	不，我不喜欢绿衬衫。*Bù, wǒ bù xǐhuan lǜ chènshān.*	No, I don't like green shirts.

EXERCISE
15·3

Answer the following questions according to real situations. Answers may vary.

1. 你喜欢穿蓝裤子吧？ *Nǐ xǐhuan chuān lán kùzi ba?*

   _____

2. 你爸爸喜欢穿黑色的西装吧？ *Nǐ bàba xǐhuan chuān hēisè de xīzhuāng ba?*

   _____

3. 你妈妈喜欢戴粉红色的围巾吧？ *Nǐ māma xǐhuan dài fěnhóngsè de wéijīn ba?*

_____

4. 你奶奶喜欢穿绿睡衣吧？ *Nǐ nǎinai xǐhuan chuān lǜ shuìyī ba?*

_____

5. 你爷爷喜欢穿灰色的拖鞋吧？ *Nǐ yéye xǐhuan chuān huīsè de tuōxié ba?*

_____

6. 你朋友喜欢黄球鞋吧？ *Nǐ péngyou xǐhuan huáng qiúxié ba?*

_____

7. 你喜欢桔黄色的雨衣吧？ *Nǐ xǐhuan jú huángsè de yǔyī ba?*

_____

8. 你爸爸喜欢穿白短裤吧？ *Nǐ bàba xǐhuan chuān bái duǎnkù ba?*

_____

9. 你妈妈喜欢买紫色的内衣吧？ *Nǐ māma xǐhuan mǎi zǐsè de nèiyī ba?*

_____

10. 你们都喜欢黑皮带吧？ *Nǐmen dōu xǐhuan hēi pídài ba?*

_____

EXERCISE
15·4

翻译成中文 Fānyì chéng Zhōngwén *Translate into Chinese and pinyin.*

1. This pair of white tennis shoes is hers.

_____

2. You do like the color red, right?

_____

3. That green raincoat is our teacher's.

_____

4. This pair of shorts is not my son's.

_____

5. These two pink scarves are mine.

_____

6. Your new leather shoes are purple, right?

_____

7. This pair of orange slippers is the actor's.

_____

8. The blue pajamas are yours, right?

_____

你知道吗? *Nǐ zhīdao ma? Do you know?*

彩虹的颜色 *cǎihóng de yánsè Colors of the rainbow*

我们都知道彩虹 (*cǎihóng*, rainbow) 是很漂亮的。可是，你知道彩虹有几种 (*zhǒng*, kind) 颜色吗? 有七种颜色! 彩虹颜色的顺序 (*shùnxù*, sequence) 是:

- 红色
- 桔黄色
- 黄色
- 绿色
- 蓝色
- 靛(*diàn*, indigo)色
- 紫色

Lessons 11–15

EXERCISE

R3·1

Answer the following questions according to real situations.
Answers may vary.

1. 你好吗？你朋友呢？ *Nǐ hǎo ma? Nǐ péngyou ne?*

   _____

2. 最近你爸爸, 妈妈身体怎么样？你爷爷, 奶奶呢？ *Zuìjìn nǐ bàba, māma shēntǐ zěnmeyàng? Nǐ yéye, nǎinai ne?*

   _____

3. 你现在忙不忙？你哥哥呢？ *Nǐ xiànzài máng bu máng? Nǐ gēge ne?*

   _____

4. 你累不累？你的朋友们呢？ *Nǐ lèi bu lèi? Nǐ de péngyoumen ne?*

   _____

5. 你很高吗？你弟弟呢？ *Nǐ hěn gāo ma? Nǐ dìdi ne?*

   _____

6. 你有没有姐姐和妹妹？ *Nǐ yǒu méiyǒu jiějie hé mèimei?*

   _____

7. 今天你高兴不高兴？ *Jīntiān nǐ gāoxìng bu gāoxìng?*

   _____

8. 香蕉酸不酸？柠檬呢？ *Xiāngjiāo suān bu suān? Níngméng ne?*

   _____

9. 你喜欢不喜欢你们学校的图书馆？ *Nǐ xǐhuan bu xǐhuan nǐmen xuéxiào de túshūguǎn?*

   _____

10. 你们学校的学生宿舍漂亮不漂亮？ *Nǐmen xuéxiào de xuésheng sùshè piàoliang bu piàoliang?*

   _____

11. 你是学生还是老师？ *Nǐ shì xuésheng háishì lǎoshī?*

_____

12. 你爸爸是工人还是军人？ *Nǐ bàba shì gōngrén háishì jūnrén?*

_____

13. Tom Cruise 是演员还是运动员？ Tom Cruise *shì yǎnyuán háishì yùndòngyuán?*

_____

14. 你想当工程师还是律师？ *Nǐ xiǎng dāng gōngchéngshī háishì lǜshī?*

_____

15. 你想喝咖啡还是想喝茶？ *Nǐ xiǎng hē kāfēi háishì xiǎng hē chá?*

_____

16. 你不是警察吧？ *Nǐ bú shì jǐngchá ba?*

_____

17. 你喜欢穿白衬衫和蓝裤子吧？ *Nǐ xǐhuan chuān bái chènshān hé lán kùzi ba?*

_____

18. 现在意大利皮鞋很贵吧？ *Xiànzài Yìdàlì píxié hěn guì ba?*

_____

EXERCISE
R3·2

Complete the sentences with the appropriate measure words.

个	件	条	副	顶	双
gè	*jiàn*	*tiáo*	*fù*	*dǐng*	*shuāng*

1. 我喜欢那 _____ 黄短裤和这 _____ 蓝雨衣。

   Wǒ xǐhuan nà _____ huáng duǎnkù hé zhè _____ lán yǔyī.

2. 那 _____ 美国人有一 _____ 黑球鞋和两 _____ 绿拖鞋。

   Nà _____ Měiguórén yǒu yì _____ hēi qiúxié hé liǎng _____ lǜ tuōxié.

3. 我先生喜欢穿那 _____ 灰西装, 戴那 _____ 红领带。

   Wǒ xiānsheng xǐhuan chuān nà _____ huī xīzhuāng, dài nà _____ hóng lǐngdài.

4. 这 _____ 皮带和那 _____ 围巾都是桔黄色的。

   Zhè _____ pídài hé nà _____ wéijīn dōu shì júhuángsè de.

5. 他太太想买两 _____ 粉红色的睡衣和一 _____ 黄毛衣。

   Tā tàitai xiǎng mǎi liǎng _____ *fěnhóngsè de shuìyī hé yī* _____
   huáng máoyī.

6. 她奶奶想买三 _____ 白手套和四 _____ 红帽子。

   Tā nǎinai xiǎng mǎi sān _____ *bái shǒutào hé sì* _____
   hóng màozi.

EXERCISE
R3·3

Insert the particle 的 **de** *into the following phrases when necessary.*

1. 老师好朋友 *lǎoshī hǎo péngyou*

   _____

2. 他爸爸和妈妈 *tā bàba hé māma*

   _____

3. 医生办公室 *yīshēng bàngōngshì*

   _____

4. 漂亮体育馆 *piàoliang tǐyùguǎn*

   _____

5. 今天早饭 *jīntiān zǎofàn*

   _____

6. 很大电脑室 *hěn dà diànnǎoshì*

   _____

7. 学校教室 *xuéxiào jiàoshì*

   _____

8. 很小体育场 *hěn xiǎo tǐyùchǎng*

   _____

9. 工程师实验室 *gōngchéngshī shíyànshì*

   _____

10. 图书馆阅览室 *túshūguǎn yuèlǎnshì*

    _____

翻译成英文 **Fānyì chéng Yīngwén**   *Translate into English.*

1. 柠檬是酸的, 可是香蕉是甜的。 *Níngméng shì suān de, kěshì xiāngjiāo shì tián de.*

_____

2. 咖啡是苦的, 茶也是苦的。 *Kāfēi shì kǔ de, chá yě shì kǔ de.*

_____

3. 这个新办公室是我们中文老师的。 *Zhè ge xīn bàngōngshì shì wǒmen Zhōngwén lǎoshī de.*

_____

4. 我有一条黑色的皮带和一条白色的皮带，可是我喜欢那条黑色的。 *Wǒ yǒu yì tiáo hēi sè de pídài hé yì tiáo bái sè de pídài, kěshì Wǒ xǐhuan nà tiáo hēi sè de.*

_____

5. 这两双黄球鞋都是她的吗？ *Zhè liǎng shuāng huáng qiúxié dōu shì tā de ma?*

_____

6. 这条绿围巾和那件灰西装都是我朋友的。 *Zhè tiáo lǜ wéijīn hé nà jiàn huí xīzhuāng dōu shì Wǒ péngyou de.*

_____

7. 这条红短裤是他弟弟的。 *Zhè tiáo hóng duǎnkù shì tā dìdi de.*

_____

8. 那双蓝拖鞋不是你的吧？ *Nà shuāng lán tuōxié bú shì nǐ de ba?*

_____

翻译成中文 **Fānyì chéng Zhōngwén**   *Translate into Chinese and pinyin.*

1. How is your grandfather's health? What about your grandmother's?

_____

2. Are you busy now? (*use affirmative-negative question*)

_____

3. I'm very tired. What about you?

_____

4. Are you American? (*use affirmative-negative question*) What about your father and mother?

_____

5. His grandfather is very thin, but his grandmother is very fat.

_____

6. All of these dishes are very salty and very spicy!

_____

7. Is he a musician or a lawyer?

_____

8. My younger sister likes this pair of slippers.

_____

9. Both of these two gray leather belts are his.

_____

10. You like wearing white sneakers, right?

_____

EXERCISE
R3·6

True or False? *After reading the following Chinese dialogue, mark each of the English statements as either* **true** *or* **false**.

Anna drops in to see her friend Mary at her dormitory.

A: 你好, Mary! 你最近怎么样? 忙不忙? *Nǐ hǎo, Mary! Nǐ zuìjìn zěnmeyàng? Máng bu máng?*

M: 我很好, 不太忙。你呢, Anna? *Wǒ hěn hǎo, bú tài máng. Nǐ ne, Anna?*

A: 我也很好, 也不太忙。Mary, 最近你爸爸, 妈妈身体怎么样? *Wǒ yě hěn hǎo, yě bú tài máng. Mary, zuìjìn nǐ bàba, māma shēntǐ zěnmeyàng?*

M: 他们身体都很好, 谢谢(*xièxie*, to thank)。*Tāmen shēntǐ dōu hěn hǎo, xièxie.*

Anna sees a photograph on Mary's desk.

A: Mary, 这是你家里人的照片(*zhàopiàn*, photograph)吧? *Mary, zhè shì nǐ jiālǐrén de zhàopiàn ba?*

M: 是, 这是我家里人的照片。你看, 这个穿黑西装的是我爸爸, 这个戴绿围巾的是我妈妈。

Shì, zhè shì wǒ jiālǐrén de zhàopiàn. Nǐ kàn, zhè ge chuān hēi xīzhuāng de shì wǒ bàba, zhè ge dài lǜ wéijīn de shì wǒ māma.

A: 你爸爸是不是律师? *Nǐ bàba shì bu shì lǜshī?*

M: 不是, 他是工程师。*Bú shì, tā shì gōngchéngshī.*

A: 你妈妈呢? *Nǐ māma ne?*

M: 她是中文老师。*Tā shì Zhōngwén lǎoshī.*

A: 她喜欢不喜欢当中文老师？ *Tā xǐhuan bu xǐhuan dāng Zhōngwén lǎoshī?*

M: 她很喜欢！ *Tā hěn xǐhuan!*

A: Mary, 这个穿白衬衫, 红裙子的是你妹妹吧？ *Mary, zhè ge chuān bái chènshān, hóng qúnzi de shì nǐ mèimei ba?*

M: 是, 她是我妹妹。 *Shì, tā shì wǒ mèimei.*

A: 她很漂亮！ *Tā hěn piàoliang!*

M: 她是一个很好的演员。 *Tā shì yí ge hěn hǎo de yǎnyuán.*

A: Mary, 这个戴黄帽子的是谁？ *Mary, zhè ge dài huáng màozi de shì shéi?*

M: 他是我哥哥。 *Tā shì wǒ gēge.*

A: 他很高大。他是军人吗？ *Tā hěn gāodà. Tā shì jūnrén mā?*

M: 不是, 他是运动员。 *Bú shì, tā shì yùndòngyuán.*

A: 他也很漂亮！ *Tā yě hěn piàoliang!*

M: 谢谢！ *Xièxie!*

1. _____ Both Mary and Anna are doing very well now.

2. _____ Mary is very busy, and so is Anna.

3. _____ Mary's parents are not in good shape now.

4. _____ The person who wears a green scarf in the picture is Mary's father.

5. _____ Her father is an engineer.

6. _____ Her mother is a language teacher, but she does not like her job at all.

7. _____ Mary's younger sister wears a white blouse and a red skirt in the picture.

8. _____ Mary's younger sister is not a good actress.

9. _____ Her brother is a policeman, not an athlete.

10. _____ Both Mary's younger sister and older brother are very good looking.

Grammar

Vocabulary

Do you know?

The verb 有 *yǒu* (II) indicating existence • More measure words • The classroom

16

The verb 有 *yǒu* (II)

	SUBJECT	+	PREDICATE		
			(PLACE/TIME PHRASE + (没)有 + OBJECT)		
STATEMENT	教室里 *Jiàoshì lǐ*		有 *yǒu*	二十张桌子。 *èrshí zhāng zhuōzi.*	There are 20 desks in the classroom.
	明天 *Míngtiān*		有 *yǒu*	汉语课。 *Hànyǔ kè.*	There is a Chinese class tomorrow.
NEGATION	教室里 *Jiàoshì lǐ*		没有 *méi yǒu*	桌子。 *zhuōzi.*	There is no desk in the classroom.
	明天 *Míngtiān*		没有 *méi yǒu*	汉语课。 *Hànyǔ kè.*	There is no Chinese class tomorrow.

生词 *SHĒNGCÍ* (VOCABULARY)

More measure words

Things they refer to

张	*zhāng*	objects with a flat surface, e.g., desks, tables, and maps
把	*bǎ*	objects with a handle, e.g., chairs
扇	*shàn*	doors and windows
本	*běn*	printed and bound things, e.g., books
枝	*zhī*	pens and writing brushes
盏	*zhǎn*	lamps and lights
台	*tái*	objects that sit on a platform, e.g., computers, air conditioners
块	*kuài*	chunk-like objects, e.g., blackboard, rocks

The classroom

里	*lǐ*	in; inside
[张]地图	*[zhāng]dìtú*	map
[张]桌子	*[zhāng]zhuōzi*	table; desk
[把]椅子	*[bǎ]yǐzi*	chair
[扇]门	*[shàn]mén*	door
[扇]窗户	*[shàn]chuānghu*	window

[枝]笔	[zhī]bǐ	pen; writing brush
[台]电脑	[tái]diànnǎo	computer
[盏]灯	[zhǎn]dēng	lamp; light
[台]空调机	[tái] kōngtiáojī	air conditioner
[块]黑板	[kuài]hēibǎn	blackboard
[块]黑板擦	[kuài]hēibǎncā	blackboard eraser

EXERCISE 16·1

First, complete the sentences with the appropriate measure words, and then translate the phrases into English.

EXAMPLES 一 _____ 教室 yì _____ jiàoshì

一个教室 yí **gè** jiàoshì   one classroom

1. 两 _____ 窗户 liǎng _____ chuānghu _____

2. 五 _____ 椅子 wǔ _____ yǐzi _____

3. 一 _____ 钟 yī _____ zhōng _____

4. 三十 _____ 桌子 sānshí _____ zhuōzi _____

5. 三 _____ 地图 sān _____ dìtú _____

6. 一百 _____ 灯 yì bǎi _____ dēng _____

7. 两百 _____ 书 liǎng bǎi _____ shū _____

8. 四 _____ 门 sì _____ mén _____

9. 五 _____ 黑板 wǔ _____ hēibǎn _____

10. 九十 _____ 笔 jiǔshí _____ bǐ _____

11. 十 _____ 空调机 shí _____ kōngtiáojī _____

12. 六 _____ 黑板擦 liù _____ hēibǎncā _____

生词 SHĒNGCÍ (VOCABULARY)

Everyday word

节 jié measure word for classes; period

Answer the following questions according to real situations. Answers may vary. Note that in a question, measure words are optional after the question word 多少 **duōshao**, *especially when there are two or more nouns that require special measure words.*

EXAMPLES 你们教室里有电脑吗? *Nǐmen jiàoshì lǐ yǒu diànnǎo ma?*

有, 我们教室里有三台电脑。*Yǒu, wǒmen jiàoshì lǐ yǒu sān tái diànnǎo.*

没有, 我们教室里没有电脑。*Méiyǒu, wǒmen jiàoshì lǐ méi yǒu diànnǎo.*

1. 你们教室里有椅子吗? *Nǐmen jiàoshì lǐ yǒu yǐzi ma?*

_____

2. 你们教室里有多少桌子? *Nǐmen jiàoshì lǐ yǒu duōshao zhuōzi?*

_____

3. 你们教室里有空调机吗? *Nǐmen jiàoshì lǐ yǒu kōngtiáojī ma?*

_____

4. 你们教室里有多少书? *Nǐmen jiàoshì lǐ yǒu duōshao shū?*

_____

5. 你们教室里有多少门和窗户? *Nǐmen jiàoshì lǐ yǒu duōshao mén hé chuānghu?*

_____

6. 你们教室里有多少黑板和黑板擦? *Nǐmen jiàoshì lǐ yǒu duōshao hēibǎn hé hēibǎncā?*

_____

7. 你们教室里有地图吗? *Nǐmen jiàoshì lǐ yǒu dìtú ma?*

_____

8. 今天有中文课吗? *Jīntiān yǒu Zhōngwén kè ma?*

_____

9. 明天有课吗? *Míngtiān yǒu kè ma?*

_____

10. 晚上有几节英文课? *Wǎnshàng yǒu jǐ jié Yīngwén kè?*

_____

生词 SHĒNGCÍ (VOCABULARY)

Everyday word

家　　*jiā*　　home; house; family

翻译成中文 **Fānyì chéng Zhōngwén**   *Translate into Chinese and pinyin.*

1. There are 36 chairs in our classroom.

   _____

2. There are 2 blackboards in their classroom.

   _____

3. There are 10 windows and 3 doors in my home.

   _____

4. There are 500 books in her home.

   _____

5. Is there a clock in your grandmother's home?

   _____

6. There is no air conditioner in my friend's home.

   _____

7. There is a map of China in his home.

   _____

8. Is there a French class this week?

   _____

9. There will be no Chinese class next week.

   _____

10. How many computers are there in your home?

   _____

你知道吗? *Nǐ zhīdao ma?* Do you know?

计量时间 *jìliáng shíjiān* Measuring time

◆ 阳历 (*yánglì*, the Gregorian calendar) 一年有三百六十五天五时 (*shí*, hour) 四十八分四十六秒 (*miǎo*, second)。
◆ 中国农历 (*nónglì*, lunar calendar) 一年有三百五十四天或者 (*huòzhě*, or) 三百五十五天。
◆ 中国农历闰月 (*rùnyuè*, leap month) 有二十九天。
◆ 中国农历二月只 (*zhǐ*, only) 有二十八天。

Location words • Verbs 有 *yǒu*, 是 *shì*, 在 *zài* indicating existence

17

Location words

Monosyllabic location words are always attached to a noun. They cannot stand alone.

| 桌子**上** | *zhuōzi**shang*** | on the table |
| 宿舍**前** | *sùshè**qián*** | in front of the dormitory |

MONOSYLLABIC LOCATION WORDS

上	*shàng*	up
下	*xià*	down
前	*qián*	front
后	*hòu*	back
左	*zuǒ*	left
右	*yòu*	right
里	*lǐ*	inside
外	*wài*	outside

Disyllabic location words are nouns. They can stand alone.

| 他在**里面** | *Tā zài **lǐmiàn**.* | He is inside |
| 谁在**外面?** | *Shéi zài **wàimiàn**?* | Who is outside? |

DISYLLABIC LOCATION WORDS

~边 ~*bian*	上边	下边	前边	后边	左边	右边	里边	外边
~面 ~*mian*	上面	下面	前面	后面	左面	右面	里面	外面
	up	down	front	back	left	right	inside	outside

These words have two forms; they can be formed by either **-biān** *side* or **-miàn** *surface*. The three words below only have one form:

旁边	*pángbiān*	beside; next to
对面	*duìmiàn*	opposite to; facing
中间	*zhōngjiān*	in between

Match each Chinese location word with its English equivalent.

1. _____ 前边 *qiánbian*   a. left

2. _____ 右边 *yòubian*   b. inside

3. _____ 对面 *duìmiàn*   c. beside

4. _____ 中间 *zhōngjiān*   d. above

5. _____ 上边 *shàngbian*   e. front

6. _____ 旁边 *pángbiān*   f. right

7. _____ 下边 *xiàbian*   g. outside

8. _____ 后边 *hòubian*   h. between

9. _____ 里边 *lǐbian*   i. opposite

10. _____ 左边 *zuǒbian*   j. behind

11. _____ 外边 *wàibian*   k. under

Translate the following Chinese location phrases into English.

1. 家里 *jiā lǐ* _____

2. 体育馆里边 *tǐyùguǎn lǐbian* _____

3. 宿舍旁边 *sùshè pángbiān* _____

4. 学校外面 *xuéxiào wàimian* _____

5. 食堂左边 *shítáng zuǒbian* _____

6. 桌子上 *zhuōzi shang* _____

7. 图书馆右面 *túshūguǎn yòumian* _____

8. 书店和礼堂中间 *shūdiàn hé lǐtáng zhōngjiān* _____

9. 办公室里 *bàngōngshì lǐ* _____

10. 教学楼对面 *jiàoxué lóu duìmiàn* _____

11. 教室前边 *jiàoshì qiánbian* _____

12. 体育场上 *tǐyùchǎng shang* _____

Verbs 有 *yǒu*, 是 *shì*, 在 *zài* indicating existence

In patterns 1 and 2, the location phrase precedes 有 *yǒu* and 是 *shì*. The two types of sentences have similar meanings. Both indicate the existence of something or someone. Between the two, 有 *yǒu* sentences focus more on existence (as opposed to nonexistence), while 是 *shì* sentences focus more on the identity of the thing (e.g., *a bookstore* rather than *a shoe store*).

In 在 *zài* sentences the location phrase follows 在 *zài*. The focus of these sentences is on the location of a person or a thing, rather than the existence of something.

SUBJECT	+		PREDICATE		
location phrase	+	有	+	Obj.	
学校前边		有		一个书店。	**There is** a bookstore in front of the school.
Xuéxiào qiánbian		*yǒu*		*yí ge shūdiàn.*	
location phrase	+	是	+	Obj.	
学校前边		是		一个书店。	In front of the school **is** a bookstore.
Xuéxiào qiánbian		*shì*		*yí ge shūdiàn.*	
Subject	+	在	+	location phrase	
书店		在		学校前边。	The bookstore is in front of the school.
Shūdiàn		*zài*		*xuéxiào qiánbian.*	

Locations on campus

生词　SHĒNGCÍ (VOCABULARY)

Location verb

在	*zài*	to be in/at/on/upon

On campus

行政	*xíngzhèng*	administration
厕所	*cèsuǒ*	restroom; toilet
数学	*shùxué*	mathematics
物理	*wùlǐ*	physics
生物	*shēngwù*	biology
历史	*lìshǐ*	history
地理	*dìlǐ*	geography
外语	*wàiyǔ*	foreign language
教育	*jiàoyù*	education
政治	*zhèngzhì*	political science
化学	*huàxué*	chemistry
工程	*gōngchéng*	engineering
人文	*rénwén*	liberal arts
理工	*lǐgōng*	science and engineering

Everyday word

就	*jiù*	exactly; precisely

翻译成英文 **Fānyì chéng Yīngwén** *Translate into English.*

1. 行政楼和政治楼中间有一个书店。*Xíngzhèng lóu hé zhèngzhì lóu zhōngjiān yǒu yí ge shūdiàn.*

_____

2. 工程楼对面是数学楼吗？*Gōngchéng lóu duìmiàn shì shùxué lóu ma?*

_____

3. 教育楼左边有一个学生食堂。*Jiàoyù lóu zuǒbian yǒu yí ge xuésheng shítáng.*

_____

4. 外语楼右边就是地理楼。*Wàiyǔ lóu yòubian jiù shì dìlǐ lóu.*

_____

5. 生物楼在历史楼后边吗？*Shēngwù lóu zài lìshǐ lóu hòubian ma?*

_____

6. 人文楼前边是理工楼。*Rénwén lóu qiánbian shì lǐgōng lóu.*

_____

7. 化学楼在物理楼旁边。*Huàxué lóu zài wùlǐ lóu pángbiān.*

_____

8. 体育馆外面有一个厕所吗？*Tǐyùguǎn wàimian yǒu yí ge cèsuǒ ma?*

_____

9. 阅览室在图书馆里。*Yuèlǎnshì zài túshūguǎn lǐ.*

_____

10. 实验室上面就是电脑室。*Shíyànshì shàngmian jiù shì diànnǎoshì.*

_____

11. 电脑室下面有一个实验室。*Diànnǎoshì xiàmian yǒu yí ge shíyànshì.*

_____

翻译成中文 **Fānyì chéng Zhōngwén** *Translate into Chinese and pinyin.*

1. There is a small bookstore beside the math building.

_____

2. The physics building is precisely on the left of the chemistry building.

_____

3. Between the biology building and the history building is the geography building.

_____

4. Is there a computer room inside the foreign language building?

_____

5. The education building is opposite the engineering building.

_____

6. Precisely on the right of the Chinese building is the library.

_____

7. Is the liberal arts building behind the administrative building?

_____

8. There is a restroom above the lab.

_____

9. Is the political science building in front of the science and engineering building?

_____

10. There is a bookstore outside the school.

_____

11. My office is right below the new reading room.

_____

你知道吗? *Nǐ zhīdao ma?* Do you know?

地点, 地点, 地点 *dìdiǎn dìdiǎn dìdiǎn* Location, location, location

- 天安门 (*Tiān'ānmén*, Tian'anmen Square) 就在紫禁城 (*Zǐjìnchéng*, the Forbidden City) 前边。
- 紫禁城在北京城 (*Běijīng chéng*, the city of Beijing) 里边, 但是长城 (*Chángchéng*, the Great Wall) 在北京城外边。
- 法国的卢浮宫 (*Lúfúgōng*, Louvre) 就在塞纳河 (*Sàinàhé*, Seine River) 旁边。
- 火星 (*Huǒxīng*, Mars) 上有水。
- 在太阳系 (*tàiyáng xì*, the solar system) 里, 金星 (*Jīnxīng*, Venus) 和火星中间就是地球。

Verb reduplication • Tag questions with 好吗 *hǎo ma* • Activities and chores

Verb reduplication

Some verbs in Chinese can be reduplicated to indicate brevity of an event, or casualness of a situation. It gives the meaning "doing something a little bit."

MONOSYLLABIC WORDS		
A	→ AA / A yi A	= A *yíxiàr*
看 *look*	→ 看看/看一看	= 看一下儿 *take a look*

DISYLLABIC WORDS		
AB	→ ABAB	= AB *yíxiàr*
运动 *work out* →	运动运动	= 运动一下儿 *work out for a little while*

NOTE Verbs that indicate existence (such as 是 *shì*), emotion (such as 喜欢 *xǐhuan*), and changes (such as 开始 *kāishǐ*, to begin) cannot be reduplicated.

Verb + Object expressions

A number of monosyllabic verbs form a close relationship with their object, which sometimes does not carry much meaning by itself. The meaning of a Verb + Object expression or VO-verbs often corresponds to the meaning of a verb in English, e.g., 睡觉 *shuìjiào to sleep* consists of the verb 睡 *shuì to sleep* and the object 觉 *jiào sleep*.

Reduplication of the VO-verbs follows the same pattern for monosyllabic verbs, as described earlier.

睡觉　sleep　睡睡觉 / 睡一睡觉　＝睡一下儿觉　to sleep for a little while
shuì jiào　shuìshui jiào/shuì yí shuì jiào = shuì yíxiàr jiào

生词　SHĒNGCÍ (VOCABULARY)		

Activities and chores

跑步 (v.o.)	*pǎobù*	to jog
游泳 (v.o.)	*yóuyǒng*	to swim
唱歌 (v.o.)	*chànggē*	to sing

跳舞(v.o.)	*tiàowǔ*	to dance
介绍	*jièshào*	to introduce
学/学习	*xué/xuéxí*	to study; to learn
听	*tīng*	to listen
休息	*xiūxi*	to rest
收拾	*shōushi*	to tidy up
整理	*zhěnglǐ*	to put in order
扫	*sǎo*	to sweep
用	*yòng*	to use
洗	*xǐ*	to wash
擦	*cā*	to wipe
吸	*xī*	to vacuum; to suck

Everyday word

一下儿	*yíxiàr*	for a little while; briefly

EXERCISE
18·1

Change the following verbal phrases into the reduplicated verbs.

EXAMPLE 看一下儿 *kàn yíxiàr*   看看 *kànkan*

1. 吃一下儿 *chī yíxiàr* _____

2. 跑一下儿步 *pǎo yíxiàr bù* _____

3. 想一下儿 *xiǎng yíxiàr* _____

4. 游一下儿泳 *yóu yíxiàr yǒng* _____

5. 喝一下儿 *hē yíxiàr* _____

6. 唱一下儿歌 *chàng yíxiàr gē* _____

7. 问一下儿 *wèn yíxiàr* _____

8. 跳一下儿舞 *tiào yíxiàr wǔ* _____

9. 穿一下儿 *chuān yíxiàr* _____

10. 介绍一下儿 *jièshào yíxiàr* _____

11. 洗一洗 *xǐ yi xǐ* _____

12. 休息一下儿 *xiūxi yíxiàr* _____

13. 擦一擦 *cā yi cā* _____

14. 运动一下儿 *yùndòng yíxiàr* _____

15. 扫一扫 *sǎo yi sǎo* _____

16. 学习一下儿 *xuéxí yíxiàr* _____

17. 吸一吸 *xī yi xī* _____

18. 收拾一下儿 *shōushi yíxiàr* _____

19. 用一用 *yòng yi yòng* _____

20. 整理一下儿 *zhěnglǐ yíxiàr* _____

Translate the following English verbal phrases into reduplicated verbs in Chinese.

1. to think for a while _____

2. to study for a while _____

3. to take a look _____

4. to sing for a while _____

5. to take a break _____

6. to tidy up briefly _____

7. to use for a while _____

8. to run for a while _____

9. to swim for a while _____

10. to have a dance _____

11. to put in an order _____

12. to give a good sweep _____

13. to give an introduction _____

14. to listen for a while _____

15. to give a good wipe _____

16. to have a wash _____

Tag questions with 好吗 *hǎo ma*

Questions with 好吗 *hǎo ma*? are often used to make a request or suggestion, or ask for one's opinion in a polite way. Oftentimes, it can be replaced by 好不好 *hǎo bu hǎo*? One usually answers the question affirmatively with 好 *hǎo*! or 好啊 *hǎo a*!

你洗洗那些脏衣服，好吗？—好！ *Nǐ xǐxi nàxiē zāng yīfu, **hǎo ma**?—hǎo!*	Would you wash those dirty clothes?—OK!
我们收拾收拾屋子，好不好？—好啊！ *Wǒmen shōushishōushi wūzi, **hǎo bu hǎo**? —hǎo a!*	Shall we tidy up the room?—OK!

生词 *SHĒNGCÍ* (VOCABULARY)

Housekeeping

脏	*zāng*	dirty
吸尘器	*xīchénqì*	vacuum cleaner
地	*dì*	floor; ground
时候	*shíhou*	(a point in) time
屋子	*wūzi*	room
碗	*wǎn*	bowl
时间	*shíjiān*	(the concept of) time
要是	*yàoshi*	if

EXERCISE 18·3

First, answer the following questions in Chinese with 好 **hǎo!** or 好啊 **hǎo a!**, and then translate them into English.

1. 你下午洗洗那些脏袜子, 好吗? *Nǐ xiàwǔ xǐxi nàxiē zāng wàzi, hǎo ma?*

_____

2. 我们现在用吸尘器吸吸地, 好吗? *Wǒmen xiànzài yòng xīchénqì xīxi dì, hǎo ma?*

_____

3. 你们上午收拾收拾屋子, 好不好? *Nǐmen shàngwù shōushishōushi wūzi, hǎo bu hǎo?*

_____

4. 你有时间的时候洗洗这些脏碗, 好吗? *Nǐ yǒu shíjiān de shíhòu xǐxi zhèxiē zāng wǎn, hǎo ma?*

_____

5. 我们现在有时间, 休息休息, 好不好? *Wǒmen xiànzài yǒu shíjiān, xiūxixiūxi, hǎo bu hǎo?*

_____

6. 我们整理整理这些书, 好吗? *Wǒmen zhěnglǐzhěnglǐ zhèxiē shū, hǎo ma?*

_____

7. 要是有时间, 你们擦擦窗户, 好吗? *Yàoshì yǒu shíjiān, nǐmen cāca chuānghu, hǎo ma?*

_____

8. 你明天上午扫扫地, 好不好? *Nǐ míngtiān shàngwù sǎosao dì, hǎo bu hǎo?*

_____

9. 我们擦擦那些桌子和椅子, 好吗? *Wǒmen cāca nàxiē zhuōzi hé yǐzi, hǎo ma?*

_____

10. 你洗洗这些脏衬衫和裤子, 好吗? *Nǐ xǐxi zhèxiē zāng chènshān hé kùzi, hǎo ma?*

_____

翻译成中文 **Fānyì chéng Zhōngwén** *Translate into Chinese and pinyin using the reduplicated verbs in your translation.*

1. You guys wash these dirty clothes, OK?

_____

2. Shall we sweep the floor now?

_____

3. Could you put those Chinese books in order?

_____

4. Would you use the new vacuum cleaner to vacuum the floor?

_____

5. Let's take a break now, OK?

_____

6. Tomorrow, could you guys tidy up your rooms?

_____

7. If you have time, would you wipe those tables?

_____

8. If we have time, let's have a dance, shall we?

_____

9. Give these dirty bowls a good wash, OK?

_____

10. Would you look at this new shirt?

_____

11. Now that we have some free time, shall we study Chinese for a while?

_____

12. Would you guys listen to this new music CD for a little bit?

_____

13. Would you briefly introduce your new friend?

_____

14. Let's sing for a while, shall we?

_____

15. You think (about it), OK?

_____

你知道吗？ *Nǐ zhīdao ma?* Do you know?

这些名人 (*míngrén*, the famous people) 周末 (*zhōumò*, weekend) 喜欢做什么？
What do famous people like to do on weekends?

◆ 中国政治家 (*zhèngzhìjiā*, statesman) 邓小平 (*Dèng Xiǎopíng*, Deng Xiaoping) 休息的
时候喜欢游游泳，打打桥牌 (*qiáopái*, bridge) 什么的 (*shénmede*, and what not)。

◆ 中国运动员姚明 (*Yáo Míng*, Yao Ming) 有时间的时候喜欢上网玩玩 (*wán*, to play)
游戏 (*yóuxì*, game)，听听音乐什么的。

◆ 中国女演员巩俐 (*Gǒng Lì*, Gong Li) 有的时侯喜欢在家里做做饭，看看书什么的。

◆ 美国演员 Brad Pitt 常喜欢运动运动，骑骑 (*qí*, to ride) 摩托车 (*mótuōchē*, motorcycle)
什么的。

◆ 美国演员 Julia Roberts 有时间的时候喜欢做做缝纫 (*féngrèn*, sewing)，弹弹 (*tán*,
to play) 钢琴 (*gāngqín*, piano) 什么的。

·19· The complement of state • Classroom activities

The complement of state

In Chinese, a complement follows the main verb or adjective of the sentence. There are various forms of complements. The complement of state is usually formed by an adjective or an adjectival phrase. The particle 得 **de** is used as a marker of the complement.

1. When there is no object, the sentences are as follows:

SUBJECT	+	PREDICATE			
		(VERB	+	得	+	COMPLEMENT)

STATEMENT				
白教授	讲	得	很清楚。	Professor Bai explains clearly.
Bái jiàoshòu	*jiǎng*	*de*	*hěn qīngchu.*	
QUESTION				
白教授	讲	得	清楚不清楚?	Does Professor Bai explain clearly?
Bái jiàoshòu	*jiǎng*	*de*	*qīngchu bu qīngchu?*	
= 白教授	讲	得	清楚吗?	
Bái jiàoshòu	*jiǎng*	*de*	*qīngchu ma?*	
NEGATION				
白教授	讲	得	不清楚。	Professor Bai doesn't explain clearly.
Bái jiàoshòu	*jiǎng*	*de*	***bù** qīngchu.*	

2. When there is an object, the verb occurs twice, and the first occurrence is optional.

SUBJECT	+	PREDICATE				
		(VERB)	+ OBJ.	+ VERB	+ 得	+ COMPLEMENT

STATEMENT						
白教授	讲	语法	讲	得	很清楚。	Professor Bai explains grammar clearly.
Bái jiàoshòu	*jiǎng*	*yǔfǎ*	*jiǎng*	*de*	*hěn qīngchu.*	
白教授		语法	讲	得	很清楚。	Professor Bai explains grammar clearly.
Bái jiàoshòu		*yǔfǎ*	*jiǎng*	*de*	*hěn qīngchu.*	

As a rule, no adverbs (such as 很 *hěn*, 也 *yě* and 都 *dōu*) are used in the affirmative-negative questions. In negation, what is negated is the complement, i.e., the adjective, not the verb. Therefore, 不 *bù* is placed before the adjective and not before the verb. It is incorrect to say 白教授不讲得清楚 *Bái jiàoshòu bù jiǎng de qīngchu.*

生词 SHĒNGCÍ (VOCABULARY)

Classroom activities

讲	*jiǎng*	to explain; to speak	念	*niàn*	to read aloud
语法	*yǔfǎ*	grammar	生词	*shēngcí*	new word; vocabulary
得	*de*	a particle	流利	*liúlì*	fluent
清楚	*qīngchu*	clear	准备	*zhǔnbèi*	to prepare; preparation
回答	*huídá*	to answer	快	*kuài*	fast; quick
问题	*wèntí*	question; problem	慢	*màn*	slow
练习	*liànxí*	exercise; to practice	复习	*fùxí*	to review; review
考试	*kǎoshì*	test; to take a test	功课	*gōngkè*	school work; homework
写	*xiě*	to write	认真	*rènzhēn*	conscientious
汉字	*Hànzì*	Chinese character	录音 (v.o)	*lùyīn*	recording; to record
说	*shuō*	to speak	录像 (v.o)	*lùxiàng*	VCR; video recording
汉语	*Hànyǔ*	Chinese language	课文	*kèwén*	text
教	*jiāo*	to teach	少	*shǎo*	little; few
多	*duō*	many; much			

EXERCISE 19·1

Rephrase the following sentences according to the example given.

EXAMPLE 白老师**语法讲**得很清楚。 *Bái lǎoshī **yǔfǎ jiǎng** de hěn qīngchu.*

白老师**讲语法讲**得很清楚。 *Bái lǎoshī **jiǎng yǔfǎ jiǎng** de hěn qīngchu.*

1. 学生们语法学得很好。 *Xuéshengmen yǔfǎ xué de hěn hǎo.*

_____

2. 学生问题问得很多吗? *Xuésheng wèntí wèn de hěn duō ma?*

_____

3. 这些学生问题回答得很快。 *Zhèxiē xuésheng wèntí huídá de hěn kuài.*

_____

4. 他们语法练习做得很慢。 *Tāmen yǔfǎ liànxí zuò de hěn màn.*

_____

5. 你们考试准备得很认真吗? *Nǐmen kǎoshì zhǔnbèi de hěn rènzhēn ma?*

_____

6. 那些学生新课文念得很流利。 *Nàxiē xuésheng xīn kèwén niàn de hěn liúlì.*

_____

7. 黄老师汉语说得很快吗？ *Huáng lǎoshī Hànyǔ shuō de hěn kuài ma?*

_____

8. 法国学生录音听得很少。 *Fǎguó xuésheng lùyīn tīng de hěn shǎo.*

_____

EXERCISE
19·2

Negate the following sentences with the complement of state.

1. 日本学生汉语考试都考得很好。 *Rìběn xuésheng Hànyǔ kǎoshì dōu kǎo de hěn hǎo.*

_____

2. 那个学生生词念得很清楚。 *Nà ge xuésheng shēngcí niàn de hěn qīngchu.*

_____

3. 俄国学生学汉语学得很慢。 *Éguó xuésheng xué Hànyǔ xué de hěn màn.*

_____

4. 他们汉语功课复习得很认真。 *Tāmen Hànyǔ gōngkè fùxí de hěn rènzhēn.*

_____

5. 这些美国学生汉语说得很流利。 *Zhèxiē Měiguó xuésheng Hànyǔ shuō de hěn liúlì.*

_____

6. 黄老师汉语语法教得很少。 *Huáng lǎoshī Hànyǔ yǔfǎ jiāo de hěn shǎo.*

_____

7. 他们看录像看得很多。 *Tāmen kàn lùxiàng kàn de hěn duō.*

_____

8. 你们汉字写得很快。 *Nǐmen Hànzì xiě de hěn kuài.*

_____

Change the following 吗 ma *questions into affirmative-negative questions according to the example given.*

EXAMPLE   白老师讲语法讲得**很清楚吗**?   *Bái lǎoshī jiǎng yǔfǎ jiǎng de **hěn qīngchu ma**?*

白老师讲语法讲得**清楚不清楚**?   *Bái lǎoshī jiǎng yǔfǎ jiǎng de **qīngchu bu qīngchu**?*

1. 学生们考试准备得很认真吗？ *Xuéshengmen kǎoshì zhǔnbèi de hěn rènzhēn ma?*

_____

2. 黄教授汉语说得很快吗？ *Huáng jiàoshòu Hànyǔ shuō de hěn kuài ma?*

_____

3. 法国学生汉语考试考得好吗？ *Fǎguó xuésheng Hànyǔ kǎoshì kǎo de hǎo ma?*

_____

4. 这些日本学生汉语说得流利吗？ *Zhèxiē Rìběn xuésheng Hànyǔ shuō de liúlì ma?*

_____

5. 新学生语法学得很好吗？ *Xīn xuésheng yǔfǎ xué de hěn hǎo ma?*

_____

6. 学生录音听得很多吗？ *Xuésheng lùyīn tīng de hěn duō ma?*

_____

7. 这个学生生词念得清楚吗？ *Zhè ge xuésheng shēngcí niàn de qīngchu ma?*

_____

8. 那些学生问题回答得很慢吗？ *Nàxiē xuésheng wèntí huídá de hěn màn ma?*

_____

9. 学生们看录像看得很多吗？ *Xuéshengmen kàn lùxiàng kàn de hěn duō ma?*

EXERCISE
19·4

翻译成中文 Fānyì chéng Zhōngwén   *Translate into Chinese and pinyin.*

1. He asks a lot of grammar questions.

_____

2. The American student reads the text very fluently.

_____

3. Do the new students watch recorded television shows very much?

   _____

4. These students listen to recordings quite a lot.

   _____

5. Do you guys review the school work quickly? (*use the affirmative-negative question*)

   _____

6. Those Russian students are preparing for the Chinese test very conscientiously.

   _____

7. They read the new words aloud very well.

   _____

8. Do you speak Chinese fluently now? (*use the affirmative-negative question*)

   _____

9. These Japanese students write characters very fast.

   _____

10. I do a lot of grammar exercises.

    _____

11. Did that Chinese student answer the questions very fast?

    _____

12. Professor Bai explained today's grammar very clearly.

    _____

你知道吗? *Nǐ zhīdao ma?* Do you know?

太多和太少 *tài duó hé tài shǎo* Too much and too little

- 两岁到十七岁的美国孩子看电视看得太 (*tài*, too) 多了: 他们每 (*měi*, every) 个星期平均 (*píngjūn*, on average) 看二十个小时 (*xiǎoshí*, hour) 的电视!
- 美国人做运动做得太少了: 他们每个星期平均只 (*zhǐ*, only) 做两个小时!
- 现在美国人吃肉吃得太多了: 他们平均每个人每年吃两百磅 (*bàng*, pound) 的肉 (*ròu*, meat)!
- 美国大学生睡觉睡得太少了: 平均每天只睡六个小时!

Sentences with subject-predicate as predicate • Adjective reduplication • Parts of the body

·20·

Sentences with subject-predicate as predicate

In this pattern, what the second subject refers to is usually part of what the first subject refers to.

SUBJECT₁	+	PREDICATE	
		(SUBJECT₂ + PREDICATE PHRASE)	
她	眼睛	很大。	Her eyes are very large.
Tā	*yǎnjing*	*hěn dà.*	
我爷爷	腰	疼。	My grandfather's lower back hurts.
Wǒ yéye	*yāo*	*téng.*	

> ## 生词 SHĒNGCÍ (VOCABULARY)
>
> ### Parts of the body
>
> | 眼睛 | *yǎnjing* | eye |
> |---|---|---|
> | 头 | *tóu* | head |
> | 头发 | *tóufa* | hair |
> | 鼻子 | *bízi* | nose |
> | 耳朵 | *ěrduo* | ear |
> | 脖子 | *bózi* | neck |
> | 肩膀 | *jiānbǎng* | shoulder |
> | 手 | *shǒu* | hand |
> | 胳膊 | *gēbo* | arm |
> | 腿 | *tuǐ* | leg |
> | 脚 | *jiǎo* | foot |
> | 嘴巴 | *zuǐba* | mouth |
> | 腰 | *yāo* | waist; lower back |
> | 肚子 | *dùzi* | belly; stomach |

Match each Chinese word with its English equivalent.

1. _____ 胳膊 *gēbo*		a.	head
2. _____ 脚 *jiǎo*		b.	nose
3. _____ 耳朵 *ěrduo*		c.	eye
4. _____ 肩膀 *jiānbǎng*		d.	hand
5. _____ 头 *tóu*		e.	shoulder
6. _____ 眼睛 *yǎnjing*		f.	ear
7. _____ 腰 *yāo*		g.	arm
8. _____ 腿 *tuǐ*		h.	belly
9. _____ 鼻子 *bízi*		i.	hair
10. _____ 肚子 *dùzi*		j.	waist
11. _____ 头发 *tóufa*		k.	foot
12. _____ 手 *shǒu*		l.	leg
13. _____ 嘴巴 *zuǐba*		m.	neck
14. _____ 脖子 *bózi*		n.	mouth

生词 SHĒNGCÍ (VOCABULARY)

Everyday words

个子	*gèzi*	height
最	*zuì*	most
疼	*téng*	to be in pain; to hurt
粗	*cū*	thick; wide (in diameter)
宽	*kuān*	broad; wide (width and breadth)

Answer the following questions according to real situations. Answers may vary.

1. 你家里人，谁眼睛最漂亮？ *Nǐ jiālǐrén, shéi yǎnjing zuì piàoliang?*

_____

2. 你家里人，谁耳朵最大？ *Nǐ jiālǐrén, shéi ěrduo zuì dà?*

_____

3. 你家里人, 谁个子最高? *Nǐ jiālǐrén, shéi gèzi zuì gāo?*

_____

4. 你家里人, 谁头发最长? *Nǐ jiālǐrén, shéi tóufa zuì cháng?*

_____

5. 你家里人, 谁鼻子最小? *Nǐ jiālǐrén, shéi bízi zuì xiǎo?*

_____

6. 你家里人, 谁肩膀最宽? *Nǐ jiālǐrén, shéi jiānbǎng zuì kuān?*

_____

7. 你家里人, 谁肚子最胖? *Nǐ jiālǐrén, shéi dùzi zuì pàng?*

_____

8. 你家里人, 谁胳膊最粗? *Nǐ jiālǐrén, shéi gēbo zuì cū?*

_____

9. 你家里人, 谁脚最大? *Nǐ jiālǐrén, shéi jiǎo zuì dà?*

_____

10. 你家里人, 谁手最长? *Nǐ jiālǐrén, shéi shǒu zuì cháng?*

_____

11. 现在你头疼吗? *Xiànzài nǐ tóu téng ma?*

_____

12. 昨天你腰很疼吗? *Zuótiān nǐ yāo hěn téng ma?*

_____

Adjective reduplication

In Chinese, certain adjectives can be reduplicated to soften or intensify the meaning. Usually, a reduplicated adjective provides a vivid description of the noun it modifies. Reduplication has a softening function for monosyllabic adjectives, but it has an intensifying function for disyllabic adjectives.

A → AA
大 *dà* large → 大大 *dàdà* largish
高 *gāo* tall → 高高 *gāogāo* tallish

AB → AABB
漂亮 *piàoliang* pretty → 漂漂亮亮 *piàopiàoliàngliàng* very pretty
高兴 *gāoxìng* happy → 高高兴兴 *gāogāoxìngxìng* very happy

Reduplicated adjectives function in the same way as adjectives in general. They are almost always followed by the particle 的 *de*.

As the modifier of a noun

她有一双大大的眼睛。 She has largish eyes.
Tā yǒu yìshuāng dàdà de yǎnjing.

As the predicate

我妹妹个子高高的。 My younger sister is tallish.
Wǒ mèimei gèzi gāogāo de.

As the complement of a verb

她穿得漂漂亮亮的。 She is dressed very prettily.
Tā chuānde piàopiàoliàngliàng de.

生词　SHĒNGCÍ (VOCABULARY)

Everyday words

整齐	*zhěngqí*	**tidy; orderly**
干净	*gānjìng*	**clean**
细	*xì*	**slender; thin**

EXERCISE
20·3

Reduplicate the following adjectives.

1. 长 *cháng* _____

2. 漂亮 *piàoliang* _____

3. 短 *duǎn* _____

4. 高兴 *gāoxìng* _____

5. 早 *zǎo* _____

6. 宽 *kuān* _____

7. 高 *gāo* _____

8. 清楚 *qīngchu* _____

9. 矮 *ǎi* _____

10. 整齐 *zhěngqí* _____

11. 慢 *màn* _____

12. 干净 *gānjìng* _____

13. 瘦 *shòu* _____

14. 胖 *pàng* _____

15. 红 *hóng* _____

16. 白 *bái* _____

17. 蓝 *lán* _____

18. 绿 *lǜ* _____

19. 粗 *cū* _____

20. 细 *xì* _____

First, complete the sentences with an appropriate reduplicated adjective according to the English equivalent, and then translate into English.

短短的	大大的	漂漂亮亮的	瘦瘦小小的
duǎnduǎn de	*dàdà de*	*piàopiàoliàngliàng de*	*shòushòuxiǎoxiǎo de*

红红的	细细的	长长的	宽宽的	清清楚楚的
hónghóng de	*xìxì de*	*chángcháng de*	*kuānkuān de*	*qīngqīngchǔchǔ de*

1. 我们都喜欢她那双 _____ 眼睛。(largish)

   Wǒmen dōu xǐhuan tā nà shuāng _____ yǎnjing.

   _____

2. 他妹妹今天晚上穿得 _____。(very prettily)

   Tā mèimei jīntiān wǎnshang chuān de _____.

   _____

3. 那个头发 _____ 的姑娘是你的朋友吗？(longish)

   Nà ge tóufa _____ de gūniang shì nǐ de péngyou ma?

   _____

4. 这件 _____ 毛衣是谁的？(reddish)。

   Zhè jiàn _____ máoyī shì shéi de?

   _____

5. 那个肩膀 _____ 先生是他弟弟。(broad-ish)

   Nà ge jiānbǎng _____ xiānsheng shì tā dìdi.

   _____

6. 他们都喜欢这个腰 _____ 女演员。(slenderish)

   Tāmen dōu xǐhuan zhè ge yāo _____ nǚ yǎnyuán.

   _____

7. 那个腿 _____ 人是一个作家吗？(shortish)

   Nà ge tuǐ _____ rén shì yí ge zuòjiā ma?

   _____

8. 白老师今天的语法讲得 _____ 的。(very clearly)

   Bái lǎoshī jīntiān de yǔfǎ jiǎng de _____ *de.*

   _____

9. 他爸爸个子 _____。(thinish and smallish)

   Tā bàba gèzi _____.

   _____

生词　SHĒNGCÍ (VOCABULARY)

Everyday word

| 总是 | *zǒngshì* | **always** |

EXERCISE
20·5

翻译成中文 Fānyì chéng Zhōngwén　*Translate into Chinese and pinyin.*

1. That tallish engineer is my older brother.

   _____

2. Does this slender-necked girl have a headache now?

   _____

3. (Among) your family members, whose eyes are the most beautiful?

   _____

4. Does she like that athlete whose shoulders are broadish?

   _____

5. That police officer's mouth is largish.

   _____

6. Her doctor's hands are longish.

   _____

7. Now I don't have a stomachache, but I have lower back pain.

   _____

8. That server's sweater is yellowish, (and) I don't like it.

   _____

9. These very clean clothes are my younger sister's.

   _____

10. My room is always tidied up and in good order.

_____

11. Is that fatish manager your father's friend?

_____

你知道吗? *Nǐ zhīdao ma? Do you know?*

特征 *tèzhēng* Physical traits

◆ 毛泽东 (*Máo Zedōng*, Mao Zedong) 个子高高大大的, 可是邓小平 (*Dèng Xiǎopíng*, Deng Xiaoping) 个子矮矮小小的。

◆ Pinocchio 个子瘦瘦小小的, 可是他鼻子长长的。

◆ 美国女演员 Audrey Hepburn 眼睛大大的, 头发短短的, 很漂亮!

Lessons 16–20

Complete the sentences with appropriate measure words from the following list.

个	张	把	扇	本	枝	盏	台	块
gè	*zhāng*	*bǎ*	*shàn*	*běn*	*zhī*	*zhǎn*	*tái*	*kuài*

1. 教室里有三 _____ 黑板和三 _____ 黑板擦。
   Jiàoshì lǐ yǒu sān _____ hēibǎn hé sān _____ hēibǎn cā.

2. 礼堂里有四 _____ 门和十 _____ 窗户。*Lǐtáng lǐ yǒu sì _____ mén hé shí _____ chuānghu.*

3. 你们宿舍里有多少 _____ 灯？*Nǐmen sùshè lǐ yǒu duōshao _____ dēng?*

4. 他家里有一 _____ 桌子和六 _____ 椅子。*Tā jiā lǐ yǒu yī _____ zhuōzi hé liù _____ yǐzi.*

5. 图书馆里现在有多少 _____ 书？*Túshūguǎn lǐ xiànzài yǒu duōshao _____ shū?*

6. 阅览室里有几 _____ 地图？*Yuèlǎnshì lǐ yǒu jǐ _____ dìtú?*

7. 我的办公室里有五 _____ 笔。*Wǒ de bàngōngshì lǐ yǒu wǔ _____ bǐ.*

8. 实验室里有两 _____ 钟。*Shíyànshì lǐ yǒu liǎng _____ zhōng.*

9. 教学楼里有十五 _____ 空调机。*Jiàoxuélóu lǐ yǒu shíwǔ _____ kōngtiáojī.*

10. 电脑室里有五十 _____ 电脑。*Diànnǎoshì lǐ yǒu wǔshí _____ diànnǎo.*

Reduplicate the following adjectives, verbs, and VO-verbs.

1. 整齐 zhěngqí _____

2. 胖 pàng _____

3. 干净 gānjìng _____

4. 说 shuō _____

5. 清楚 qīngchu _____

6. 写 xiě _____

7. 高兴 gāoxìng _____

8. 休息 xiūxi _____

9. 粗 cū _____

10. 跑步 (v.o.) pǎobù _____

11. 宽 kuān _____

12. 游泳 (v.o.) yóuyǒng _____

13. 慢 màn _____

14. 跳舞 (v.o.) tiàowǔ _____

15. 整理 zhěnglǐ _____

16. 练习 liànxí _____

17. 大 dà _____

18. 介绍 jièshào _____

19. 高 gāo _____

20. 唱歌 (v.o.) chànggē _____

翻译成英文 Fānyì chéng Yīngwén   *Translate into English.*

1. 行政楼在图书馆和体育场中间。 *Xíngzhèng lóu zài túshūguǎn hé tǐyùchǎng zhōngjiān.*

_____

2. 外语楼旁边是体育馆。 *Wàiyǔ lóu pángbiān shì tǐyùguǎn.*

_____

3. 地理楼对面有一个礼堂。 *Dìlǐ lóu duìmiàn yǒu yí ge lǐtáng.*

_____

4. 政治楼在生物楼左边。 *Zhèngzhì lóu zài shēngwù lóu zuǒbian.*

_____

5. 化学楼前边是历史楼。 *Huàxué lóu qiánbian shì lìshǐ lóu.*

_____

6. 物理楼右边有一个食堂。 *Wùlǐ lóu yòubian yǒu yí ge shítáng.*

_____

7. 老师们的办公室在厕所上边。 *Lǎoshīmen de bàngōngshì zài cèsuǒ shàngbian.*

_____

8. 人文楼后边是理工楼。 *Rénwén lóu hòubian shì lǐgōnglóu.*

_____

9. 学校外面有一个书店。 *Xuéxiào wàimian yǒu yí ge shūdiàn.*

_____

10. 我们教室里有两台空调机。 *Wǒmen jiàoshì lǐ yǒu liǎng tái kōngtiáojī.*

_____

11. 实验室在电脑室下面。 *Shíyànshì zài diànnǎoshì xiàmian.*

_____

12. 数学楼左面是工程楼。 *Shùxué lóu zuǒmiàn shì gōngchéng lóu.*

_____

EXERCISE
R4·4

Answer the following questions according to real situations. Answers may vary.

1. 现在你汉语学得好不好？ *Xiànzài nǐ Hànyǔ xué de hǎo bu hǎo?*

_____

2. 你们老师语法讲得清楚不清楚？ *Nǐmen lǎoshī yǔfǎ jiǎng de qīngchu bu qīngchu?*

_____

3. 现在你说汉语说得流利不流利？ *Xiànzài nǐ shuō Hànyǔ shuō de liúlì bu liúlì?*

_____

4. 你们语法练习做得多不多？ *Nǐmen yǔfǎ liànxí zuò de duō bu duō?*

_____

5. 你汉语考试考得好不好？ *Nǐ Hànyǔ kǎoshì kǎo de hǎo bu hǎo?*

_____

6. 你看录像看得很少吗？ *Nǐ kàn lùxiàng kàn de hěn shǎo ma?*

_____

7. 你们汉语课文念得很流利吗？ *Nǐmen Hànyǔ kèwén niàn de hěn liúlì ma?*

_____

8. 他学习得很认真吗？ *Tā xuéxí de hěn rènzhēn ma?*

_____

9. 你看得清楚吗？ *Nǐ kàn de qīngchu ma?*

_____

10. 你家里人，谁个子最高？ *Nǐ jiālǐrén, shéi gèzi zuì gāo?*

_____

11. 你家里人，谁眼睛最漂亮？ *Nǐ jiālǐrén, shéi yǎnjing zuì piàoliang?*

_____

12. 你家里人，谁肩膀最宽？ *Nǐ jiālǐrén, shéi jiānbǎng zuì kuān?*

_____

13. 你家里人，谁腿最长？ *Nǐ jiālǐrén, shéi tuǐ zuì cháng?*

_____

14. 你家里人，谁胳膊最粗？ *Nǐ jiālǐrén, shéi gēbo zuì cū?*

_____

15. 你现在肚子疼吗？腰呢？脖子呢？ *Nǐ xiànzài dùzi téng ma? Yāo ne? Bózi ne?*

_____

EXERCISE R4·5

翻译成中文 Fānyì chéng Zhōngwén *Translate into Chinese and pinyin.*

1. There are 200 Chinese books and 30 pens in our dormitory.

_____

2. There are two air conditioners and 20 lights in their classroom.

_____

3. There is no Chinese class next week.

_____

4. Are there 15 desks and 16 chairs in your classroom?

_____

5. There is a restroom on the right of the chemistry building.

_____

6. Is the liberal arts building at the back of the science and engineering building?

_____

7. Precisely in front of the math building is the physics building.

_____

8. Now let's go to the stadium to have a run, OK?

_____

9. You guys will wipe these doors and windows tomorrow, OK?

_____

10. You wash these dirty bowls, OK?

_____

11. Let's take a break now, OK?

_____

12. The students answered the teacher's questions very quickly.

_____

13. Does your friend speak Chinese fluently?

_____

14. Professor Huang explained today's grammar very clearly! (*use the reduplicated adjective*)

_____

15. Is that gentleman with long hair your father? (*use the reduplicated adjective*)

_____

16. Our teacher is neatly dressed tonight. (*use the reduplicated adjective*)

_____

True or False? *After reading the following Chinese dialogue, mark each of the English statements as either **true** or **false**.*

Mark [马克 *Mǎkè*] shows his friend Lily [莉莉 *Lìlì*] around on campus.

马克: 这就是我们的校园。*Zhè jiù shì wǒmen de xiàoyuán.*

莉莉: 啊！你们的校园太漂亮了！马克，你介绍介绍，好吗？*Ā! Nǐmen de xiàoyuán tài piàoliang le! Mǎkè, nǐ jièshaojièshao, hǎo ma?*

马克: 好啊！你看，那栋(*dòng*, a m. w. for buildings)高高的楼是行政楼。行政楼的左边是大礼堂，右边是图书馆。*Hǎo a! Nǐ kàn, nà dòng gāogāo de lóu shì xíngzhèng lóu. Xíngzhèng lóu de zuǒbian shì dà lǐtáng, yòubian shì túshūguǎn.*

莉莉: 你们图书馆里有中文书吗？*Nǐmen túshūguǎn lǐ yǒu Zhōngwén shū ma?*

马克: 当然(*dāngrán*, of course)有！还有不少呢。*Dāngrán yǒu! Hái yǒu bù shǎo ne.*

莉莉: 外语楼在哪儿呢？*Wàiyǔ lóu zài nǎr ne?*

马克: 外语楼就在大礼堂旁边。我们中文系(*xì*, department)就在外语楼里。*Wàiyǔ lóu jiù zài dà lǐtáng pángbiān. Wǒmen Zhōngwén xì jiù zài wàiyǔ lóu lǐ.*

莉莉: 我们现在去看看中文系的教室，好吗？*Wǒmen xiànzài qù kànkàn Zhōngwén xì de jiàoshì, hǎo ma?*

马克: 好啊！(他们慢慢地走进[*zǒu jìn*, to enter]中文系的一个教室里。) 你看，这就是我们上课(to attend class)的教室。*Hǎo a! (Tāmen mànman de zǒu jìn Zhōngwén xì de yí ge jiàoshì lǐ.) Nǐ kàn, zhè jiù shì wǒmen shàngkè de jiàoshì.*

莉莉: 这个教室不太新，可是收拾得干干净净的。教室里有没有空调机？*Zhè ge jiàoshì bú tài xīn, kěshì shōushi de gāngānjìngjìng de. Jiàoshì lǐ yǒu méi yǒu kōngtiáojī?*

马克: 有，有两台。你看，那两台空调机都是新的。*Yǒu, yǒu liǎngtái. Nǐ kàn, nà liǎng tái kōngtiáojī dōu shì xīn de.*

莉莉: 马克，你觉得(*juéde*, to think) 你们的老师教得好不好？*Mǎkè, nǐ juéde nǐmen de lǎoshī jiāo de hǎo bù hǎo?*

马克: 我觉得他们都教得很好！…… *Wǒ jué de tāmen dōu jiāo de hěn hǎo!* … (在外语楼外面。*Zài wàiyǔ lóu wàimian.*)

莉莉: 你们的体育场在哪儿？*Nǐmen de tǐyùchǎng zài nǎr?*

马克: 体育场在行政楼后边。*Tǐyùchǎng zài xíngzhèng lóu hòubian.*

莉莉: 学生食堂呢? *Xuésheng shítáng ne?*

马克: 你看，那栋红红的大楼是我们的宿舍楼，学生食堂就在宿舍楼前边。*Nǐ kàn, nà dòng hónghóng de dà lóu shì wǒmen de sùshè lóu, xuésheng shítáng jiù zài sùshè lóu qiánbian.*

莉莉: 你们学校里有书店吗？*Nǐmen xuéxiào lǐ yǒu shūdiàn ma?*

马克: 有两个，一个大的和一个小的。大的在食堂对面，小的在体育馆和宿舍中间。*Yǒu liǎng ge, yí ge dà de hé yí ge xiǎo de. Dà de zài shítáng duìmiàn, xiǎo de zài tǐyùguǎn hé sùshè zhōngjiān.*

莉莉: 我们去看看你们的宿舍，好不好？*Wǒmen qù kànkàn nǐmen de sùshè, hǎo bù hǎo?*

马克: 好啊！…… (他们慢慢地走进马克的房间。) 这就是我的房间。*Hǎo a! … (Tāmen mànmàn de zǒu jìn Mǎkè de fángjiān.) Zhè jiù shì wǒ de fángjiān.*

莉莉: 你的房间不太大，可是收拾得整整齐齐的嘛 (*ma*, a modal particle)。*Nǐ de fángjiān bú tài dà, kěshi shōushi de zhěngzhěngqíqí de ma.*

马克: 谢谢！我喜欢整齐的房间。*Xièxie! Wǒ xǐhuan zhěngqí de fángjiān.*

莉莉: 这是你家里人的照片吧？这个个子高高的先生是你爸爸吧？*Zhè shì nǐ jiālǐrén de zhàopiàn ba? Zhè ge gèzi gāogāo de xiānsheng shì nǐ bàba ba?*

马克: 是，他是我爸爸。这个头发短短的是我妈妈。*Shì, tā shì wǒ bàba. Zhè ge tóufa duǎnduǎn de shì wǒ māma.*

莉莉: 这个腿长长的小姐是你妹妹吧？*Zhè ge tuǐ chángcháng de xiǎojie shì nǐ mèimei ba?*

马克: 不是，她是我姐姐。这个穿得漂漂亮亮的小姐才(*cái*, instead)是我妹妹。*Bú shì, tā shì wǒ jiějie. Zhè ge chuān de piàopiàoliàngliàng de xiǎojie cái shì wǒ mèimei.*

莉莉: 她们都很漂亮嘛！* *Tāmen dōu hěn piàoliang ma!*

马克: 哪里(*nǎli*, I feel flattered)！哪里！*Nǎli! Nǎli!*

*In spoken Chinese, the particle 嘛 *ma* is often used at the end of a declarative sentence to indicate that a reasoning or an excuse is obvious.

1. _____ Mark's school campus is not pretty at all.

2. _____ Lily is, apparently, a total stranger to the campus.

3. _____ The administrative building is quite tall.

4. _____ On the right of administrative building is the grand auditorium.

5. _____ There are quite a few Chinese books in the library.

6. _____ The Chinese department is inside the foreign language building.

7. _____ The classroom of the Chinese department is very tidy and air-conditioned.

8. _____ Mark does not think that all of his teachers teach well.

9. _____ The administrative building is in front of the stadium.

10. _____ The dormitory building where Mark lives is red.

11. _____ There is only one bookstore on campus.

12. _____ The small bookstore is between the stadium and the dorm.

13. _____ Mark's room is not too big, but very tidy.

14. _____ Mark's father is very short.

15. _____ His mother has short hair.

16. _____ His younger sister has long legs.

17. _____ Both of his sisters are very pretty.

18. _____ His younger sister is not well dressed.

Grammar

Vocabulary

Do you know?

Pivotal sentences • Sentences with double objects • Entertainment

21

Pivotal sentences

In a pivotal sentence, the pivot serves as the object of the first verb and, at the same time, as the subject of the second verb. The first verb is a **causative verb**, (a verb that indicates that some person or thing causes something to happen).

SUBJECT₁ + PREDICATE

	(VERB₁ +	OBJECT₁/SUBJECT₂ +	VERB₂ +	OBJECT₂)	
他 *Tā*	教 *jiāo*	我们 *wǒmen*	跳舞 *tiàowǔ*		He teaches us how to dance.
我 *Wǒ*	请 *qǐng*	他们 *tāmen*	吃 *chī*	中国饭。 *Zhōngguó fàn.*	I invite them to eat Chinese food.

生词　SHĒNGCÍ (VOCABULARY)

Causative verbs and entertainment

请	*qǐng*	to invite
让	*ràng*	to let
叫	*jiào*	to ask
帮助	*bāngzhù*	to help
打麻将	*dǎ májiàng*	to play mahjong
做游戏	*zuò yóuxì*	to play games
下围棋	*xià wéiqí*	to play Go

EXERCISE 21·1

*First fill in the blanks with the appropriate causative verbs (请 **qǐng**, 教 **jiāo**, 让 **ràng**, 帮助 **bāngzhù**, 叫 **jiào**), and then translate into English.*

1. 下个星期他 _____ 谁吃饺子？ *Xià ge xīngqī tā*
_____ *shéi chī jiǎozi?* (invite)

_____

2. 老师每天都 _____ 学生们跳舞。*Lǎoshī měi tiān dōu* _____

   xuéshengmen tiàowǔ. (teach)

   _____

3. 她爸爸 _____ 她喝啤酒吗？*Tā bàba* _____ *tā hē píjiǔ ma?* (let)

   _____

4. 我爷爷 _____ 我下围棋。*Wǒ yéye* _____ *wǒ xià wéiqí.* (teach)

   _____

5. 他的女朋友 _____ 他去她家打麻将。*Tā de nǚ péngyou* _____

   tā qù tā jiā dǎ májiàng. (invite)

   _____

6. 妈妈不 _____ 我听法国音乐。*Māma bú* _____ *wǒ tīng Fǎguó*

   yīnyuè. (let)

   _____

7. 那个漂亮的女演员 _____ 我跳舞。*Nà ge piàoliàng de nǚ yǎnyuán*

   _____ *wǒ tiàowǔ.* (invite)

   _____

8. 老师 _____ 学生们做游戏。*Lǎoshī* _____ *xuéshengmen zuò*

   yóuxì. (help)

   _____

9. 明天你不 _____ 朋友们喝酒吗？*Míngtiān nǐ bù* _____

   péngyoumen hē jiǔ ma? (invite)

   _____

10. 那个音乐家 _____ 她去礼堂唱歌。*Nà ge yīnyuèjiā* _____ *tā qù*

    lǐtáng chànggē. (ask)

    _____

生词　SHĒNGCÍ (VOCABULARY)

Everyday word

小时候	*xiǎoshíhou*	**in one's childhood**

Answer the following questions according to real situations. Answers may vary.

1. 小时候，谁教你唱歌？ *Xiǎoshíhou, shéi jiāo nǐ chànggē?*

_____

2. 小时候，谁教你跳舞？ *Xiǎoshíhou, shéi jiāo nǐ tiàowǔ?*

_____

3. 小时候，老师常教你们做游戏吗？ *Xiǎoshíhou, lǎoshī cháng jiāo nǐmen zuò yóuxì ma?*

_____

4. 小时候，你爸爸让你喝酒吗？ *Xiǎoshíhou, nǐ bàba ràng nǐ hē jiǔ ma?*

_____

5. 小时候，你爸爸常让你看电视吗？ *Xiǎoshíhou, nǐ bàba cháng ràng nǐ kàn diànshì ma?*

_____

6. 小时候，你妈妈常让你上网吗？ *Xiǎoshíhou, nǐ māma cháng ràng nǐ shàng wǎng ma?*

_____

7. 小时候，你妈妈常让你听音乐吗？ *Xiǎoshíhou, nǐ māma cháng ràng nǐ tīng yīnyuè ma?*

_____

8. 最近你朋友常请你去打麻将吗？ *Zuìjìn nǐ péngyou cháng qǐng nǐ qù dǎ májiàng ma?*

_____

9. 星期天你朋友常请你去下围棋吗？ *Xīngqītiān nǐ péngyou cháng qǐng nǐ qù xià wéiqí ma?*

_____

10. 现在你常请你朋友去喝酒吗？ *Xiànzài nǐ cháng qǐng nǐ péngyou qù hē jiǔ ma?*

_____

11. 中文老师常请学生吃饭吗？ *Zhōngwén lǎoshī cháng qǐng xuésheng chī fàn ma?*

_____

12. 在家里，你常帮助妈妈做饭吗？ *Zài jiā lǐ, nǐ cháng bāngzhù māma zuòfàn ma?*

_____

Sentences with double objects

In a sentence with double objects, the first object is usually animate, while the second object is usually inanimate.

SUBJECT	+	PREDICATE			
		(TRANSITIVE VERB + 1ST OBJECT + 2ND OBJECT)			
我朋友		给	我	一张电影票。	My friend gave me a
Wǒ péngyou		*gěi*	*wǒ*	*yì zhāng diànyǐng piào.*	movie ticket.

生词 SHĒNGCÍ (VOCABULARY)

Transitive verbs and more entertainment

给	*gěi*	to give
送	*sòng*	to give as a gift
还	*huán*	to return
告诉	*gàosu*	to tell
音乐会	*yīnyuèhuì*	concert
电影	*diànyǐng*	movie; film
票	*piào*	ticket
晚会	*wǎnhuì*	evening party
歌剧	*gējù*	opera
舞会	*wǔhuì*	dance party; ball

EXERCISE 21·3

First, complete the sentences with the appropriate transitive verbs (送 sòng, 给 gěi, 告诉 gàosu, 还 huán, 问 wèn), and then translate into English.

1. 我 _____ 他两张舞会票。*Wǒ _____ tā liǎng zhāng wǔhuì piào.* (give)

_____

2. 那个作家 _____ 我们歌剧的名字。*Nà ge zuòjiā _____ wǒmen gējù de míngzi.* (tell)

_____

3. 他明天 _____ 黄教授中文书。*Tā míngtiān _____ Huáng jiàoshòu Zhōngwén shū.* (return)

_____

4. 爸爸 _____ 我一张音乐会的票。*Bàba _____ wǒ yì zhāng yīnyuèhuì de piào.* (give as a gift)

_____

5. 学生们常 _____ 音乐老师问题。*Xuéshengmen cháng _____ yīnyuè lǎoshī wèntí.* (ask)

_____

6. 我不 _____ 你那个电影的名字。 *Wǒ bú _____ nǐ nà ge diànyǐng de míngzi.* (tell)

_____

7. 那个律师想 _____ 你什么票？ *Nà ge lǜshī xiǎng _____ nǐ shénme piào?* (give)

_____

8. 警察 _____ 那个演员几个问题。 *Jǐngchá _____ nà ge yǎnyuán jǐ ge wèntí.* (ask)

_____

9. 我姐姐 _____ 我一张晚会票。 *Wǒ jiějie _____ wǒ yì zhāng wǎnhuì piào.* (give as a gift)

_____

10. 你下个星期 _____ 我弟弟麻将吗？ *Nǐ xià ge xīngqī _____ wǒ dìdi májiàng ma?* (return)

_____

EXERCISE
21·4

翻译成中文 **Fānyì chéng Zhōngwén** *Translate into Chinese and pinyin.*

1. Did the actors invite those American soldiers to dance today?

_____

2. My older brother gave me a movie ticket.

_____

3. The teacher often teaches the students to sing Chinese songs.

_____

4. My mother does not let my younger sister listen to French music.

_____

5. His good friend gave him two tickets for the Italian opera as a gift.

_____

6. Will the clerk return the mahjong to my older brother tomorrow?

_____

7. Did Mom ask us to play games today?

_____

8. The lawyer did not tell them the name of the new movie.

_____

9. His father did not teach him how to play Go.

_____

10. The musician asked you the name of the concert.

_____

Prepositional phrases with 在 *zài*, 从 *cóng*, 到 *dào* • Public places

22

Prepositional phrases with 在 *zài*, 从 *cóng*, 到 *dào*

SUBJECT	+	PREDICATE			
		(ADVERB) +	PREP. PHRASE +	VERB +	(OBJECT)
学生们 *Xuéshengmen*			从宿舍 *cóng sùshè*	来。 *lái*	The students come from the dorm.
她 *Tā*		不 *bú*	到学校 *dào xuéxiào*	去。 *qù.*	She won't go to school.
他 *Tā*		常 *cháng*	在我这儿 *zài wǒ zhèr*	看 *kàn*	电视 He often watches *diànshì.* TV at my place.

NOTE The negative adverb 不 *bù* is placed **before** the preposition. As a rule, a pronoun cannot be used alone as the object of a preposition that indicates location, and it must combine with either 这儿 *zhèr,* here or 那儿 *nàr,* there to form a location phrase before combining with the preposition. For example, 我这儿 *wǒ zhèr,* my place; 他们那儿 *tāmen nàr,* their place.

生词 SHĒNGCÍ (VOCABULARY)

Prepositions and public places

从	*cóng*	from
到	*dào*	to
银行	*yínháng*	bank
邮局	*yóujú*	post office
医院	*yīyuàn*	hospital
商店	*shāngdiàn*	shop; store
酒吧	*jiǔbā*	bar; tavern
商场	*shāngchǎng*	shopping mall
餐馆	*cānguǎn*	restaurant
超市	*chāoshì*	supermarket
博物馆	*bówùguǎn*	museum
电影院	*diànyǐngyuàn*	movie theater
剧场	*jùchǎng*	opera house

Rearrange each group of fragments into a grammatically correct sentence.

1. 从宿舍 *cóng sùshè* /学生们 *xuéshengmen* /去银行 *qù yínháng* /现在 *xiànzài*

_____

2. 到邮局去吗? *dào yóujú qù ma?* /明天 *míngtiān* /也 *yě* /你朋友 *nǐ péngyou*

_____

3. 在那个医院 *zài nà ge yīyuàn* /这些新医生 *zhèxiē xīn yīshēng* /上班 *shàngbān* /都 *dōu*

_____

4. 常到 *cháng dào* /那个演员 *nà ge yǎnyuán* /那个小商店 *nà ge xiǎo shāngdiàn* /去 *qù*

_____

5. 常在酒吧 *cháng zài jiǔbā* /这个老警察 *zhè ge lǎo jǐngchá* /喝酒 *hē jiǔ* /周末 *zhōumò*

_____

6. 来 *lái* /他们 *tāmen* /没从黄先生那儿 *méi cóng Huáng xiānsheng nàr* /我们这儿 *wǒmen zhèr*

_____

7. 职员们 *zhíyuánmen* /从商场 *cóng shāngchǎng* /来 *lái* /今天 *jīntiān*

_____

8. 中午 *zhōngwǔ* /我这儿 *wǒ zhèr* /想到 *xiǎng dào* /来吗? *lái ma?* /你们 *nǐmen*

_____

First, complete the sentences with the appropriate prepositions (在 **zài**, 从 **cóng**, 到 **dào**), and then translate into English.

1. 今天他哥哥不 _____ 家里去超市。 *Jīntiān tā gēge bù _____ jiālǐ qù chāoshì.*

_____

2. 我妹妹下午不 _____ 博物馆去。 *Wǒ mèimei xiàwǔ bú _____ bówùguǎn qù.*

_____

3. 她们都 _____ 白老师那儿吃晚饭吗? *Tāmen dōu _____ Bái lǎoshī nàr chī wǎnfàn ma?*

_____

4. 这些工人现在 _____ 哪儿去? *Zhèxiē gōngrén xiànzài _____ nǎr qù?*

_____

5. 老师们常 _____ 那个餐馆吃饭。 *Lǎoshīmen cháng* _____ *nà ge cānguǎn chīfàn.*

_____

6. 你们 _____ 哪儿来？ *Nǐmen* _____ *nǎr lái?*

_____

7. 你哥哥明天也 _____ 电影院去吗？ *Nǐ gēge míngtiān yě* _____ *diànyǐngyuàn qù ma?*

_____

8. 我不常 _____ 那个剧场去。 *Wǒ bù cháng* _____ *nà ge jùchǎng qù.*

_____

EXERCISE 22·3

翻译成中文 **Fānyì chéng Zhōngwén** *Translate into Chinese and pinyin.*

1. My father works at the post office now.

_____

2. I'll go to the Bank of China from the store tomorrow.

_____

3. The lawyers often drink beer in that small bar.

_____

4. Will the musicians go to the opera house in the evening?

_____

5. These soldiers do not often go to the movie theater now.

_____

6. Did that old farmer come from your place?

_____

7. This writer often dines in that restaurant.

_____

8. These waiters will go to the museum from the supermarket this morning.

_____

9. Do those nurses all work in that hospital?

_____

10. These workers do not go to the shopping mall in the afternoon.

_____

你知道吗? *Nǐ zhīdao ma?* Do you know?

百分比 *bǎifēnbǐ* Percentages

◆ 现在百分之三十 (*bǎifēnzhī sānshí,* 30%) 的美国年轻人 (*niánqīngrén,* youth) 在他们的爸爸, 妈妈家里居住 (*jūzhù,* to reside)。

◆ 从 2009 年到 2010 年, 从中国来美国的大学学习的留学生 (*liúxuésheng,* foreign students) 一共 (*yígòng,* totally) 有 158,000 人, 占 (*zhàn,* to occupy) 留学生总数 (*zǒngshù,* total number) 的百分之二十二!

◆ 从 1999 年到 2000 年, 从美国到中国的大学学习的留学生只有 (*zhǐyǒu,* only) 3,000 人, 可是从 2009 年到 2010 年, 从美国到中国的大学学习的留学生一共有 14,000 人!

◆ 美国现在大约 (*dàyuē,* about) 有百分之八十的人口 (*rénkǒu,* population) 在城市 (*chéngshì,* city) 里居住。

Adverbials • Sentences with serial verb phrases • Daily routines

·23·

Adverbials

An adverbial is a word or phrase that functions like an adverb. In Chinese, an adverbial, regardless of what it denotes, always occurs before the verb. The particle 地 *de* is usually placed immediately after a descriptive adverbial and is used as a marker of the adverbial.

SUBJECT +	PREDICATE				
	ADVERBIAL +	(地 DE) +	VERB +	(OBJECT/OTHER)	
他们 *Tāmen*	都认认真真 *dōu* *rènrènzhēnzhēn*	地 *de*	学习 *xuéxí*	汉语。 *Hànyǔ.*	They study Chinese conscientiously.
弟弟 *Dìdi*	高兴 *gāoxìng*	地 *de*	来 *lái*	了。 *le.*	My younger brother happily came.
我们 *Wǒmen*	在家里 *zài jiālǐ*		吃 *chī*	午饭。 *wǔ fàn.*	We eat lunch at home.
他 *Tā*	也 *yě*		回答 *huídá*	得很好。 *de hěn hǎo.*	He also answers well.
我们 *Wǒmen*	明天 *míngtiān*		上课。 *shàng kè.*		We will have class tomorrow.

NOTE   A time phrase can also be placed before the subject. For example, 明天我们上课。 *Míngtiān wǒmen shàngkè. We will have class tomorrow.*

生词 SHĒNGCÍ (VOCABULARY)

Daily routines

上课	*shàng kè*	to attend class
下课	*xià kè*	to get out of class
洗澡	*xǐzǎo*	to take a shower
工作	*gōngzuò*	work; job

Everyday words

了	*le*	particle
女	*nǚ*	female; woman
男	*nán*	male; man

翻译成英文 **Fānyì chéng Yīngwén**   *Translate into English.*

1. 你每天早上几点起床？ *Nǐ měi tiān zǎoshang jǐ diǎn qǐchuáng?*

_____

2. 我们今天九点上课，十点半下课。 *Wǒmen jīntiān jiǔ diǎn shàngkè, shí diǎn bàn xià kè.*

_____

3. 那些女护士都在食堂吃午饭。 *Nàxiē nǚ hùshi dōu zài shítáng chī wǔfàn.*

_____

4. 这些学生每天晚上都洗澡吗？ *Zhèxiē xuésheng měi tiān wǎnshang dōu xǐzǎo ma?*

_____

5. 那些老警察这个星期不喝咖啡。 *Nàxiē lǎo jǐngchá zhè ge xīngqī bù hē kāfēi.*

_____

6. 这些新医生都认认真真地工作。 *Zhèxiē xīn yīshēng dōu rènrènzhēnzhēn de gōngzuò.*

_____

7. 她哥哥是商人, 她弟弟也是商人。 *Tā gēge shì shāngrén, tā dìdi yě shì shāngrén.*

_____

8. 我爷爷每天晚上都早早地睡觉。 *Wǒ yéye měi tiān wǎnshang dōu zǎozǎo de shuìjiào.*

_____

9. 那个男演员现在不工作。 *Nà ge nán yǎnyuán xiànzài bù gōngzuò.*

_____

10. 那个女律师最喜欢红色的领带。 *Nà ge nǚ lùshī zuì xǐhuan hóngsè de lǐngdài.*

_____

Sentences with serial verb phrases

Two or more verb phrases can be used together in a sentence. Often the second verb phrase (e.g., 看她 *kàn tā see her*) indicates the purpose of the first event; and the first verb phrase (e.g., 骑自行车 *qí zìxíngchē ride a bike*) indicates the means of the second event.

SUBJECT	+	PREDICATE			
	VERB₁ +	(OBJ.₁) +	VERB₂ +	(OBJ.₂)	
他们	去	宿舍	看	她。	They go to the dorm to see her.
Tāmen	*qù*	*sùshè*	*kàn*	*tā*	
他们	骑	自行车	去	学校。	They ride a bike to school.
Tāmen	*qí*	*zìxíngchē*	*qù*	*xuéxiào.*	

More daily routines and means of transportation

脸	liǎn	face
刷	shuā	to brush
牙/牙齿	yá/yáchǐ	tooth
刮	guā	to shave
胡子	húzi	beard; mustache
化妆	huàzhuāng	to apply make-up
上床	shàngchuáng	to go to bed
回(家)	huí(jiā)	to return (home)
公司	gōngsī	company
下班	xià bān	to get off work
坐	zuò	to ride; to sit
公共汽车	gōnggòngqìchē	bus
飞机	fēijī	airplane
船	chuán	boat
开(车)	kāi(chē)	to drive (auto)
走(路)	zǒu(lù)	to walk; to go on foot
路	lù	road

EXERCISE

23·2

Answer the following questions according to real situations. Answers may vary.

1. 你每天都刷牙, 洗脸吗？ *Nǐ měitiān dōu shuā yá, xǐ liǎn ma?*

   _____

2. 你每天早上都刮胡子吗？ *Nǐ měitiān zǎoshang dōu guā húzi ma?* (for men)

   _____

3. 你每天都化妆吗？ *Nǐ měitiān dōu huàzhuāng ma?* (for women)

   _____

4. 你上午几点去学校上学？ *Nǐ shàngwǔ jǐ diǎn qù xuéxiào shàngxué?*

   _____

5. 你坐公共汽车去还是开汽车去？ *Nǐ zuò gōnggòng qìchē qù háishì kāi qìchē qù?*

   _____

6. 你也常骑自行车去吗？ *Nǐ yě cháng qí zìxíngchē qù ma?*

   _____

7. 你每天几点下班回家？ *Nǐ měitiān jǐ diǎn xià bān huíjiā?*

   _____

8. 你坐车回家, 开车回家还是骑车回家？ *Nǐ zuò chē huíjiā, kāi chē huíjiā háishì qíchē huíjiā?*

   _____

9. 你也常走路回家吗？ *Nǐ yě cháng zǒu lù huíjiā ma?*

_____

10. 你在哪儿吃晚饭？你常在家里吃还是常在外边吃？ *Nǐ zài nǎr chī wǎnfàn? Nǐ cháng zài jiālǐ chī háishì cháng zài wàibian chī?*

_____

11. 星期天你常去餐馆吃晚饭吗？ *Xīngqītiān nǐ cháng qù cānguǎn chī wǎnfàn ma?*

_____

12. 你晚上几点上床睡觉？ *Nǐ wǎnshang jǐ diǎn shàng chuáng shuìjiào?*

_____

EXERCISE 23·3

Complete the following sentences with appropriate serial verb phrases. Answers may vary.

1. 职员们每天都去公司 _____。 *Zhíyuánmen měitiān dōu qù gōngsī _____.*

2. 爸爸和妈妈晚上不常回家 _____。 *Bàba hé māma wǎnshang bù cháng huí jiā _____.*

3. 那些新护士上午去医院 _____。 *Nàxiē xīn hùshi shàngwǔ qù yīyuàn _____.*

4. 现在学生们都来图书馆 _____。 *Xiànzài xuéshengmen dōu lái túshūguǎn _____.*

5. 这些工人都回宿舍 _____。 *Zhèxiē gōngrén dōu huí sùshè _____.*

6. 我弟弟晚上十点上床 _____。 *Wǒ dìdi wǎnshang shí diǎn shàng chuáng _____.*

7. 他的女朋友常走路 _____吗？ *Tā de nǚ péngyou cháng zǒu lù _____ ma?*

8. 那些律师都开汽车 _____。 *Nàxiē lǜshī dōu kāi qìchē _____.*

9. 医生们常坐飞机 _____吗？ *Yīshēngmen cháng zuò fēijī _____ ma?*

10. 这个警察不常坐船 _____。 *Zhè ge jǐngchá bù cháng zuò chuán _____.*

EXERCISE 23·4

翻译成中文 **Fānyì chéng Zhōngwén**   *Translate into Chinese and pinyin.*

1. The students attend Chinese class in the big classroom from 8:00 a.m. to 10:00 a.m.

_____

2. The new manager will drive his car to work tomorrow.

_____

3. Do you wash your face and brush your teeth every day?

_____

4. Does his father go to work by bus or by bike?

_____

5. The writer rarely goes home to eat supper.

_____

6. Do those athletes go to the gymnasium to work out every day?

_____

7. This musician goes to bed at eleven o'clock.

_____

8. That businessperson will not go to France by boat, (and) he will go by plane.

_____

9. These farmers do not have an automobile now, (and) they often go home on foot.

_____

10. Do the musicians usually go to the new opera house to sing on Saturdays?

_____

你知道吗? *Nǐ zhīdao ma? Do you know?*

上班的交通工具 *shàngbān de jiāotōng gōngjù Means of transportation*

在美国的大城市里，几乎 (*jīhū*, almost) 没有人坐船去上班，也很少人坐飞机去上班。可是有很多人开汽车或者 (*huòzhě*, or) 坐公共汽车去上班，也有一些人骑自行车、骑摩托车 (*mótuōchē*, motor bike) 或者走路去上班。从 2005 年到 2009 年，在洛杉矶县 (*Luòshānjī xiàn*, Los Angeles county), 大约 (*dàyuē*, about)

◆ 百分之七十二 (*bǎifēnzhī qīshí'èr*, 72%) 的人独自 (*dúzì*, alone) 开车去上班。
◆ 百分之十点八 (10.8%) 的人合伙 (*héhuǒ*, to carpool) 开车去上班。
◆ 百分之七点二 (7.2%) 的人坐公共汽车去上班。
◆ 百分之二点九 (2.9%) 的人走路去上班。
◆ 百分之零点九 (0.9%) 的人骑自行车去上班。
◆ 百分之一 (1.0%) 的人骑摩托车去上班。
◆ 百分之五 (5%) 的人在家里上班。

◆24◆ Auxiliary verbs (I) 想 *xiǎng*, 要 *yào*, 会 *huì*, 能 *néng*, 可以 *kěyǐ* • Sports and games

Auxiliary verbs (I) 想 *xiǎng*, 要 *yào*, 会 *huì*, 能 *néng*, 可以 *kěyǐ*

Auxiliary verbs are placed before verbs to indicate intention, ability, possibility, or permission.

生词 SHĒNGCÍ (VOCABULARY)

Auxiliary verbs

想	*xiǎng*	want
要	*yào*	must; want
会	*huì*	to know how to
能	*néng*	can; to be able to
可以	*kěyǐ*	may; can

SUBJECT + PREDICATE

	[TIME WORD]	+ AUX.VERB +	VERB PHRASE	
你们	今天	要不要	打篮球?	Do you want to play basketball today?
Nǐmen	*jīntiān*	*yào bu yào*	*dǎ lánqiú?*	(*strong will or desire*)
我们	今天	不想	打篮球。	We don't want to play basketball today.
Wǒ	*jīntiān*	*bù xiǎng*	*dǎ lánqiú*	
你们	今天	想	打篮球吗?	Do you intend to play basketball today?
Nǐmen	*jīntiān*	*xiǎng*	*dǎ lánqiú?*	(*volition or intention*)
我们	今天	不想	打篮球。	We don't intend to play basketball today.
Wǒmen	*jīntiān*	*bù xiǎng*	*dǎ lánqiú.*	
她		会不会	游泳?	Does she know how to swim?
Tā		*huì bu huì*	*yóuyǒng?*	(*acquired skill or ability*)
她		会	游泳。	She knows how to swim.
Tā		*huì*	*yóuyǒng.*	
她		能	去游泳吗?	Can she go swimming?
Tā		*néng*	*qù yóuyǒng ma?*	(*ability depending on circumstances*)

她		不能	去游泳。	She cannot go swimming.
Tā		*bù néng*	*qù yóuyǒng.*	
她		可以	去游泳吗?	Can she go swimming?
Tā		*kěyǐ*	*qù yóuyǒng ma?*	(*ability depending on circumstances*)
她		不能	去游泳。	She cannot go swimming.
Tā		*bù néng*	*qù yóuyǒng.*	
我	现在	可以	去游泳吗?	May I go swimming now?
Wǒ	*xiànzài*	*kěyǐ*	*qù yóuyǒng ma?*	(*permission*)
你	现在	不能	去游泳。	You may not go swimming now.
Nǐ	*xiànzài*	*bù néng*	*qù yóuyǒng.*	

NOTE   The negative form of 要 *yào* is 不想 *bù xiǎng*, not 不要 *bú yào*. 不要 *bú yào*, is used to indicate strong will of not wanting to do something. For example, 我不要去! *Wǒ bú yào qù!* *I don't want to go!* 不要 *bú yào* is also used in an imperative sentence to indicate prohibition or dissuasion. For example, 你不要去! *Nǐ bú yào qù!* *Don't go!* The negative form of 可以 *kěyǐ* is 不能 *bù néng*, not 不可以 *bù kěyǐ*. 不可以 *bù kěyǐ* is used to indicate prohibition, as in 你不可以进来! *Nǐ bù kěyǐ jìnlài!* *You are not allowed to come in!*

生词   SHĒNGCÍ (VOCABULARY)

Sports and games

打(球)	*dǎ(qiú)*	to play (ball)
篮球	*lánqiú*	basketball
冰球	*bīngqiú*	ice hockey
排球	*páiqiú*	volleyball
网球	*wǎngqiú*	tennis
乒乓球	*pīngpāngqiú*	ping-pong
高尔夫球	*gāo'ěrfūqiú*	golf
踢	*tī*	to kick
足球	*zúqiú*	soccer; football
滑雪	*huáxuě*	to ski
滑冰	*huábīng*	to skate
象棋	*xiàngqí*	chess
扑克	*pūkè*	poker

Everyday words

| 跟 | *gēn* | with |
| 一起 | *yìqǐ* | together |

EXERCISE

24·1

Answer the following questions according to real situations. Answers may vary.

1. 你今天想去体育馆打冰球吗? *Nǐ jīntiān xiǎng qù tǐyùguǎn dǎ bīngqiú ma?*

_____

2. 你下午要去体育场踢足球吗? *Nǐ xiàwǔ yào qù tǐyùchǎng tī zúqiú ma?*

_____

3. 你爸爸会不会打篮球和排球？ *Nǐ bàba huì bu huì dǎ lánqiú hé páiqiú?*

_____

4. 你朋友明天可以打乒乓球吗？ *Nǐ péngyou míngtiān kěyǐ dǎ pīngpāngqiú ma?*

_____

5. 一个眼睛不好的人能打网球吗？ *Yí ge yǎnjing bù hǎo de rén néng dǎ wǎngqiú ma?*

_____

6. 你明年要不要学打高尔夫球？ *Nǐ míngnián yào bu yào xué dǎ gāo'ěrfūqiú?*

_____

7. 你妈妈能不能教你滑冰？ *Nǐ māma néng bu néng jiāo nǐ huábīng?*

_____

8. 今年你想不想学滑雪？ *Jīnnián nǐ xiǎng bu xiǎng xué huáxuě?*

_____

9. 你朋友今天可以跟你一起去打球吗？ *Nǐ péngyou jīntiān kěyǐ gēn nǐ yìqǐ qù dǎ qiú ma?*

_____

10. 你爸爸, 妈妈会不会打扑克？ *Nǐ bàba, māma huì bu huì dǎ pūkè?*

_____

EXERCISE
24·2

First, provide negative answers to following questions, and then translate the negative sentences into English.

1. 你晚上要不要跟哥哥一起下象棋？ *Nǐ wǎnshang yào bu yào gēn gēge yìqǐ xià xiàngqí?*

_____

_____

2. 他们下午可以去体育场踢足球吗？ *Tāmen xiàwǔ kěyǐ qù tǐyùchǎng tī zúqiú ma?*

_____

_____

3. 他爸爸会不会打高尔夫球？ *Tā bàba huì bu huì dǎ gāo'ěrfūqiú?*

_____

_____

4. 演员们明天想去体育馆滑冰吗？ *Yǎnyuánmen míngtiān xiǎng qù tǐyùguǎn huábīng ma?*

_____

_____

5. 那些律师星期天能去打网球吗？ *Nàxiē lǜshī Xīngqītiān néng qù dǎ wǎngqiú ma?*

_____

_____

6. 你们要跟那些军人一起打篮球吗？ *Nǐmen yào gēn nàxiē jūnrén yìqǐ dǎ lánqiú ma?*

_____

_____

7. 白先生想不想学打冰球？ *Bái Xiānsheng xiǎng bu xiǎng xué dǎ bīngqiú?*

_____

_____

8. 您下个月能不能教我们打排球？ *Nín xià ge yuè néng bu néng jiāo wǒmen dǎ páiqiú?*

_____

_____

9. 我可以跟你一起下围棋吗？ *Wǒ kěyǐ gēn nǐ yìqǐ xià wéiqí ma?*

_____

_____

10. 在上班时间，护士们可以打扑克吗？ *Zài shàngbān shíjiān, hùshimen kěyǐ dǎ pūkè ma?*

_____

_____

EXERCISE
24·3

翻译成中文 **Fānyì chéng Zhōngwén**   *Translate into Chinese and pinyin.*

1. I don't know how to play Go, (and) I don't know how to play chess, either.

_____

2. Can you guys play the game with us today?

_____

3. She'd like to learn how to play mahjong next month.

_____

4. My friend wants to go to the gymnasium to play basketball this afternoon.

_____

5. May I play poker with you guys? (*use the affirmative-negative question*)

_____

6. The old writer knows how to play volleyball and basketball.

_____

7. Would you like to play ice hockey with the teachers? (*use the affirmative-negative question*)

_____

8. These athletes can play tennis and ping-pong in our school's gymnasium.

_____

9. Mom, may we go skiing this Sunday?—No, you may not go.

_____

10. Professor Bai wants to teach those lawyers to play golf next week.

_____

你知道吗? *Nǐ zhīdao ma?* Do you know?

运动, 麻将和下棋 *yùndòng májiàng hé xiàqí* Sports and games

- 无数 (*wúshù*, countless) 中国人都会打麻将。据说 (*jùshuō*, it is said) 百分之九十的中国人都会打麻将。不少外国人 (*wàiguórén*, foreigner) 也会打麻将。你也会吗?
- 无数的中国人都会下中国象棋。据说, 百分之五十的中国人会下中国象棋。很多越南人 (*Yuènánrén*, Vietnamese) 也都会下中国象棋。据说, 百分之三十的越南人会下中国象棋。
- 很多中国人都会下围棋, 而且 (*érqiě*, and) 也很喜欢下围棋。不少日本人和韩国人也会下围棋, 而且他们下得很好。
- 在中国, 很少人会打冰球和网球, 可是每 (*měi*, every) 个人都会打乒乓球! 而且他们都打得很好!

Events that are going to take place • Future plans

Events that are going to take place

	AFFIRMATION	NEGATION
With time words	他明天上课。 *Tā míngtiān shàngkè.* He'll attend class tomorrow.	他明天不上课。 *Tā míngtiān bú shàngkè.* He won't attend class tomorrow.
With 会 *huì* or 要 *yào*	他(明天)**会**上课。 *Tā (míngtiān) **huì** shàngkè.* He'll attend class (tomorrow). 他(明天)**要**上课。 *Tā (míngtiān) **yào** shàngkè.* He'll attend class (tomorrow).	他(明天)(**还**)**不会**上课。 *Tā (míngtiān)(**hái**) **bú huì** shàngkè.* He won't attend class (tomorrow) (yet).
With (**就**)要…了 (**jiù**) *yào…le,* or "**快要**…了 *kuài yào …le* (Immediacy is emphasized.)	他(明天) (**就**)**要**上课**了**。 *Tā (míngtiān) (**jiù**) **yào** shàngkè **le.*** He's going to attend class (tomorrow). 他**快要**上课**了**。 *Tā **kuài yào** shàngkè **le.*** He's going to attend class very soon.	他(明天)(**还**)**不会**上课。 *Tā (míngtiān)(**hái**) **bú huì** shàngkè.* He's not going to attend class (tomorrow) (yet). 他(**还**)**不会**上课。 *Tā (**hái**) **bú huì** shàngkè.* He's not going to attend class (yet).

Usually no time word is used with **快要**…了 *kuài yào…le*.

生词 SHĒNGCÍ (VOCABULARY)

Future plans, vacations, and four seasons

周末	zhōumò	weekend
结婚	jiéhūn	to get married
海滩	hǎitān	(sea) beach
房子	fángzi	house
旅游	lǚyóu	to travel
北京	Běijīng	Beijing
打算	dǎsuàn	to intend; to plan
计划	jìhuà	to plan
准备	zhǔnbèi	to be going to
找	zhǎo	to look for
开会	kāihuì	to attend/hold a meeting
毕业	bìyè	to graduate
到	dào	to arrive
开始	kāishǐ	to begin; to start
春天	chūntiān	spring
夏天	xiàtiān	summer
秋天	qiūtiān	autumn; fall
冬天	dōngtiān	winter

EXERCISE 25·1

Answer the following questions according to real situations. Answers may vary.

1. 你明天会去体育馆打球吗？ *Nǐ míngtiān huì qù tǐyùguǎn dǎqiú ma?*

_____

2. 你晚上要跟你朋友一起打扑克吗？ *Nǐ wǎnshang yào gēn nǐ péngyou yìqǐ dǎ pūkè ma?*

_____

3. 你星期六打算去中国餐馆吃饭吗？ *Nǐ Xīngqīliù dǎsuàn qù Zhōngguó cānguǎn chīfàn ma?*

_____

4. 你周末准备收拾一下儿你的屋子吗？ *Nǐ zhōumò zhǔnbèi shōushi yíxiàr nǐ de wūzi ma?*

_____

5. 下个星期你打算去海滩游泳吗？ *Xià ge xīngqī nǐ dǎsuàn qù hǎitān yóuyǒng ma?*

_____

6. 你计划明年秋天买房子吗？ *Nǐ jìhuà míngnián qiūtiān mǎi fángzi ma?*

_____

7. 你准备明年找新工作吗？ *Nǐ zhǔnbèi míngnián zhǎo xīn gōngzuò ma?*

_____

8. 今年夏天你就要去意大利旅游了吗？ *Jīnnián xiàtiān nǐ jiù yào qù Yìdàlì lǚyóu le ma?*

_____

9. 你计划明年春天结婚吗？ *Nǐ jìhuà míngnián chūntiān jiéhūn ma?*

_____

10. 你快要去中国开会了吗？ *Nǐ kuàiyào qù Zhōngguó kāihuì le ma?*

_____

EXERCISE
25·2

Reword sentences 1–5 with 快要…了 **kuài yào…le** and sentences 6–10 with 就要…了 **jiù yào…le**.

EXAMPLES   电影开始。 *Diànyǐng kāishǐ.*

电影**快要**开始**了**。 *Diànyǐng **kuài yào** kāishǐ **le**.*

电影七点一刻开始。 *Diànyǐng qīdiǎn yí kè kāishǐ.*

电影七点一刻**就要**开始**了**。 *Diànyǐng qīdiǎn yí kè **jiù yào** kāishǐ **le**.*

1. 他们到北京去工作。 *Tāmen dào Běijīng qù gōngzuò.*

_____

2. 经理们开会。 *Jīnglǐmen kāihuì.*

_____

3. 那些学生从大学毕业。 *Nàxiē xuésheng cóng dàxué bìyè.*

_____

4. 爸爸和妈妈回家。 *Bàba hé māma huíjiā.*

_____

5. 新护士上班吗？ *Xīn hùshi shàngbān ma?*

_____

6. 音乐会两点半开始。 *Yīnyuèhuì liǎng diǎn bàn kāishǐ.*

_____

7. 这些律师明年夏天去北京学习。 *Zhèxiē lǜshī míngnián xiàtiān qù Běijīng xuéxí.*

_____

8. 这个星期六她跟他结婚吗？ *Zhè ge Xīngqīliù tā gēn tā jiéhūn ma?*

_____

9. 老师们下个月去旅游。 *Lǎoshīmen xià ge yuè qù lǚyóu.*

_____

10. 黄先生明年春天买房子。 *Huáng xiānsheng míngnián chūntiān mǎi fángzi.*

_____

First, negate the following sentences, and then translate into English.

1. 这些老师明天要开会。*Zhèxiē lǎoshī míngtiān yào kāihuì.*

   _____

   _____

2. 那个服务员会去上班。*Nà ge fúwùyuán huì qù shàngbān.*

   _____

   _____

3. 公共汽车会来。*Gōnggòng qìchē huì lái.*

   _____

   _____

4. 我姐姐快要结婚了。*Wǒ jiějie kuài yào jiéhūn le.*

   _____

   _____

5. 这个星期六我妈妈就要来看我了。*Zhè ge Xīngqīliù wǒ māma jiù yào lái kàn wǒ le.*

   _____

   _____

6. 那个律师快要到北京了。*Nà ge lǜshī kuài yào dào Běijīng le.*

   _____

   _____

7. 舞会快要开始了。*Wǔhuì kuài yào kāishǐ le.*

   _____

   _____

8. 这些运动员现在要休息。*Zhèxiē yùndòngyuán xiànzài yào xiūxi.*

   _____

   _____

9. 我弟弟今年秋天会毕业。*Wǒ dìdi jīnnián qiūtiān huì bìyè.*

   _____

   _____

10. 白教授计划明年春天买新房子。*Bái jiàoshòu jìhuà míngnián chūntiān mǎi xīn fángzi.*

   _____

   _____

11. 那些职员想去海滩游泳。*Nàxiē zhíyuán xiǎng qù hǎitān yóuyǒng.*

_____

_____

12. 他打算去中国找工作。*Tā dǎsuàn qù Zhōngguó zhǎo gōngzuò.*

_____

_____

13. 我爸爸准备下个星期去上海开会。*Wǒ bàba zhǔnbèi xià ge xīngqī qù Shànghǎi kāihuì.*

_____

_____

14. 今年冬天我们要到中国去旅游。*Jīnnián dōngtiān wǒmen yào dào Zhōngguó qù lǚyóu.*

_____

_____

EXERCISE
25·4

翻译成中文 Fānyì chéng Zhōngwén   *Translate into Chinese and pinyin.*

1. These teachers will go to China for a tour next year.

_____

2. The concert will start very soon.

_____

3. His younger sister will be graduating soon.

_____

4. My younger brother is going to look for a new job next month.

_____

5. Does Professor Huang plan to buy a new car next autumn?

_____

6. She won't marry me this winter. (*use* 跟我结婚 *gēn wǒ jiéhūn*)

_____

7. Are the actors going (*prepared*) to come to the beach to swim this weekend?

_____

8. Do you guys intend to go to China to study Chinese this summer?

_____

9. This spring my friend will buy a house in Beijing.

    _____

10. The professors are not going to have a meeting at 10:00 a.m.

    _____

你知道吗? *Nǐ zhīdao ma? Do you know?*

未来 *wèilái The future*

- 预计 2040 年印度的人口会达到十五点二亿，超越 (*chāoyuè*, to surpass) 那个时候的中国人口(十四点五亿)。
- 再过 (*guò*, pass) 五十年，也许 (*yěxǔ*, maybe) 家家 (each household) 都有机器人 (*jīqìrén*, robot) 了。
- 将来 (*jiānglái*, in the future) 有一天，人类 (*rénlèi*, mankind) 可能登上 (*dēngshàng*, land on) 火星 (*Huǒxīng*, Mars)。

Lessons 21–25

EXERCISE
R5·1

Match each VO-verb or the verbal phrase in Chinese with its English equivalent.

1. _____ 洗澡 *xǐzǎo*

2. _____ 化妆 *huàzhuāng*

3. _____ 跳舞 *tiàowǔ*

4. _____ 结婚 *jiéhūn*

5. _____ 滑雪 *huáxuě*

6. _____ 滑冰 *huábīng*

7. _____ 唱歌 *chànggē*

8. _____ 起床 *qǐchuáng*

9. _____ 洗脸 *xǐ liǎn*

10. _____ 刷牙 *shuā yá*

11. _____ 刮胡子 *guā húzi*

12. _____ 打球 *dǎ qiú*

13. _____ 踢足球 *tī zúqiú*

14. _____ 打扑克 *dǎ pūkè*

15. _____ 走路 *zǒu lù*

16. _____ 坐公共汽车 *zuò gōnggòng qìchē*

17. _____ 骑自行车 *qí zìxíngchē*

18. _____ 坐船 *zuò chuán*

19. _____ 坐飞机 *zuò fēijī*

20. _____ 做游戏 *zuò yóuxì*

21. _____ 下围棋 *xià wéiqí*

22. _____ 下班 *xià bān*

a. to ski

b. to dance

c. to sing

d. to take a bath

e. to put on makeup

f. to get up

g. to skate

h. to play a ballgame

i. to play poker

j. to get married

k. to wash one's face

l. to take a plane; by air

m. to walk; on foot

n. to shave the beard

o. to brush one's teeth

p. to play Go

q. to play soccer

r. to get off work

s. to take a bus

t. to go home

u. to take a boat

v. to ride a bike

23. _____ 回家 huí jiā   w. to play chess

24. _____ 打麻将 dǎ májiàng   x. to attend class

25. _____ 下象棋 xià xiàngqí   y. to play a game

26. _____ 上课 shàng kè   z. to play mahjong

◆ EXERCISE
R5·2

*Complete the pivotal sentences 1–8 with appropriate **VO-verbs** or **verbal phrases** and the last four double-object sentences (9–12) with appropriate **nouns** or **noun phrases**. Answers may vary.*

1. 我明天想请您到我家 _____。

   Wǒ míngtiān xiǎng qǐng nín dào wǒ jiā _____.

2. 下个星期一老师准备让学生们在教室 _____。

   Xià ge Xīngqīyī lǎoshī zhǔnbèi ràng xuéshengmen zài jiàoshì _____.

3. 爸爸打算今年夏天叫我跟他一起 _____。

   Bàba dǎsuàn Jīnnián xiàtiān jiào wǒ gēn tā yìqǐ _____.

4. 他朋友今天要帮助他 _____。

   Tā péngyou jīntiān yào bāngzhù tā _____.

5. 白老师计划明年春天教他们 _____。

   Bái lǎoshī jìhuà míngnián chūntiān jiāo tāmen _____.

6. 他以后会教这些新工人 _____。

   Tā yǐhòu huì jiāo zhèxiē xīn gōngrén _____.

7. 她现在可以帮助这些新演员 _____。

   Tā xiànzài kěyǐ bāngzhù zhèxiē xīn yǎnyuán _____.

8. 那个作家明天要给 _____ 两张电影票。

   Nà ge zuòjiā míngtiān yào gěi _____ *liǎng zhāng diànyǐng piào.*

9. 他妈妈今天告诉他 _____。

   Tā māma jīntiān gàosu tā _____.

10. 那个警察现在要问 _____ 几个问题。

    Nà ge jǐngchá xiànzài yào wèn _____ *jǐ ge wèntí.*

11. 黄老师星期三送 _____ 一本中文书。

    Huáng lǎoshī Xīngqīsān sòng _____ *yì běn Zhōngwén shū.*

First, complete the sentences with the appropriate prepositions (在 zài, 从 cóng, 到 dào, 跟 gēn), and then translate into English.

1. 他朋友不 _____ 他一起去酒吧喝酒。 *Tā péngyou bù _____ tā yìqǐ qù jiǔbā hē jiǔ.*

   _____

2. 明天他不 _____ 他家里去公司上班。 *Míngtiān tā bù _____ tā jiālǐ qù gōngsī shàngbān.*

   _____

3. 学生们现在都 _____ 我这儿吃午饭。 *Xuéshengmen xiànzài dōu _____ wǒ zhèr chī wǔfàn.*

   _____

4. 我今天不想 _____ 医生那儿去。 *Wǒ jīntiān bù xiǎng _____ yīshēng nàr qù.*

   _____

5. 这些农民 _____ 哪儿来北京旅游？ *Zhèxiē nóngmín _____ nǎr lái Běijīng lǚyóu?*

   _____

6. 律师们常 _____ 这个中国餐馆吃饭。 *Lǜshīmen cháng _____ zhè ge Zhōngguó cānguǎn chī fàn.*

   _____

7. 我不常 _____ 他一起去那个商店。 *Wǒ bù cháng _____ tā yìqǐ qù nà ge shāngdiàn.*

   _____

8. 她妹妹星期六下午也要 _____ 邮局去吗？ *Tā mèimei Xīngqīliù xiàwǔ yě yào _____ yóujú qù ma?*

   _____

翻译成英文 Fānyì chéng Yīngwén *Translate into English.*

1. 他们每天早上都开车去学校上课。 *Tāmen měitiān zǎoshang dōu kāichē qù xuéxiào shàngkè.*

   _____

2. 我妈妈下午五点要坐公共汽车回家。 *Wǒ māma xiàwǔ wǔ diǎn yào zuò gōnggòng qìchē huíjiā.*

   _____

3. 他们今天在学生食堂吃晚饭吗？ *Tāmen jīntiān zài xuésheng shítáng chī wǎnfàn ma?*

_____

4. 你们每天都可以走路去体育馆打篮球。 *Nǐmen měi tiān dōu kěyǐ zǒu lù qù tǐyùguǎn dǎ lánqiú.*

_____

5. 这些医生明天不会去体育场运动。 *Zhèxiē yīshēng míngtiān bú huì qù tǐyùchǎng yùndòng.*

_____

6. 她毕业以后也想到北京去找工作。 *Tā bìyè yǐhòu yě xiǎng dào Běijīng qù zhǎo gōngzuò.*

_____

7. 那些新护士都认认真真地工作。 *Nàxiē xīn hùshi dōu rènrènzhēnzhēn de gōngzuò.*

_____

8. 她哥哥也常骑自行车去公司上班。 *Tā gēge yě cháng qí zìxíngchē qù gōngsī shàngbān.*

_____

9. 爸爸每个星期天都很早地来宿舍看我。 *Bàba měi ge Xīngqītiān dōu hěn zǎo de lái sùshè kàn wǒ.*

_____

10. 演员们能不能在剧场里化妆？ *Yǎnyuánmen néng bu néng zài jùchǎng lǐ huàzhuāng?*

_____

11. 这个女律师现在很喜欢坐船去旅游。 *Zhè ge nǚ lǜshī xiànzài hěn xǐhuan zuò chuán qù lǚyóu.*

_____

12. 他明天上午不会有时间刮胡子。 *Tā míngtiān shàngwǔ bú huì yǒu shíjiān guā húzi.*

_____

EXERCISE R5·5

Provide negative answers to the following questions.

1. 你要不要跟弟弟一起下中国象棋？ *Nǐ yào bu yào gēn dìdi yìqǐ xià Zhōngguó xiàngqí?*

2. 他们星期六可以不可以去体育场踢足球？ *Tāmen Xīngqīliù kěyǐ bu kěyǐ qù tǐyùchǎng tī zúqiú?*

_____

3. 你们经理会不会打高尔夫球？ *Nǐmen jīnglǐ huì bu huì dǎ gāo'ěrfūqiú?*

4. 她妹妹明天想不想去体育馆滑冰？ *Tā mèimei míngtiān xiǎng bu xiǎng qù tǐyùguǎn huábīng?*

_____

5. 那些军人星期天能不能去打篮球？ *Nàxiē jūnrén Xīngqītiān néng bu néng qù dǎ lánqiú?*

_____

6. 你们明天要跟那些律师一起打网球吗？ *Nǐ men míngtiān yào gēn nàxiē lǜshī yìqǐ dǎ wǎngqiú ma?*

_____

7. 那些职员下午会去体育馆打排球吗？ *Nàxiē zhíyuán xiàwǔ huì qù tǐyùguǎn dǎ páiqiú ma?*

_____

8. 下个月这些学生就要毕业了吗？ *Xià ge yuè zhèxiē xuésheng jiù yào bìyè le ma?*

_____

9. 学生们快要去中国旅游了吗？ *Xuéshengmen kuài yào qù Zhōngguó lǚyóu le ma?*

_____

10. 现在姑娘们快下班了吗？ *Xiànzài gūniangmen kuài xià bān le ma?*

_____

11. 那个警察要结婚了吗？ *Nà ge jǐngchá yào jiéhūn le ma?*

_____

12. 你爸爸今年夏天打算买新房子吗？ *Nǐ bàba jīnnián xiàtiān dǎsuàn mǎi xīn fángzi ma?*

_____

EXERCISE
R5·6

翻译成中文 Fānyì chéng Zhōngwén *Translate into Chinese and pinyin.*

1. Professor Huang does not let his students play poker in the classroom.

_____

2. I may ask him to go to China with you next year.

_____

3. My older sister will give me a ticket for the ball tomorrow.

_____

4. Can you tell me the name of the opera?

_____

5. Does the actress often go the museum?

_____

6. The old nurse will go to the hospital from her place tonight.

_____

7. The workers won't have their lunch in the cafeteria today.

_____

8. Your mother wants you to work conscientiously in the new company.

_____

9. Do you guys want to play mahjong at my place over the weekend?

_____

10. You may go to the shopping mall by bus with her on Saturday.

_____

11. The farmer is going to France on a tour by air this Sunday.

_____

12. Is your older brother going to get married soon?—No, he is not going to get married yet.

_____

13. Our manager does not know how to play Chinese chess.

_____

14. Do you want to go to play soccer with us?—No, we don't want to play soccer with you.

_____

15. Mom, may I go play tennis this afternoon?—No, you may not go play tennis.

_____

16. This winter Professor Bai plans to teach the students to ski.

_____

EXERCISE
R5·7

True or False? *After reading the following Chinese dialogue, mark each of the English statements as either **true** or **false**.*

Xiao Wang [小王 *Xiǎo Wáng*, Mr. Wang] runs into Xiao Li [小李 *Xiǎo Lǐ*, Mr. Li], his good friend, on campus.

小王：你好，小李！你最近怎么样？ *Nǐ hǎo, Xiǎo Lǐ! Nǐ zuìjìn zěnmeyàng?*

小李：我很好，你呢？ *Wǒ hěn hǎo, nǐ ne?*

小王：我也很好。你现在要去哪儿？ *Wǒ yě hěn hǎo. Nǐ xiànzài yào qù nǎr?*

小李：我要去体育馆打篮球。你想不想跟我一起去？*Wǒ yào qù tǐyùguǎn dǎ lánqiú. Nǐ xiǎng bu xiǎng gēn wǒ yìqǐ qù?*

小王：对不起(duìbuqǐ, I'm sorry)，小李，我不会打篮球。你知道的，我只(zhǐ, only)会打乒乓球。你去找会打篮球的同学(tóngxué, classmate)跟你一起去吧。*Duìbuqǐ, Xiǎo Lǐ, wǒ bú huì dǎ lánqiú. Nǐ zhīdao de, wǒ zhǐ huì dǎ pīngpāngqiú. Nǐ qù zhǎo huì dǎ lánqiú de tóngxué gēn nǐ yìqǐ qù ba.*

小李：好吧，我现在就回宿舍去找别的(biéde, other)同学。*Hǎo ba, wǒ xiànzài jiù huí sùshè qù zhǎo biéde tóngxué.*

小王：对了，小李，我要告诉你一个好消息(xiāoxi, news)：北京京剧团(jīngjù tuán, Beijing Opera Troupe)就要来上海(Shànghǎi, Shanghai)演出(yǎnchū, to perform)了。*Duìle, Xiǎo Lǐ, wǒ yào gàosu nǐ yí ge hǎo xiāoxi: Běijīng Jīngjùtuán jiù yào lái Shànghǎi yǎnchū le.*

小李：是吗？太好了！演出时间是在哪一天？几点？*Shì ma? Tài hǎo le! Yǎnchū shíjiān shì zài nǎ yì tiān? Jǐ diǎn?*

小王：下个星期六晚上七点半。*Xià ge Xīngqīliù wǎnshang qī diǎn bàn.*

小李：他们要在哪儿演出？*Tāmen yào zài nǎr yǎnchū?*

小王：他们要在上海剧场演出。我想请你跟我一起去看这个京剧演出。*Tāmen yào zài Shànghǎi Jùchǎng yǎnchū. Wǒ xiǎng qǐng nǐ gēn wǒ yìqǐ qù kàn zhè ge jīngjù yǎnchū.*

小李：好啊！可是你能搞到(gǎodào, to get)票吗？*Hǎo a! Kěshì nǐ néng gǎodào piào ma?*

小王：没问题(no problem)！我爸爸认识京剧团的经理。他说他明天要给我两张好的票。*Méi wèntí! Wǒ bàba rènshi jīngjùtuán de jīnglǐ. Tā shuō tā míngtiān yào gěi wǒ liǎng zhāng hǎo de piào.*

小李：太好了！谢谢你，小王！*Tài hǎo le! Xièxie nǐ, Xiǎo Wáng!*

小王：不客气(búkèqi, you're welcome!)！对了，从我们学校到上海剧场不近(jìn, close)，我们怎么去那儿呢？我们骑自行车去还是坐公共汽车去？*Bú kèqi! Duì le, cóng wǒmen xuéxiào dào Shànghǎi Jùchǎng bù jìn, wǒmen zěnme qù nàr ne? Wǒmen qí zìxíngchē qù háishì zuò gōnggòng qìchē qù?*

小李：我们开车去！*Wǒmen kāi chē qù!*

小王：什么？开车去？你有汽车吗？*Shénme? Kāichē qù? Nǐ yǒu qìchē ma?*

小李：小王，我也告诉你一个好消息吧：我上个月买汽车了*。下个星期六晚上，你可以坐我的新汽车去上海剧场看京剧。*Xiǎo Wáng, wǒ yě gàosu nǐ yí ge hǎo xiāoxi ba: wǒ shàng ge yuè mǎi qìchē le. Xià ge Xīngqīliù wǎnshang, nǐ kěyǐ zuò wǒ de xīn qìchē qù Shànghǎi Jùchǎng kàn jīngjù.*

小王：你刚(gāng, just)买车，会开车吗？我们还是骑自行车去吧。*Nǐ gāng mǎi chē, huì kāi chē ma? Wǒmen háishì qí zìxíngchē qù ba.*

小李：没问题！我来大学上学以前(yǐqián, before)就学会开车了。*Méi wèntí! Wǒ lái dàxué shàngxué yǐqián jiù xué huì kāi chē le.*

小王：是吗？*Shì ma?*

小李：那当然(dāngrán, of course)！哦(ò, Oh)，时间不早了，我现在要回宿舍找几个同学一起去打篮球。再见，小王！*Nà dāngrán! Ò, shíjiān bù zǎo le, wǒ xiànzài yào huí sùshè zhǎo jǐ ge tóngxué yìqǐ qù dǎ lánqiú. Zài jiàn, Xiǎo Wáng!*

小王：再见，小李！*Zàijiàn, Xiǎo Lǐ!*

The particle 了 *le* is used at the end of a sentence to confirm the completion or realization of a nonconsecutive or non-scenic action or event in the past. Please see Lesson 26 for the detailed explanation and usage.

1. _____ Both Mr. Li and Mr. Wang have been doing very well recently.

2. _____ Mr. Li is going to the stadium to work out now.

3. _____ Mr. Wang has decided to go play basketball with Mr. Li.

4. _____ Mr. Wang knows how to play both basketball and table tennis.

5. _____ The Beijing Opera Troupe is going to give a performance in Shanghai very soon.

6. _____ The performance will be held in the Shanghai Opera House at 7:30 p.m. next Saturday.

7. _____ Mr. Li would like to invite Mr. Wang to go to see the performance with him.

8. _____ Mr. Wang's father has met the manager of the Beijing Opera Troupe before.

9. _____ Mr. Li was given two tickets for the Beijing opera early today.

10. _____ The opera house is so close to the school that they can go there on foot.

11. _____ Mr. Li owns a car.

12. _____ Mr. Wang suggests that they should go to the opera house by bus next Saturday.

13. _____ Mr. Li has not learned how to drive yet.

14. _____ They will go to the opera house by car next Saturday.

15. _____ Mr. Wang is now going directly to the gymnasium to play basketball.

Grammar

Vocabulary

Do you know?

The sentence-final particle 了 *le* (I) • Shopping

The sentence-final particle 了 *le* (I)

The sentence-final particle 了 *le* is placed at the end of a sentence. It emphatically confirms the completion or realization of a action or event in the past.

SUBJECT + PREDICATE
(ADVERB + VERB + OBJECT + 了 + …)

Questions

吗 *ma* question

你	买	衣服	了	吗?	Have you bought any clothes?
Nǐ	*mǎi*	*yīfu*	*le*	*ma?*	/Did you buy any clothes?

affirmative-negative question

	你	有没有		买 衣服?	Have you bought any clothes?
	Nǐ	*yǒu méi yǒu*		*mǎi yīfu?*	/Did you buy any clothes?
or	你	买	衣服	了 没有?	Have you bought any clothes?
	Nǐ	*mǎi*	*yīfu*	*le méiyǒu?*	/Did you buy any clothes?
or	你	买没买		衣服?	Have you bought any clothes?
	Nǐ	*mǎi mei mǎi*		*yīfu?*	/Did you buy any clothes?

Affirmation

我	买	衣服	了。	I (have) bought some clothes.
Wǒ	*mǎi*	*yīfu*	*le.*	

Negation

我	没(有)	买	衣服。	I haven't bought any clothes.
Wǒ	*méi(yǒu)*	*mǎi*	*yīfu.*	/I didn't buy any clothes.

NOTE   In the negative form, the adverb 没(有) *méi(yǒu)* is placed before the verb, and the particle 了 *le* is **not** used.

179

Shopping

买东西	mǎi dōngxi	to do shopping
东西	dōngxi	thing; stuff
电器	diànqì	electric appliance
店	diàn	store; shop
逛	guàng	to stroll around
减	jiǎn	to reduce
价/价格	jià/jiàgé	price
顾客	gùkè	customer
杂志	zázhì	magazine
付	fù	to pay
钱	qián	money
家具	jiājù	furniture
用品	yòngpǐn	articles for use
文具	wénjù	stationery
铅笔	qiānbǐ	pencil
纸	zhǐ	paper

EXERCISE
26·1

Rephrase the following sentences according to the examples given.

EXAMPLE　他们**要**去商店买东西。　*Tāmen **yào** qù shāngdiàn mǎi dōngxi.*

他们去商店买东西**了**。　*Tāmen qù shāngdiàn mǎi dōngxi **le**.*

1. 我哥哥要去电器店买吸尘器。*Wǒ gēge yào qù diànqì diàn mǎi xīchénqì.*

   _____

2. 姑娘们要去逛商场。*Gūniangmen yào qù guàng shāngchǎng.*

   _____

3. 这些意大利皮鞋都要减价。*Zhèxiē Yìdàlì píxié dōu yào jiǎnjià.*

   _____

4. 那些女顾客都要付钱。*Nàxiē nǚ gùkè dōu yào fù qián.*

   _____

5. 他朋友要去家具店买桌子和椅子。*Tā péngyou yào qù jiājù diàn mǎi zhuōzi hé yǐzi.*

   _____

EXAMPLE   他们**不**去商店买东西。 *Tāmen bú qù shāngdiàn mǎi dōngxi.*

他们**没(有)**去商店买东西。 *Tāmen méi (yǒu) qù shāngdiàn mǎi dōngxi.*

6. 他们不去体育用品店买篮球。*Tāmen bú qù tǐyù yòngpǐn diàn mǎi lánqiú.*

_____

7. 那个律师不去文具店买纸和铅笔。*Nà ge lǜshī bú qù wénjù diàn mǎi zhǐ hé qiānbǐ.*

_____

8. 爸爸不去水果店买香蕉和苹果。*Bàba bú qù shuǐguǒ diàn mǎi xiāngjiāo hé píngguǒ.*

_____

9. 黄先生不跟太太一起去逛商店。*Huang xiānsheng bù gēn tàitai yìqǐ qù guàng shāngdiàn.*

_____

10. 白老师不去书店买英文杂志。*Bái lǎoshī bú qù shūdiàn mǎi Yīngwén zázhì.*

_____

EXERCISE
26·2

First, turn the following affirmative-negative questions into 吗 **ma** questions, and then negate them.

EXAMPLE   他昨天**有没有**买东西？ *Tā zuótiān **yǒu méi yǒu** mǎi dōngxi?*

他昨天买东西**了吗**？ *Tā zuótiān mǎi dōngxi **le ma**?*

他昨天**没(有)**买东西。 *Tā zuótiān **méi(yǒu)** mǎi dōngxi。*

1. 她昨天有没有买电器？*Tā zuótiān yǒu méi yǒu mǎi diànqì?*

_____

_____

2. 他们上个周末有没有去逛商场？*Tāmen shàng ge zhōumò yǒu méi yǒu qù guàng shāngchǎng?*

_____

_____

3. 日本空调机有没有减价？*Rìběn kōngtiáojī yǒu méi yǒu jiǎn jià?*

_____

_____

4. 那个俄国顾客付钱了没有？*Nà ge Éguó gùkè fù qián le méiyǒu?*

_____

_____

5. 那个作家上午买杂志了没有？ *Nà ge zuòjiā shàngwǔ mǎi zázhì le méiyǒu?*

   _____

   _____

6. 今天他去体育用品店买篮球了没有？ *Jīntiān tā qù tǐyù yòngpǐn diàn mǎi lánqiú le méiyǒu?*

   _____

   _____

7. 小白今天逛没逛商店？ *Xiǎo Bái jīntiān guàng mei guàng shāngdiàn?*

   _____

   _____

8. 上个星期电器减没减价？ *Shàng ge xīngqī diànqì jiǎn mei jiǎn jià?*

   _____

   _____

9. 今天下午他弟弟去没去文具店？ *Jīntiān xiàwǔ tā dìdi qù mei qù wénjù diàn?*

   _____

   _____

EXERCISE
26·3

Answers the following questions according to real situations. Answers may vary.

1. 上个周末你去超市买东西了吗？ *Shàng ge zhōumò nǐ qù chāoshì mǎi dōngxi le ma?*

   _____

   如果去了, 你有没有买牛奶？ *Rúguǒ qù le, nǐ yǒu méi yǒu mǎi niúnǎi?*

   _____

2. 上个周末你去衣服店买衣服了吗？ *Shàng ge zhōumò nǐ qù yīfu diàn mǎi yīfu le ma?*

   _____

   如果去了, 你有没有买毛衣？ *Rúguǒ qù le, nǐ yǒu méi yǒu mǎi máoyī?*

   _____

3. 上个周末你去电器店买电器了吗？ *Shàng ge zhōumò nǐ qù diànqì diàn mǎi diànqì le ma?*

   _____

   如果去了, 你有没有买吸尘器？ *Rúguǒ qù le, nǐ yǒu méi yǒu mǎi xīchénqì?*

   _____

4. 上个周末你去家具店买家具了吗? *Shàng ge zhōumò nǐ qù jiājù diàn mǎi jiājù le ma?*

_____

如果去了, 你有没有买桌子? *Rúguǒ qù le, nǐ yǒu méi yǒu mǎi zhuōzi?*

_____

5. 你昨天去体育用品店买东西了没有? *Nǐ zuótiān qù tǐyù yòngpǐn diàn mǎi dōngxi le méiyǒu?*

_____

如果去了, 你买没买足球? *Rúguǒ qù le, nǐ mǎi mei mǎi zúqiú?*

_____

6. 你昨天去文具店买文具了没有? *Nǐ zuótiān qù wénjù diàn mǎi wénjù le méiyǒu?*

_____

如果去了, 你买没买纸和铅笔? *Rúguǒ qù le, nǐ mǎi mei mǎi zhǐ hé qiānbǐ?*

_____

7. 你昨天去书店买书了没有? *Nǐ zuótiān qù shūdiàn mǎi shū le méiyǒu?*

_____

如果去了, 你买没买杂志? *Rúguǒ qù le, nǐ mǎi mei mǎi zázhì?*

_____

8. 你昨天去水果店买水果了没有? *Nǐ zuótiān qù shuǐguǒ diàn mǎi shuǐguǒ le méiyǒu?*

_____

如果去了, 你买没买苹果? *Rúguǒ qù le, nǐ mǎi mei mǎi píngguǒ?*

_____

EXERCISE
26·4

翻译成中文 **Fānyì chéng Zhōngwén**   *Translate into Chinese and pinyin.*

1. Did Mom buy any fruit yesterday?

_____

2. The male customer has not paid (did not pay) any money.

_____

3. This writer went to the stationery store in the afternoon to buy some paper and pencils.

_____

4. Did he go to that electronics store to buy a computer this morning?

_____

5. Did you buy any Chinese magazines last weekend?

   _____

6. The female students strolled the shopping mall last night.

   _____

7. Have those athletes bought any basketballs in the sports equipment store?

   _____

8. Last Sunday did they go to the mall to do any shopping?

   _____

你知道吗？ *Nǐ zhīdao ma?* Do you know?

早逝的诗人 *zǎoshì de shīrén* Poets who died young

很多有名 (*yǒumíng*, famous) 的英国和美国诗人 (*shīrén*, poet) 很早就去世 (*qùshì*, to pass away) 了：

◆ 英国诗人　　Percy Bysshe Shelley　　二十九岁就去世了。
◆ 英国诗人　　George Gordon Byron　　三十六岁就去世了。
◆ 英国诗人　　John Keats　　二十五岁就去世了。
◆ 美国诗人　　Edgar Allan Poe　　四十岁就去世了。
◆ 美国女诗人　Sylvia Plath　　三十岁就去世了。

可是他们都留下 (*liúxià*, to leave behind) 了不朽 (*bùxiǔ*, eternal) 的诗篇 (*shīpiān*, poem)

The perfective particle 了 *le* • Expressing completed actions

·27·

The perfective particle 了 *le*

The perfective particle 了 *le* is placed immediately after the verb. It denotes the completion or realization of an action.

When the perfective particle 了 *le* is present, the sentence-final particle 了 *le* can also be used at the end of the sentence. See Lesson 28 for more information on the sentence-final 了 *le*.

SUBJECT + PREDICATE
(ADVERBIAL + VERB + 了 + ATTRIBUTIVE + OBJECT + ...)

Questions

吗 *ma* question

| 你 | 买 | 了 | 白 | 衬衫 | 了 吗? | Have you bought a white shirt? |
| *Nǐ* | *mǎi* | *le* | *bái* | *chènshān* | *le ma?* | /Did you buy a white shirt? |

affirmative-negative question

| 你 | 有 没有 | 买 | 白 | 衬衫? | Have you bought a white shirt? |
| *Nǐ* | *yǒu méiyǒu* | *mǎi* | *bái* | *chènshān?* | /Did you buy a white shirt? |

| or 你 | 买 | 了 | 白 | 衬衫 | 没有? | Have you bought a white shirt? |
| *Nǐ* | *mǎi* | *le* | *bái* | *chènshān* | *méiyǒu?* | /Did you buy a white shirt? |

| or 你 | 买 没 买 白 | 衬衫? | Have you bought a white shirt? |
| *Nǐ* | *mǎi mei mǎi bái* | *chènshān?* | /Did you buy a white shirt? |

Affirmation

买了,	我	已经	买	了	一	Yes, I've bought a white shirt
Mǎi le,	*wǒ*	*yǐjīng*	*mǎi*	*le*	*yí*	(already). / Yes, I bought a
件	白	衬衫	(了)。	white shirt (already).
jiàn	*bái*	*chènshān*	*(le).*	

185

Negation

没有,	我	没(有)买	白	衬衫。	No, I haven't bought a white shirt.
Méiyǒu,	*wǒ*	*méi(yǒu) mǎi bái*		*chènshān.*	No, I didn't buy a white shirt.

NOTE In the negative form, the adverb 没(有) *méi(yǒu)* is placed right before the verb, and the perfective particle 了 *le* is **not** used.

生词 SHĒNGCÍ (VOCABULARY)

Common verbs and more measure words

给	*gěi*	to give; for; to
参加	*cānjiā*	to attend; to join
认识	*rènshi*	to meet; to know
借	*jiè*	to borrow
租	*zū*	to rent
场	*chǎng*	measure word (m.w.) for movies
首	*shǒu*	m.w. for songs and poems
间	*jiān*	m.w. for rooms
栋	*dòng*	m.w. for buildings
瓶	*píng*	m.w.; bottle
一些	*yìxiē*	m.w.; some; a few

Everyday words

上	*shàng*	in; on; upon
已经	*yǐjīng*	already
刚才	*gāngcái*	just now

EXERCISE 27·1

First, rephrase the following sentences according to the example given, and then translate into English.

EXAMPLE 他今天**要**买一公斤苹果。 *Tā jīntiān **yào** mǎi yì gōngjīn píngguǒ.*

他今天买**了**一公斤苹果。 *Tā jīn tiān mǎi **le** yì gōngjīn píngguǒ.*

He (has) bought a kilo of apples today.

1. 我姐姐上午要洗那些脏衣服。 *Wǒ jiějie shàngwǔ yào xǐ nàxiē zāng yīfu.*

   _____

   _____

2. 妈妈要给我做一条黑裤子。 *Māma yào gěi wǒ zuò yì tiáo hēi kùzi.*

   _____

   _____

3. 她星期六要戴姐姐的红帽子。 *Tā Xīngqīliù yào dài jiějie de hóng màozi.*

_____

_____

4. 他朋友今天要看两本中文杂志。 *Tā péngyou jīntiān yào kàn liǎng běn Zhōngwén zázhì.*

_____

_____

5. 白教授要给我们介绍一些朋友。 *Bái jiàoshòu yào gěi wǒmen jièshào yìxiē péngyou.*

_____

_____

6. 这个学生要买几枝铅笔。 *Zhè ge xuésheng yào mǎi jǐ zhī qiānbǐ.*

_____

_____

7. 我要参加她的生日晚会。 *Wǒ yào cānjiā tā de shēngrì wǎnhuì.*

_____

_____

8. 这个周末我弟弟要借很多英文书。 *Zhè ge zhōumò wǒ dìdi yào jiè hěn duō Yīngwén shū.*

_____

_____

EXERCISE
27·2

Negate the following sentences according to the example given.

EXAMPLE   我喝了一杯美国咖啡。   *Wǒ hē **le yì bēi** Měiguó kāfēi.*

我没(有)喝美国咖啡。   *Wǒ **méi(yǒu)** hē Měiguó kāfēi.*

1. 他们晚上看了一场美国电影。 *Tāmen wǎnshang kàn le yì chǎng Měiguó diànyǐng.*

_____

2. 爸爸刚才喝了一杯热茶。 *Bàba gāngcái hē le yì bēi rè chá.*

_____

3. 这个月他学了很多英文生词。 *Zhè ge yuè tā xué le hěn duō Yīngwén shēngcí.*

_____

4. 我在晚会上唱了几首中国歌。 *Wǒ zài wǎnhuì shang chàng le jǐ shǒu Zhōngguó gē.*

_____

5. 白教授上午上了两节语法课。 *Bái jiàoshòu shàngwǔ shàng le liǎng jié yǔfǎ kè.*

_____

6. 妹妹在医院外面租了一栋房子。 *Mèimei zài yīyuàn wàimian zū le yí dòng fángzi.*

_____

7. 他弟弟今天穿了一件白衬衫。 *Tā dìdi jīntiān chuān le yí jiàn bái chènshān.*

_____

8. 我们已经认识了一些法国朋友。 *Wǒmen yǐjīng rènshi le yìxiē Fǎguó péngyou.*

_____

EXERCISE
27·3

Answer the first five questions in the negative and the last five sentences in the affirmative.

EXAMPLES 你买没买那本杂志？ *Nǐ mǎi mei mǎi nà běn zázhì?*

negative   我没(有)买那本杂志。 *Wǒ méi(yǒu) mǎi nà běn zázhì.*

你买没买那本杂志？ *Nǐ mǎi mei mǎi nà běn zázhì?*

affirmative   我买了那本杂志。 *Wǒ mǎi le nà běn zázhì.*

1. 你有没有看我家的新家具？ *Nǐ yǒu méiyǒu kàn wǒ jiā de xīn jiājiù?*

_____

2. 这个运动员吃没吃那些馒头？ *Zhè ge yùndòngyuán chī mei chī nàxiē mántou?*

_____

3. 他今天逛了这个商场没有？ *Tā jīntiān guàng le zhè ge shāngchǎng méiyǒu?*

_____

4. 刚才服务员有没有擦桌子？ *Gāngcái fú wùyuán yǒu méiyǒu cā zhuōzi?*

_____

5. 白老师去了那个小商店吗？ *Bái lǎoshī qù le nà ge xiǎo shāngdiàn ma?*

_____

6. 她喝没喝那杯咖啡？ *Tā hē mei hē nà bēi kāfēi?*

_____

7. 你找了他们经理没有？ *Nǐ zhǎo le tāmen jīnglǐ méiyǒu?*

_____

8. 刚才她有没有回答老师的问题？ *Gāngcái tā yǒu méiyǒu huídá lǎoshī de wèntí?*

_____

9. 你哥哥上午收拾了他的屋子没有？ *Nǐ gēge shàngwǔ shōushi le tā de wūzi méiyǒu?*

_____

10. 你租没租那栋大房子？ *Nǐ zū mei zū nà dòng dà fángzi?*

_____

EXERCISE
27·4

翻译成中文 **Fānyì chéng Zhōngwén**   *Translate into Chinese and pinyin.*

1. Has Miss Bai already bought that pair of leather shoes?

_____

2. The lawyer (has) borrowed three English magazines from the library.

_____

3. How many cups of coffee has he drunk today?

_____

4. Did he see those new electric appliances last weekend?

_____

5. I have already rented that small house.

_____

6. Those waiters did not go shopping at the mall just now.

_____

7. Mom has made some winter clothes for us.

_____

8. Last night they watched a Chinese movie.

_____

你知道吗? *Nǐ zhīdao ma?* Do you know?

四大发明 sì dà fāmíng *Four great inventions*

中国古代 (*gǔdài*, ancient times) 的四大发明 (*fāmíng*, invention; to invent):

◆ 中国人在汉朝 (*Hàncháo*, Han Dynasty, 206 B.C.-A.D. 25) 的时候 (*de shíhou*, during) 就发明了指南针 (*zhǐnánzhēn*, compass)。

◆ 公元 (*gōngyuán*, A.D.) 二世纪 (*shìjì*, century), 科学家 (*kēxuéjiā*, scientist) 蔡伦 (*Cài Lún*, Cai Lun) 发明了造纸 (*zàozhǐ*, paper making) 术 (*shù*, technology)。

◆ 公元九世纪, 中国人就发明了黑火药 (*huǒyào*, gunpowder)。

◆ 公元十一世纪, 科学家毕升 (*Bì Shēng*, Bi Sheng) 发明了活字印刷 (*huózì yìnshuā*, movable type printing) 术。

The sentence-final particle 了 *le* (II) • Auxiliary verbs (II) 会 *huì*, 可能 *kěnéng*, 必须 *bìxū*, 应该 *yīnggāi*, 要 *yào*, 得 *děi* • Weather conditions

The sentence-final particle 了 *le* (II)

Besides indicating completion (Lesson 26), the sentence-final particle 了 *le* also indicates emergence of a new situation or changed circumstances.

SUBJECT + PREDICATE					
(ADV. + VERB/ADJ. + OBJ + 了)					
现在 天气 热 了 吗? *Xiànzài tiānqì rè le ma?*					Is it (getting) hot now?
现在 天气 热 了。 *Xiànzài tiānqì rè le*					It's (getting) hot now. *(It was not hot before.)*
现在 天气 (还) 没有 热 (呢)。 *Xiànzài tiānqì (hái) méiyǒu rè (ne).*					Now it's not hot (yet).
现在 天气 不 热 了。 *Xiànzài tiānqì bú rè le*					Now it's not hot anymore. *(It was hot before.)*
他 喜欢 热天气 了吗? *Tā xǐhuan rè tiānqì le ma?*					Does he like the hot weather (now)?
他 喜欢 热天气 了。 *Tā xǐhuan rè tiānqì le.*					He likes the hot weather (now). *(He didn't like the hot weather before.)*
他 (还) 没有 喜欢 热天气 (呢)。 *Tā (hái) méiyǒu xǐhuan rè tiānqì (ne).*					He does not like the hot weather (yet).
他 不 喜欢 热天气 了。 *Tā bù xǐhuan rè tiānqì le.*					He doesn't like the hot weather anymore. *(He used to like the hot weather before.)*

NOTE The negative form (还)没有(呢) *(hái) méiyǒu (ne)* means *not… (yet)*, whereas 不…了 *bù….le* means *not…anymore* or *no longer*.

191

生词 SHĒNGCÍ (VOCABULARY)

Weather conditions

天气	*tiānqì*	weather
热	*rè*	hot
冷	*lěng*	cold
暖和	*nuǎnhuo*	nice and warm
凉快	*liángkuai*	nice and cool
刮风	*guāfēng*	to be windy
风	*fēng*	wind
下雪	*xiàxuě*	to snow
雪	*xuě*	snow
下雨	*xiàyǔ*	to rain
雨	*yǔ*	rain
下雾	*xiàwù*	to be foggy; to be misty
雾	*wù*	fog; mist
太阳	*tàiyáng*	the sun

Western cities

巴黎	*Bālí*	Paris
伦敦	*Lúndūn*	London
纽约	*Niǔyuē*	New York
洛杉矶	*Luòshānjī*	Los Angeles

EXERCISE
28·1

Provide negative answers to the following questions.

EXAMPLE   现在天气热了吗? *Xiànzài tiānqì rè le ma?*

现在天气还没有热呢。*Xiànzài tiānqì hái méiyǒu rè ne.*

1. 现在天气冷了吗? *Xiànzài tiānqì lěng le ma?*

_____

2. 现在天气凉快了吗? *Xiànzài tiānqì liángkuai le ma?*

_____

3. 现在天气暖和了吗? *Xiànzài tiānqì nuǎnhuo le ma?*

_____

4. 现在巴黎下雨了吗? *Xiànzài Bālí xiàyǔ le ma?*

_____

5. 现在伦敦下雾了吗? *Xiànzài Lúndūn xiàwù le ma?*

_____

6. 现在纽约下雪了吗? *Xiànzài Niǔyuē xiàxuě le ma?*

_____

7. 现在洛杉矶有太阳了吗？*Xiànzài Luòshānjī yǒu tàiyáng le ma?*

_____

8. 现在北京刮风了吗？*Xiànzài Běijīng guāfēng le ma?*

_____

EXERCISE
28·2

翻译成英文 Fānyì chéng Yīngwén   *Translate into English.*

1. 现在天气不冷了。*Xiànzài tiānqì bù lěng le.*

_____

2. 现在天气不热了。*Xiànzài tiānqì bù rè le.*

_____

3. 现在不刮风了。*Xiànzài bù guāfēng le.*

_____

4. 现在不下雪了。*Xiànzài bú xiàxuě le.*

_____

5. 现在不下雨了。*Xiànzài bú xiàyǔ le.*

_____

6. 现在不下雾了。*Xiànzài bú xiàwù le.*

_____

7. 我朋友不喜欢热天气了。*Wǒ péngyou bù xǐhuan rè tiānqì le.*

_____

8. 他爸爸不喜欢冷天气了。*Tā bàba bù xǐhuan lěng tiānqì le.*

_____

Auxiliary verbs (II) 会 *huì*, 可能 *kěnéng*, 必须 *bìxū*, 应该 *yīnggāi*, 要 *yào*, 得 *děi*

SUBJECT + PREDICATE

(Aux. v. + V. + Object)

今天	会不会	下	雪?	Will it snow today?
Jīntiān	*huì bu huì*	*xià*	*xuě?*	*(expressing probability or possibility)*
下午	可能	下	雨。	It probably will rain in the afternoon.
Xiàwǔ	*kěnéng*	*xià*	*yǔ.*	
我们	必须	买	温度计了吗?	Must we buy a thermometer (now)?
Wǒmen	*bìxū*	*mǎi*	*wēndùjì le ma?*	
你们	(还)不用	买	温度计。	You needn't buy a thermometer (yet).
Nǐmen	*(hái) bú yòng*	*mǎi*	*wēndùjì.*	
我们	应该	买	温度计了吗?	Should we buy a thermometer (now)?
Wǒmen	*yīnggāi*	*mǎi*	*wēndùjì le ma?*	
你们	(还)不应该	买	温度计。	You shouldn't buy a thermometer (yet).
Nǐmen	*(hái)bù yīnggāi*	*mǎi*	*wēndùjì.*	
我们	要	买	温度计了吗?	Need we buy a thermometer (now)?
Wǒmen	*yào*	*mǎi*	*wēndùjì le ma?*	
你们	(还)不用	买	温度计。	You needn't buy a thermometer (yet).
Nǐmen	*(hái) búyòng*	*mǎi*	*wēndùjì.*	
我们	得	买	温度计了吗?	Do we have to buy a thermometer (now)?
Wǒmen	*děi*	*mǎi*	*wēndùjì le ma?*	
你们	(还)不用	买	温度计。	You don't have to buy a thermometer (yet).
Nǐmen	*(hái)bú yòng*	*mǎi*	*wēndùjì.*	

Some of the auxiliary verbs are often used together with the sentence-final particle 了 *le* to indicate emergence of a new situation or changed circumstances. If there is no time word in the sentence, it generally suggests *now*. Compare:

	我们必须买温度计	*Wǒmen bìxū mǎi wēndùjì*	We must buy a thermometer.
versus			
	我们必须买温度计了	*Wǒmen bìxū mǎi wēndùjì **le***	(due to the changed situation, it's high time that) we must buy a thermometer (now).

More auxiliary verbs

会	*huì*	(probably) will
可能	*kěnéng*	to be probable
必须	*bìxū*	must
不用	*bú yòng*	need not
应该	*yīnggāi*	should; ought to
得	*děi*	to have to

More weather

温度计	*wēndùjì*	thermometer
温度	*wēndù*	temperature
晴	*qíng*	fine; clear; sunny
阴	*yīn*	cloudy; overcast
停	*tíng*	to stop; to cease

EXERCISE
28·3

Answer the following questions by negating the auxiliary verbs, and then translate the answers into English.

1. 今天晚上北京会下雪吗？ *Jīntiān wǎnshang Běijīng huì xiàxuě ma?*

_____

_____

2. 明天上午伦敦可能下雾吗？ *Míngtiān shàngwǔ Lúndūn kěnéng xiàwù ma?*

_____

_____

3. 今天下午洛杉矶会下雨吗？ *Jīntiān xiàwǔ Luòshānjī huì xiàyǔ ma?*

_____

_____

4. 下个星期纽约可能刮大风吗？ *Xià ge xīngqī Niǔyuē kěnéng guā dà fēng ma?*

_____

_____

5. 天气还没有热呢, 他们现在就要买短裤了吗？ *Tiānqì hái méiyǒu rè ne, tāmen xiànzài jiù yào mǎi duǎnkù le ma?*

_____

_____

6. 天气还没有冷呢, 我们现在就得买毛衣了吗? *Tiānqì hái méiyǒu lěng ne, wǒmen xiànzài jiù děi mǎi máoyī le ma?*

_____

_____

7. 天气还没有凉快呢, 你们现在就必须穿T-恤衫了吗? *Tiānqì hái méiyǒu liángkuai ne, nǐmen xiànzài jiù bìxū chuān tīxùshān le ma?*

_____

_____

8. 现在天阴了, 工人们应该休息了吗? *Xiànzài tiān yīn le, gōngrénmen yīnggāi xiūxi le ma?*

_____

_____

9. 现在天晴了, 职员们要去公司上班了吗? *Xiànzài tiān qíng le, zhíyuánmen yào qù gōngsī shàngbān le ma?*

_____

_____

10. 现在雨停了, 那些运动员得去体育场运动了吗? *Xiànzài yǔ tíng le, nàxiē yùndòngyuán děi qù tǐyùchǎng yùndòng le ma?*

_____

_____

EXERCISE
28·4

翻译成中文 Fānyì chéng Zhōngwén   *Translate into Chinese and pinyin.*

1. Is it (getting) nice and cool now? —It's not (getting) nice and cool yet.

_____

2. His mother likes the hot weather now.

_____

3. It's (getting) warm now, and the girls needn't wear sweaters.

_____

4. Now it's not cold anymore, and it won't snow (now).

_____

5. Next week the students should buy thermometers.

_____

6. Will it probably snow in Los Angeles this afternoon? —It probably won't snow.

_____

7. Tomorrow morning, it will be foggy in London, (and) it will rain in Paris.

   _____

8. Will it be cloudy in New York City the day after tomorrow?

   _____

9. It's (getting) cold (now); do they have to wear overcoats? —They don't have to wear overcoats yet.

   _____

10. It's getting warm (now); shall we buy shorts now? —You needn't buy shorts yet.

   _____

你知道吗? *Nǐ zhīdao ma? Do you know?*

气候 *qìhòu Climate*

- 因为 (*yīnwèi*, because) 温室效应 (*wēnshì xiàoyìng*, warming effect)，现在的天气越来越 (*yuè lái yuè*, increasingly) 热了。
- 也因为温室效应，北极 (*běijí*, North Pole) 的冰山 (*bīngshān*, iceberg) 可能会融化 (*rónghuà*, to melt)。
- 洛杉矶的冬天很暖和，可是有时候 (*yǒushíhou*, sometimes) 也可能会下雪。

Comparative constructions • Quantity complement • Making comparisons

Comparative constructions

Subj. + 跟 + obj. + 一样 + adj. (Equality: S = O)

他	跟	她	一样	高	吗?	Is he as tall as she is?
Tā	gēn	tā	yíyàng	gāo	ma?	

他	跟	她	一样	高。	He is as tall as she is.
Tā	gēn	tā	yíyàng	gāo.	

Subj. + 比 + obj. + adj. (More than : S > O)

他	比	她	高	吗?	Is he taller than she is?
Tā	bǐ	tā	gāo	ma?	

他	比	她	高。	He is taller than she is.
Tā	bǐ	tā	gāo.	

他	不比	她	高。	He is not taller than she is.
Tā	bù bǐ	tā	gāo.	

Subj. + 没有 + obj. + (那么/这么) + adj. (Less than: S < O)

他	有	她	(那么/这么)	高	吗?	Is he as tall as she is?
Tā	yǒu	tā	(nàme/zhème)	gāo	ma?	

他	没有	她	(那么/这么)	高。	He is not as tall as she is.
Tā	méiyǒu	tā	(nàme/zhème)	gāo.	

NOTE   The difference between 他没有她高 **Tā méiyǒu tā gāo**, *He is not as tall as she is*, and 他不比她高 **Tā bù bǐ tā gāo**, *He is not taller than she is*. The former indicates that *he is shorter than she is*, whereas the latter is ambiguous: without any context, it could mean either *he is shorter than she is* or *he is as tall as she is* (that is to say, in terms of height, they could be the same).

生词 SHĒNGCÍ (VOCABULARY)

Making comparisons

比	*bǐ*	more than; to compare
跟…一样	*gēn…yíyàng*	the same as
那么	*nàme*	so; like that
这么	*zhème*	so; like this

Everyday words

旧	*jiù*	old (things)
面积	*miànjī*	area

EXERCISE

29·1

Rephrase the following sentences with the antonyms given.

EXAMPLE   哥哥比弟弟**高**。 *Gēge bǐ dìdi **gāo**.* (矮 *ǎi*)

              弟弟比哥哥**矮**。 *Dìdi bǐ gēge **ǎi**.*

1. 我比你大。 *Wǒ bǐ nǐ dà.* (小 *xiǎo*)

   _____

2. 爷爷比奶奶胖。 *Yéye bǐ nǎinai pàng.* (瘦 *shòu*)

   _____

3. 爸爸比妈妈快。 *Bàba bǐ māma kuài.* (慢 *màn*)

   _____

4. 她的扑克比我的新。 *Tā de pūkè bǐ wǒ de xīn.* (旧 *jiù*)

   _____

5. 小白的腿比小黄的长。 *Xiǎo Bái de tuǐ bǐ Xiǎo Huáng de cháng.* (短 *duǎn*)

   _____

6. 你的朋友比我的多。 *Nǐ de péngyou bǐ wǒ de duō.* (少 *shǎo*)

   _____

7. 北京的房子比洛杉矶的贵。 *Běijīng de fángzi bǐ Luòshānjī de guì.* (便宜 *piányi*)

   _____

8. 上海的春天比纽约的热。 *Shànghǎi de chūntiān bǐ Niǔyuē de rè.* (冷 *lěng*)

   _____

True or false? 对还是错? **Duì háishì cuò** *Decide whether the following statements are* 对 **duì** *true or* 错 **cuò** *false.*

1. _____ 中国的面积比美国的大。*Zhōngguó de miànjī bǐ Měiguó de dà.*

2. _____ 秋天跟冬天一样冷。*Qiūtiān gēn dōngtiān yíyàng lěng.*

3. _____ 夏天没有春天那么热。*Xiàtiān méiyǒu chūntiān nàme rè.*

4. _____ 秋天比夏天凉快。*Qiūtiān bǐ xiàtiān liángkuai.*

5. _____ 纽约的冬天没有洛杉矶的那么暖和。*Niǔyuē de dōngtiān méiyǒu Luòshānjī de nàme nuǎnhuo.*

6. _____ 柠檬跟桔子一样酸。*Níngméng gēn júzi yíyàng suān.*

7. _____ 香蕉比草莓甜。*Xiāngjiāo bǐ cǎoméi tián.*

8. _____ 法国的历史跟中国的一样长。*Fǎguó de lìshǐ gēn Zhōngguó de yíyàng cháng.*

9. _____ 美国的飞机比俄国的好。*Měiguó de fēijī bǐ Éguó de hǎo.*

10. _____ 德国的汽车没有中国的那么快。*Déguó de qìchē méiyǒu Zhōngguó de nàme kuài.*

Quantity complement

SUBJ. + 比 + OBJ. + ADJ. + QUANTITY COMPLEMENT

我	比	你	高	两公分。	I am two centimeters taller than you are.
Wǒ	*bǐ*	*nǐ*	*gāo*	*liǎng gōngfēn.*	
我	比	你	高	一点儿。	I am a little bit taller than you are.
Wǒ	*bǐ*	*nǐ*	*gāo*	*yìdiǎnr.*	
我	比	你	高	得多/多了/很多。	I am much taller than you are.
Wǒ	*bǐ*	*nǐ*	*gāo*	*de duō/duō le/hěn duō.*	

生词   **SHĒNGCÍ (VOCABULARY)**

Measurements

公分	*gōngfēn*	centimeter
英里	*yīnglǐ*	mile
英寸	*yīngcùn*	English inch
公里	*gōnglǐ*	kilometer
公斤	*gōngjīn*	kilogram
英尺	*yīngchǐ*	English foot
公尺	*gōngchǐ*	meter

Everyday words

河	*hé*	river
一点儿	*yìdiǎnr*	a little bit
住	*zhù*	to live; to reside

Complete each sentence with an appropriate quantity complement according to the English phrase given.

1. 面条比米饭贵 _____。(a little bit)

   Miàntiáo bǐ mǐfàn guì _____.

2. 妈妈比妹妹累 _____。(much)

   Māma bǐ mèimei lèi _____.

3. 我比我爸爸矮 _____。(3 cm)

   Wǒ bǐ wǒ bàba ǎi _____.

4. 这件毛衣比那件宽 _____。(1 inch)

   Zhè jiàn máoyī bǐ nà jiàn kuān _____.

5. 那条路比这条短 _____。(10 km)

   Nà tiáo lù bǐ zhè tiáo duǎn _____.

6. 数学楼比化学楼高 _____。(1 foot)

   Shùxué lóu bǐ huàxué lóu gāo _____.

7. 这条河比那条长 _____。(150 miles)

   Zhè tiáo hé bǐ nà tiáo cháng _____.

8. 这些学生比那些认真 _____。(a lot)

   Zhèxiē xuésheng bǐ nàxiē rènzhēn _____.

Answer the following questions according to real situations. Answers may vary.

1. 你比你的好朋友大吗？大几岁？ *Nǐ bǐ nǐ de hǎo péngyou dà ma? Dà jǐ suì?*

   _____

2. 你比你的好朋友高吗？高几公分？ *Nǐ bǐ nǐ de hǎo péngyou gāo ma? Gāo jǐ gōngfēn?*

   _____

3. 你比你的好朋友胖吗？胖多少公斤？ *Nǐ bǐ nǐ de hǎo péngyou pàng ma? Pàng duōshao gōngjīn?*

   _____

4. 你的腿比你好朋友的长吗？长多少公分？ *Nǐ de tuǐ bǐ nǐ hǎo péngyou de cháng ma? Cháng duōshao gōngfēn?*

   _____

5. 你的肩膀比你好朋友的宽吗？宽多少？ *Nǐ de jiānbǎng bǐ nǐ hǎo péngyou de kuān ma? Kuān duōshao?*

_____

6. 你的腰比你好朋友的粗吗？粗多少？ *Nǐ de yāo bǐ nǐ hǎo péngyou de cū ma? Cū duōshao?*

_____

7. 你住的房子比你好朋友住的新吗？新得多吗？ *Nǐ zhù de fángzi bǐ nǐ hǎo péngyou zhù de xīn ma? Xīn de duō ma?*

_____

8. 你住的房子比你好朋友住的干净吗？干净很多吗？ *Nǐ zhù de fángzi bǐ nǐ hǎo péngyou zhù de gānjìng ma? Gānjìng hěn duō ma?*

_____

EXERCISE 29·5

翻译成中文 Fānyì chéng Zhōngwén *Translate into Chinese and pinyin.*

1. This blouse is as red as that one.

_____

2. Is orange sweeter than grapefruit?

_____

3. My older brother is 2 centimeters shorter than I am.

_____

4. Coffee is a little more bitter than tea.

_____

5. The opera house is not as new as the movie theater.

_____

6. Are dumplings much more expensive than rice noodles?

_____

7. His grandfather is much thinner than his grandmother.

_____

8. This road is 50 miles longer than that road.

_____

你知道吗? *Nǐ zhīdao ma? Do you know?*

比较 *bǐjiào Making comparisons*

- 现在中国人比以前长寿 (*chángshòu*, longevity) 多了: 2011 年, 中国女人的平均 (*píngjūn*, average) 寿命 (*shòumìng*, life expectancy) 是 76.94 岁, 中国男人的平均寿命是 72.68 岁。
- 中国的长江 (*Chángjiāng*, Yangtze River) 没有尼罗 (*Níluó*, Nile) 河那么长: 可是长江比美国的密西西比 (*Mìxīxībǐ*, Mississippi) 河长一点儿, 只 (*zhǐ*, only) 长 25 公里。
- 北京的面积比上海的大, 可是北京的人口 (*rénkǒu*, population) 没有上海的那么多。
- 女人跟男人一样聪明 (*cōngmíng*, clever)。
- 在很多的国家 (*guójiā*, country) 里, 男人都比女人多; 在蒙古 (*Ménggǔ*, Mongolia) 和索马里 (*Suǒmǎlǐ*, Somali), 男人跟女人差不多 (*chàbuduō*, almost) 一样多; 可是在中国、印度和阿拉伯 (*Ālābó*, Arabia) 国家, 男人比女人多。

The progressive aspect of an action • Expressing actions in progress

The progressive aspect of an action

The progressive aspect is expressed by 在 *zài* 正 *zhèng* or 正在 *zhèngzài*. In spoken Chinese, sometimes the final particle 呢 *ne* is added to the end of a sentence, or used alone, to indicate the progression of an action.

SUBJECT + PREDICATE

在	+	verb + obj.	[+ 呢]	
正	+	verb + obj.	[+ 呢]	
正在	+	verb + obj.	[+ 呢]	
		verb + obj.	+ 呢	

Question

他们　　正在　　学习　汉语　吗?　　Are they studying Chinese (now)?
Tāmen zhèngzài xuéxí Hànyǔ ma?

Affirmation

他们　　(正)在　学习　　汉语。　They are studying Chinese (now).
Tāmen (zhèng) zài xuéxí Hànyǔ.

他们　　正　　学习　汉语　呢。　They are studying Chinese (now).
Tāmen zhèng xuéxí Hànyǔ ne.

他们　　学习　汉语　呢。　They are studying Chinese (now).
Tāmen xuéxí Hànyǔ ne.

Negation

他们　　没(有)在　学习　　汉语。　They are not studying Chinese
Tāmen méi(yǒu)zài xuéxí Hànyǔ.　　(now).

他们　　没(有)　学习　汉语。　They are not studying Chinese
Tāmen méiyǒu xuéxí Hànyǔ.　　(now).

An action in the progressive aspect may take place in the past, present or future. For example, 昨天上午八点他们正在学习汉语呢 *Zuótiān shàngwǔ bā diǎn tāmen zhèngzài xuéxí Hànyǔ ne*. *They were studying Chinese at 8:00 a.m. yesterday* and 明天上午八点他们也许正在学习汉语呢 *Míngtiān shàngwǔ bā diǎn tāmen yěxǔ zhèngzài xuéxí Hànyǔ ne*, *They will probably be studying*

Chinese at 8:00 a.m. tomorrow. Without any time word, however, the default time of the action usually refers to the present, as shown in the previous examples.

生词　SHĒNGCÍ (VOCABULARY)

Progressive marker

在	*zài*	in progress of
正(在)	*zhèng(zài)*	in progress of

More common verbs and their objects

参观	*cānguān*	to visit (a place)
访问	*fǎngwèn*	to visit
欢迎	*huānyíng*	to welcome
弹	*tán*	to play (the piano)
谈话	*tánhuà*	to talk; to chat
画	*huà*	to paint; to draw
打工	*dǎgōng*	to do manual work
修理	*xiūlǐ*	to repair
搬(家)	*bān(jiā)*	to move (to another home)
种	*zhòng*	to plant; to grow
刷	*shuā*	to paint (house or wall)
钢琴	*gāngqín*	piano
画儿	*huàr*	painting; picture
树	*shù*	tree
草	*cǎo*	grass

EXERCISE

30·1

According to the example given, rephrase three sentences 1–3 with "在…(呢) zài…(ne)", sentences 4–6 with "正在…(呢) zhèngzài…(ne)" sentences 7–9 with "正…(呢) zhèng…(ne)", and sentences 10–12 with "呢 ne".

EXAMPLE　他吃早饭。　*Tā chī zǎofàn.*

他**在**吃早饭(呢)。　*Tā **zài** chī zǎofàn (**ne**).*

/他正**在**吃早饭(呢)。　*Tā **zhèngzài** chī zǎofàn (**ne**).*

/他正吃早饭(呢)。　*Tā zhèng chī zǎofàn (**ne**).*

/他吃早饭呢。　*Tā chī zǎofàn **ne**.*

1. 学生们参观北京博物馆。*Xuéshēngmen cānguān Běijīng bówùguǎn.*

_____

2. 那个作家访问白教授。*Nà ge zuòjiā fǎngwèn Bái jiàoshòu.*

_____

3. 医院欢迎新护士。*Yīyuàn huānyíng xīn hùshi.*

_____

4. 他妹妹弹钢琴。 *Tā mèimei tán gāngqín.*

_____

5. 黄律师跟她谈话。 *Huáng lǜshī gēn tā tánhuà.*

_____

6. 这个工程师画画儿。 *Zhè ge gōngchéngshī huàhuàr.*

_____

7. 我哥哥打工。 *Wǒ gēge dǎgōng.*

_____

8. 那些职员修理旧家具。 *Nàxiē zhíyuán xiūlǐ jiù jiājiù.*

_____

9. 这些演员搬家。 *Zhèxiē yǎnyuán bānjiā.*

_____

10. 我爸爸种树。 *Wǒ bàba zhòng shù.*

_____

11. 那个军人种草。 *Nà ge jūnrén zhòng cǎo.*

_____

12. 工人们刷房子。 *Gōngrénmen shuā fángzi.*

_____

EXERCISE
30·2

Rephrase the following sentences according to the example given.

EXAMPLE 他不吃早饭。 *Tā **bù** chī zǎofàn.*

他**没在**吃早饭。 or 他**没(有)**吃早饭。

*Tā **méi zài** chī zǎofàn.* *Tā **méi(yǒu)** chī zǎofàn.*

1. 农民们不种树。 *Nóngmínmen bú zhòng shù.*

_____

2. 她们的经理不种草。 *Tāmen de jīnglǐ bú zhòng cǎo.*

_____

3. 护士们不刷房子。 *Hùshimen bù shuā fángzi.*

_____

4. 这个商人不搬家。*Zhè ge shāngrén bù bānjiā.*

_____

5. 我姐姐不弹钢琴。*Wǒ jiějie bù tán gāngqín.*

_____

6. 这些学生不参观访问工厂。*Zhèxiē xuésheng bù cānguān fǎngwèn gōngchǎng.*

_____

7. 他朋友不修理旧椅子。*Tā péngyou bù xiūlǐ jiù yǐzi.*

_____

8. 我弟弟不打工。*Wǒ dìdi bù dǎgōng.*

_____

9. 他们不欢迎那些警察。*Tāmen bù huānyíng nàxiē jǐngchá.*

_____

10. 这个音乐家不画画儿。*Zhè ge yīnyuèjiā bú huà huàr.*

_____

EXERCISE
30·3

First, turn the following statement sentences into 吗 **ma** *questions, and then answer them in the negative.*

EXAMPLE 他**在**吃早饭呢。 *Tā **zài** chī zǎofàn **ne**.*

他**在**吃早饭**吗**? *Tā **zài** chī zǎofàn **ma**?*

没有，他**没在**吃早饭。　　/没有，他**没(有)**吃早饭。
*Méiyǒu, tā **méi zài** chī zǎofàn. /Méiyǒu, tā **méi (yǒu)**chī zǎofàn.*

1. 运动员们在参观体育馆呢。*Yùndòngyuánmen zài cānguān tǐyùguǎn ne.*

_____

_____

2. 经理们正在访问白教授呢。*Jīnglǐmen zhèngzài fǎngwèn Bái jiàoshòu ne.*

_____

_____

3. 那个女演员正在弹钢琴呢。*Nà ge nǚ yǎnyuán zhèngzài tán gāngqín ne.*

_____

_____

4. 他跟那些工程师谈话呢。 *Tā gēn nàxiē gōngchéngshī tánhuà ne.*

_____

_____

5. 爸爸在修理旧桌子呢。 *Bàba zài xiūlǐ jiù zhuōzi ne.*

_____

_____

6. 那个作家正在画画儿呢。 *Nà ge zuòjiā zhèngzài huà huàr ne.*

_____

_____

7. 这些服务员搬家呢。 *Zhèxiē fúwùyuán bānjiā ne.*

_____

_____

8. 他弟弟在打工呢。 *Tā dìdi zài dǎgōng ne.*

_____

_____

9. 我正在刷房子呢。 *Wǒ zhèngzài shuā fángzi ne.*

_____

_____

10. 那些护士休息呢。 *Nàxiē hùshi xiūxi ne.*

_____

_____

EXERCISE
30·4

翻译成中文 **Fānyì chéng Zhōngwén** *Translate into Chinese and pinyin.*

1. The workers are painting the house. (在)

_____

2. Those soldiers are planting the trees. (……呢)

_____

3. Is this engineer moving houses? (正)

_____

4. We are welcoming the new students. (正在……呢)

_____

5. Professor Huang is talking with her now. (正……呢)

_____

6. Is your younger sister working now? (正在)

_____

7. These writers are painting. (正……呢)

_____

8. Is that lawyer visiting Professor Bai? (在)

_____

你知道吗? *Nǐ zhīdao ma?* Do you know?

增加与减少 *zēngjiā yǔ jiǎnshǎo* Expansion and reduction

◆ 世界上 (*shìjiè shang*, in the world) 的石油 (*shíyóu*, petroleum) 正在急剧地 (*jíjùde*, rapidly) 减少 (*jiǎnshǎo*, to decrease), 估计 (*gūjì*, to estimate) 五, 六十年以后就会用完 (*yòngwán*, to use up) 了。

◆ 因为 (*yīnwèi*, because) 世界上的石油正在急剧地减少, 现在科学家 (*kēxuéjiā*, scientist) 们正在积极 (*jījí*, actively) 寻找 (*xúnzhǎo*, to look for) 新的燃料 (*ránliào*, fuel), 比如 (*bǐrú*, for example) 可燃冰 (*kěrán bīng*, flammable ice)。

◆ 近年来 (*jìn nián lái*, in the recent years), 在美国留学 (*liúxué*, to study abroad) 的中国学生人数 (*rénshù*, number of people) 正在快速地 (*kuàisù*, quickly) 增长 (*zēngzhǎng*, to increase) 在 2012 年的时候已经达到 (*dádào*, to reach) 十六万 (*wàn*, ten thousand) 多人了。

◆ 近年来, 去中国留学的美国学生人数也正在逐步地 (*zhúbùde*, gradually) 增加, 在 2012 年的时候已经达到两万多人了。

Lessons 26–30

EXERCISE
R6·1

Answer the following questions in the negative.

EXAMPLE 他昨天去商店买东西了吗? *Tā zuótiān qù shāngdiàn mǎi dōngxi le ma?*

/他昨天去商店买东西了没有? *Tā zuótiān qù shāngdiàn mǎi dōngxi le méiyǒu?*

/他昨天去没去商店买东西? *Tā zuótiān qù mei qù shāngdiàn mǎi dōngxi?*

/他昨天有没有去商店买东西? *Tā zuótiān yǒu mei yǒu qù shāngdiàn mǎi dōngxi?*

他昨天没(有)去商店买东西。 *Tā zuótiān méi(yǒu) qù shāngdiàn mǎi dōngxi.*

1. 妈妈昨天去商店买东西了吗? *Māma zuótiān qù shāngdiàn mǎi dōngxi le ma?*

_____

2. 那个顾客刚才付钱了没有? *Nà ge gùkè gāngcái fù qián le méiyǒu?*

_____

3. 黄老师昨天下午买没买法文杂志? *Huáng lǎoshī zuótiān xiàwǔ mǎi mei mǎi Fǎwén zázhì?*

_____

4. 他们今天下午有没有去逛街? *Tāmen jīntiān xiàwǔ yǒu méiyǒu qù guàng jiē?*

_____

5. 这个星期那些体育用品都减价了吗? *Zhè ge xīngqī nàxiē tǐyù yòngpǐn dōu jiǎnjià le ma?*

_____

6. 上个星期天白老师买新电器了没有? *Shàng ge Xīngqītiān Bái lǎoshī mǎi xīn diànqì le méiyǒu?*

_____

7. 她晚上去没去文具店买纸和铅笔？ *Tā wǎnshang qù mei qù wénjùdiàn mǎi zhǐ hé qiānbǐ?*

_____

8. 上个周末那些意大利家具有没有降价？ *Shàng ge zhōumò nàxiē Yìdàlì jiājù yǒu méiyǒu jiàng jià?*

_____

EXERCISE
R6·2

Rephrase the following sentences according to the example given.

EXAMPLE 他今天**要**参加一个晚会。 *Tā jīntiān **yào** cānjiā yí ge wǎnhuì.*

他今天参加**了**一个晚会。 *Tā jīntiān cānjiā **le** yí ge wǎnhuì.*

他今天**没有**参加晚会。 *Tā jīntiān **méiyǒu** cānjiā wǎnhuì.*

1. 白小姐要认识一些德国律师。 *Bái xiǎojie yào rènshi yìxiē Déguó lǜshī.*

_____

_____

2. 黄教授上午要借五本中文杂志。 *Huáng jiàoshòu shàngwǔ yào jiè wǔ běn Zhōngwén zázhì.*

_____

_____

3. 那个经理要喝四杯法国葡萄酒。 *Nà ge jīnglǐ yào hē sì bēi Fǎguó pútao jiǔ.*

_____

_____

4. 他今天要给我介绍一个朋友。 *Tā jīntiān yào gěi wǒ jièshào yí ge péngyou.*

_____

_____

5. 他们中午要去看一场美国电影。 *Tāmen zhōngwǔ yào qù kàn yì chǎng Měiguó diànyǐng.*

_____

_____

6. 那个音乐家要唱几首中国歌。 *Nà ge yīnyuèjiā yào chàng jǐ shǒu Zhōngguó gē.*

_____

_____

7. 这个星期服务员们要扫十间屋子。*Zhè ge xīngqī fúwùyuánmen yào sǎo shí jiān wūzi.*

_____

_____

8. 他弟弟下午要上三节汉语课。*Tā dìdi xiàwǔ yào shàng sān jié Hànyǔ kè.*

_____

_____

9. 这个老农民早上要吃两碗米粉。*Zhè ge lǎo nóngmín zǎoshang yào chī liǎng wǎn mǐfěn.*

_____

_____

10. 那些工人要租一栋房子。*Nàxiē gōngrén yào zū yí dòng fángzi.*

_____

_____

EXERCISE R6·3

Answer the following questions in the negative. (Note: Some of the negative forms are irregular.)

1. 这个星期天气凉快了吗？*Zhè ge xīngqī tiānqì liángkuai le ma?*

_____

2. 她妈妈喜欢热天气了吗？*Tā māma xǐhuan rè tiānqì le ma?*

_____

3. 现在纽约下雪了吗？*Xiànzài Niǔyuē xià xuě le ma?*

_____

4. 现在伦敦下雾了吗？*Xiànzài Lúndūn xià wù le ma?*

_____

5. 明天会是晴天吗？*Míngtiān huì shì qíngtiān ma?*

_____

6. 下个星期一巴黎可能刮大风吗？*Xià ge Xīngqīyī Bālí kěnéng guā dà fēng ma?*

_____

7. 学生们下个月必须买温度计吗？*Xuéshengmen xià ge yuè bìxū mǎi wēndùjì ma?*

_____

8. 那些工人应该去上班了吗？*Nàxiē gōngrén yīnggāi qù shàngbān le ma?*

_____

9. 这些姑娘现在得去买毛衣了吗？ *Zhèxiē gūniang xiànzài děi qù mǎi máoyī le ma?*

_____

10. 运动员现在要去体育场跑步了吗？ *Yùndòngyuán xiànzài yào qù tǐyùchǎng pǎobù le ma?*

_____

翻译成英文 Fānyì chéng Yīngwén   *Translate into English.*

1. 中国的面积比美国的大一点儿。 *Zhōngguó de miànjī bǐ Měiguó de dà yìdiǎnr.*

_____

2. 这些医生比那些医生认真。 *Zhèxiē yīshēng bǐ nàxiē yīshēng rènzhēn.*

_____

3. 我朋友比我瘦，可是我比他高。 *Wǒ péngyou bǐ wǒ shòu, kěshì wǒ bǐ tā gāo.*

_____

4. 他弟弟比他哥哥矮两公分。 *Tā dìdi bǐ tā gēge ǎi liǎng gōngfēn.*

_____

5. 这个星期妈妈比爸爸累得多。 *Zhè ge xīngqī māma bǐ bàba lèi de duō.*

_____

6. 这条河比那条长十五公里。 *Zhè tiáo hé bǐ nà tiáo cháng shíwǔ gōnglǐ.*

_____

7. 奶奶比爷爷胖得多。 *Nǎinai bǐ yéye pàng de duō.*

_____

8. 物理楼跟生物楼一样漂亮。 *Wùlǐ lóu gēn shēngwù lóu yíyàng piàoliang.*

_____

9. 我穿的衣服跟他穿的一样新。 *Wǒ chuān de yīfu gēn tā chuān de yíyàng xīn.*

_____

10. 这个屋子跟那个一样宽。 *Zhè ge wūzi gēn nà ge yíyàng kuān.*

_____

11. 洛杉矶的房子没有纽约的这么贵。 *Luòshānjī de fángzi méiyǒu Niǔyuē de zhème guì.*

_____

12. 苹果没有香蕉那么甜。 *Píngguǒ méiyǒu xiāngjiāo nàme tián.*

_____

13. 秋天没有夏天这么热。 *Qiūtiān méiyǒu xiàtiān zhème rè.*

_____

14. 我姐姐不比我妹妹高。 *Wǒ jiějie bù bǐ wǒ mèimei gāo.*

_____

Rephrase the following sentences according to the example given.

EXAMPLE 他在吃早饭呢。 *Tā **zài** chī zǎofàn **ne**.*
他在吃早饭吗? *Tā **zài** chī zǎofàn **ma**?*
没有, 他没在吃早饭。 *Méiyǒu, tā **méi zài** chī zǎofàn.*

1. 黄经理在刷房子呢。 *Huáng jīnglǐ zài shuā fángzi ne.*

_____

_____

2. 农民们正种草呢。 *Nóngmínmen zhèng zhòng cǎo ne.*

_____

_____

3. 他爷爷正在种树呢。 *Tā yéye zhèngzài zhòng shù ne.*

_____

_____

4. 他朋友搬家呢。 *Tā péngyou bān jiā ne.*

_____

_____

5. 这些工人在修理汽车呢。 *Zhèxiē gōngrén zài xiūlǐ qìchē ne.*

_____

_____

6. 他妹妹正打工呢。 *Tā mèimei zhèng dǎgōng ne.*

_____

_____

7. 那个作家正在画画儿呢。 *Nà ge zuòjiā zhèngzài huàhuàr ne.*

_____

_____

8. 律师在跟她谈话呢。 *Lǜshī zài gēn tā tánhuà ne.*

_____

_____

9. 那个演员正弹钢琴呢。 *Nà ge yǎnyuán zhèng tán gāngqín ne.*

_____

_____

10. 学生们正在欢迎新老师呢。 *Xuéshengmen zhèngzài huānyíng xīn lǎoshī ne.*

_____

_____

11. 这些警察在喝啤酒呢。 *Zhèxiē jǐngchá zài hē píjiǔ ne.*

_____

_____

12. 工程师们正参观博物馆呢。 *Gōngchéngshīmen zhèng cānguān bówùguǎn ne.*

_____

_____

EXERCISE
R6·6

True or False? *After reading the following Chinese dialogue, mark each of the English statements as either* **true** *or* **false**.

星期天上午十点, 玛丽给她的男朋友马克打电话(dǎ diànhuà, to make a phone call)的时候(de shíhou, when), 他正在做语法练习。 *Xīngqītiān shàngwǔ shí diǎn, Mǎlì gěi tā de nán péngyou Mǎkè dǎ diànhuà de shíhou, tā zhèngzài zuò yǔfǎ liànxí.*

玛丽: 喂(wèi, hello)! 是马克吗？ *Wèi! Shì Mǎkè ma?*

马克: 是我, 玛丽。你早！ *Shì wǒ, Mǎlì. Nǐ zǎo!*

玛丽: 早, 马克! 现在你在做什么呢？ *Zǎo, Mǎkè! Xiànzài nǐ zài zuò shénme ne?*

马克: 我正在做语法练习呢。 *Wǒ zhèngzài zuò yǔfǎ liànxí ne.*

玛丽: 不要做了, 好吗？你也该停一下儿休息休息了。你看窗户外边, 现在天已经晴了, 不会再下雨了, 而且(érqiě, moreover)气温也没有昨天那么热了。听说(it is said)这个星期天商场里的衣服都减价了。我们上午一起去逛一下儿商场, 好吗？我想买几件新衣服。 *Bú yào zuò le, hǎo ma? Nǐ yě gāi tíng yíxiàr xiūxixiūxi le. Nǐ kàn chuānghu wàibian, xiànzài tiān yǐjīng qíng le, bú huì zài xiàyǔ le, érqiě qìwēn yě méiyǒu zuótiān nàme rè le. Tīngshuō zhè ge Xīngqītiān shāngchǎng lǐ de yīfu dōu jiǎn jià le. Wǒmen shàngwǔ yìqǐ qù guàng yíxiàr shāngchǎng, hǎo ma? Wǒ xiǎng mǎi jǐ jiàn xīn yīfu.*

马克: 好啊！可是我还没有做完 (*wán*, to finish) 这些语法练习呢。黄老师要我们明天交 (*jiāo*, to submit) 这些练习, 所以 (*suǒyǐ*, therefore) 我今天必须做完。*Hǎo a! Kěshì wǒ hái méiyǒu zuò wán zhèxiē yǔfǎ liànxí ne. Huáng lǎoshī yào wǒmen míngtiān jiāo zhèxiē liànxí, suǒyǐ wǒ jīntiān bìxū zuò wán.*

玛丽: 你还有多少题 (*tí*, problem) 没有做完呢？*Nǐ hái yǒu duōshao tí méiyǒu zuò wán ne?*

马克: 还有五个题。我十分钟就可以做完了。*Hái yǒu wǔ ge tí. Wǒ shí fēnzhōng jiù kěyǐ zuòwán le.*

玛丽: 好, 你做完了以后就开车来我家接(*jiē*, to pick up)我。我们一起去商场。*Hǎo, nǐ zuò wán le yǐhòu jiù kāichē lái wǒ jiā jiē wǒ. Wǒmen yìqǐ qù shāngchǎng.*

马克: 好的, 现在是十点五分, 我们十点半见！…… *Hǎo de, xiànzài shì shí diǎn wǔ fēn, wǒmen shí diǎn bàn jiàn!……*

(在商场的衣服店里。*Zài shāngchǎng de yīfudiàn li.*)

玛丽: 马克, 你看这件蓝衬衫怎么样？*Mǎkè, nǐ kàn zhè jiàn lán chènshān zěnmeyàng?*

马克: 是挺(*tǐng*, rather)漂亮的, 可是有点儿大。旁边的那件灰衬衫比这件小一点儿。*Shì tǐng piàoliang de, kěshì yǒu diǎnr dà. Pángbian de nà jiàn huī chènshān bǐ zhè jiàn xiǎo yì diǎnr.*

玛丽: 我不喜欢灰色的衬衫，而且它(*tā*, it)比这件蓝的贵三十块呢。*Wǒ bù xǐhuan huīsè de chènshān, érqiě tā bǐ zhè jiàn lán de guì sānshí kuài ne.*

马克: 你看, 灰衬衫旁边的那件红衬衫怎么样？*Nǐ kàn, huī chènshān pángbiān de nà jiàn hóng chènshān zěnmeyàng?*

玛丽: 让我看看。…… 啊, 是挺漂亮的！不过 (*búguò*, nevertheless), 它的价格跟那件灰色的一样贵。*Ràng wǒ kànkan. … À, shì tǐng piàoliang de! Búguò, tā de jiàgé gēn nà jiàn huīsè de yíyàng guì.*

马克: 那, 你再看看这件白色的。它的价格没有红色的那么贵了, 而且大小(size)也合适 (*héshì*, fit)。*Nà, nǐ zài kànkan zhè jiàn báisè de. Tā de jiàgé méiyǒu hóngsè de nàme guì le, érqiě dàxiǎo yě héshì.*

玛丽: 好, 那我就买这件白衬衫。…… *Hǎo, nà wǒ jiù mǎi zhè jiàn bái chènshān. …*

(他们逛了商场以后, 马克就开车送玛丽回家了。在玛丽的家里。*Tāmen guàng le shāngchǎng yǐhòu, Mǎkè jiù kāi chē sòng Mǎlì huí jiā le. Zài Mǎlì de jiālǐ.*)

妹妹: 姐姐, 你回来了！刚才你去哪儿了？*Jiějie, nǐ huílái le! Gāngcái nǐ qù nǎr le?*

玛丽: 刚才我跟马克去逛商场了。*Gāngcái wǒ gēn Mǎkè qù guàng shāngchǎng le.*

妹妹: 你们买什么了？*Nǐmen mǎi shénme le?*

玛丽: 买了几件减价的衣服。*Mǎi le jǐ jiàn jiǎnjià de yīfu.*

妹妹: 你买没买衬衫？*Nǐ mǎi mei mǎi chènshān?*

玛丽: 买了, 我买了一件白衬衫。*Mǎi le, wǒ mǎi le yí jiàn bái shènshān.*

妹妹: 你还买了一些什么？*Nǐ hái mǎi le yìxiē shénme?*

玛丽: 我还给弟弟买了一双白球鞋, 给你买了一条红裙子。*Wǒ hái gěi dìdi mǎi le yì shuāng bái qiúxié, gěi nǐ mǎi le yì tiáo hóng qúnzi.*

妹妹: 是吗？让我看看。…… 啊, 太漂亮了！谢谢你, 姐姐！*Shì ma? Ràng wǒ kànkan. … À, tài piàoliang le! Xièxie nǐ, jiějie!*

玛丽: 不谢。对了, 我还给妈妈买了一件毛衣, 给爸爸买了一条领带。 *Bú xiè. Duìle, wǒ hái gěi māma mǎi le yí jiàn máoyī, gěi bàba mǎi le yì tiáo lǐngdài.*

妹妹: 你没给马克买东西吗? *Nǐ méi gěi Mǎkè mǎi dōngxi ma?*

玛丽: 当然(dāngrán, of course)买了, 我给他买了一双黑皮鞋和一顶黄色的帽子。 *Dāngrán mǎi le, wǒ gěi tā mǎi le yì shuāng hēi píxié hé yì dǐng huángsè de màozi.*

1. _____ When Mary called Mark in the evening, he was reading a grammar book.

2. _____ The rain had already stopped when she called him.

3. _____ Mary wanted to go to the shopping mall to buy some clothes on sale.

4. _____ Mark told Mary that he would finish doing those exercises in about an hour.

5. _____ Yesterday was much hotter than today.

6. _____ The gray blouse is bigger than the blue one.

7. _____ The blue blouse is more expensive than the gray one.

8. _____ The red blouse is as expensive as the gray one.

9. _____ The white blouse is cheaper than the red one.

10. _____ None of the items Mary bought was on sale.

11. _____ Mary bought a pair of white sneakers for her younger brother and a white blouse for herself.

12. _____ She also bought a red skirt for her mother.

13. _____ Mary didn't buy anything for her parents.

14. _____ The skirt that Mary bought for her younger sister is not very pretty.

15. _____ Mary also bought a pair of black leather shoes and a yellow cap for her boyfriend.

English-Chinese glossary

Note: To indicate the parts of speech of the vocabulary, the following abbreviations are used in the glossaries: **n**—noun, **pron**—pronoun, **prep**—preposition, **v**—verb, **v.o**—verb-object, **aux.v**—auxiliary verb, **adj**—adjective, **ad**—adverb, **conj**—conjunction, **n.w**—numeral word, **m.w**—measure word, **part**—particle, **a.p**—aspect particle, **s.p**—structural particle, **ph**—phrase.

English	Pinyin	Chinese	Part of speech	Lesson
a little bit	*yìdiǎnr*	一点儿	n	29
a little bit	*yǒudiǎnr*	有点儿	ph	11
a quarter (of an hour)	*kè*	刻	n	8
actor	*yǎnyuán*	演员	n	13
add; plus	*jiā*	加	v	7
administration	*xíngzhèng*	行政	n	17
afternoon	*xiàwǔ*	下午	n	5
age; years	*suìshu*	岁数	n	8
air conditioner	*kōngtiáojī[tái]*	空调机[台]	n	16
airplane	*fēijī*	飞机	n	23
already	*yǐjīng*	已经	ad	27
also; too	*yě*	也	ad	4
always	*zǒngshì*	总是	ad	20
American person/people	*Měiguórén*	美国人	n	1
and	*hé*	和	conj	4
angry	*shēngqì*	生气	adj	12
answer; to reply	*huídá*	回答	v	19
anxious	*zháojí*	着急	adj	12
apple	*píngguǒ*	苹果	n	3
apply make-up	*huàzhuāng*	化妆	v.o	23
area	*miànjī*	面积	n	29
arm	*gēbo*	胳膊	n	20
arrive; to reach	*dào*	到	v	25
articles for use	*yòngpǐn*	用品	n	26
ask	*jiào*	叫	v	21
athlete	*yùndòngyuán*	运动员	n	13
attend a meeting; to hold a meeting	*kāihuì*	开会	v.o	25
attend class	*shàng kè*	上课	v.o	23
attend; to join	*cānjiā*	参加	v	27

English	Pinyin	Chinese	Part of speech	Lesson
auditorium	*lǐtáng*	礼堂	n	14
autumn; fall	*qiūtiān*	秋天	n	25
back	*hòu*	后	n	17
back	*hòubian*	后边	n	17
back	*hòumian*	后面	n	17
banana	*xiāngjiāo*	香蕉	n	3
bank	*yínháng*	银行	n	22
bar; tavern	*jiǔba*	酒吧	n	22
basketball	*lánqiú*	篮球	n	24
bathe; to take a shower	*xǐzǎo*	洗澡	v.o	23
be (am, is, are)	*shì*	是	v	1
be foggy	*xiàwù*	下雾	v.o	28
be in/at/on/upon; in; at; on; upon	*zài*	在	v/prep	17
be probable	*kěnéng*	可能	aux.v	28
be windy	*guāfēng*	刮风	v.o	28
beach	*hǎitān*	海滩	n	25
beard; mustache	*húzi*	胡子	n	23
become; act as	*dāng*	当	v	13
bed	*chuáng*	床	n	23
beer	*píjiǔ*	啤酒	n	6
begin; to start	*kāishǐ*	开始	v	25
Beijing	*Běijīng*	北京	n	25
belly; stomach	*dùzi*	肚子	n	20
beside; next to	*pángbiān*	旁边	n	17
between	*zhōngjiān*	中间	n	17
beverages	*yǐnliào*	饮料	n	6
big; large	*dà*	大	adj	11
biology	*shēngwù*	生物	n	17
birthday	*shēngri*	生日	n	9
bitter	*kǔ*	苦	adj	12
black; dark	*hēi*	黑	adj	15
blackboard	*hēibǎn[kuài]*	黑板 [块]	n	16
blackboard eraser	*hēibǎncā*	黑板擦	n	16
blue	*lán*	蓝	adj	15
boat	*chuán*	船	n	23
book	*shū[běn]*	书 [本]	n	14
bookstore	*shūdiàn*	书店	n	14
borrow	*jiè*	借	v	27
both; all	*dōu*	都	ad	4
bowl; m.w	*wǎn*	碗	n/m.w	18
bread	*miànbāo*	面包	n	4
breakfast	*zǎofàn*	早饭	n	5
broad; wide (width and breadth)	*kuān*	宽	adj	20
brush; to brush	*shuā*	刷	n/v	23
building	*lóu*	楼	n	14

English	Pinyin	Chinese	Part of speech	Lesson
bus	*gōnggòng qìchē*	公共汽车	n	23
businessman	*shāngrén*	商人	n	13
busy	*máng*	忙	adj	11
but; however	*kěshì*	可是	conj	11
buy	*mǎi*	买	v	4
cafeteria	*shítáng*	食堂	n	14
can; to be able to	*néng*	能	aux.v	24
centimeter	*gōngfēn*	公分	n	29
chair	*yǐzi[bǎ]*	椅子[把]	n	16
cheese	*nǎilào*	奶酪	n	4
chemistry	*huàxué*	化学	n	17
chess	*xiàngqí*	象棋	n	24
China	*Zhōngguó*	中国	n	1
Chinese (language)	*Zhōngwén*	中文	n	14
Chinese character	*Hànzì*	汉字	n	19
Chinese language	*Hànyǔ*	汉语	n	19
Chinese person/people	*Zhōngguórén*	中国人	n	1
cinema; movie theater	*diànyǐngyuàn*	电影院	n	22
classroom	*jiàoshì*	教室	n	14
clean	*gānjìng*	干净	adj	20
clear	*qīngchu*	清楚	adj	19
clerk	*zhíyuán*	职员	n	13
clock; bell; time	*zhōng*	钟	n	8
clothes	*yīfu[jiàn]*	衣服[件]	n	10
cloudy; overcast	*yīn*	阴	adj	28
coffee	*kāfēi*	咖啡	n	6
cold	*lěng*	冷	adj	28
color	*yánsè/sè*	颜色/色	n	15
company; firm	*gōngsī*	公司	n	23
computer	*diànnǎo[tái]*	电脑[台]	n	16
computer room	*diànnǎoshì*	电脑室	n	14
concert	*yīnyuèhuì*	音乐会	n	21
conscientious	*rènzhēn*	认真	adj	19
customer	*gùkè*	顾客	n	26
dance	*tiàowǔ*	跳舞	v.o	18
dance party; ball	*wǔhuì*	舞会	n	21
date	*rì*	日	n	9
date (*informal*)	*hào*	号	n	9
daughter	*nǚ'ér*	女儿	n	2
daytime	*báitiān*	白天	n	5
delighted	*gāoxìng*	高兴	adj	12
dirty	*zāng*	脏	adj	18
disappointed	*shīwàng*	失望	adj	12
dish (of Chinese food)	*cài*	菜	n	12
do manual work	*dǎgōng*	打工	v.o	30
doctor	*yīshēng*	医生	n	13

English	Pinyin	Chinese	Part of speech	Lesson
door	mén[shàn]	门[扇]	n	16
dormitory	sùshè	宿舍	n	14
down	xià	下	n	17
down	xiàbian	下边	n	17
down	xiàmian	下面	n	17
drink	hē	喝	v	6
drive (auto)	kāi(chē)	开(车)	v	23
dumpling	jiǎozi	饺子	n	4
ear	ěrduo	耳朵	n	20
eat	chī	吃	v	3
education	jiàoyù	教育	n	17
eight	bā	八	n.w	7
electrical appliance	diànqì	电器	n	26
engineer	gōngchéngshī	工程师	n	13
engineering	gōngchéng	工程	n	17
English foot	yīngchǐ	英尺	n	29
English inch	yīngcùn	英寸	n	29
English mile	yīnglǐ	英里	n	29
English person/people	Yīngguórén	英国人	n	1
equal	děngyú	等于	v	7
evening	wǎnshang	晚上	n	5
evening party	wǎnhuì	晚会	n	21
exactly; precisely	jiù	就	ad	17
excited	jīdòng	激动	adj	12
exercise; to practice	liànxí	练习	n/v	19
expensive	guì	贵	adj	11
explain; to speak	jiǎng	讲	v	19
eye	yǎnjing	眼睛	n	20
face	liǎn	脸	n	23
family members	jiālǐrén	家里人	n	6
farmer	nóngmín	农民	n	13
fast; quick	kuài	快	adj	19
fat (people)	pàng	胖	adj	11
father; dad	bàba	爸爸	n	2
female; woman	nǚ	女	adj	23
fine; clear; sunny	qíng	晴	adj	28
five	wǔ	五	n.w	7
floor; ground	dì	地	n	18
fluent	liúlì	流利	adj	19
fog	wù	雾	n	28
food; meal	cān	餐	n	4
foot	jiǎo	脚	n	20
for a little while; briefly	yíxiàr	一下儿	ad	18
for; to; to give	gěi	给	prep/v	27
foreign language	wàiyǔ	外语	n	17
four	sì	四	n.w	7
France	Fǎguó	法国	n	1

English	Pinyin	Chinese	Part of speech	Lesson
French person/people	*Fǎguórén*	法国人	n	1
Friday	*Xīngqīwǔ*	星期五	n	9
friend	*péngyou*	朋友	n	8
from	*cóng*	从	prep	22
front	*qián*	前	n	17
front	*qiánbian*	前边	n	17
front	*qiánmian*	前面	n	17
fruit juice	*guǒzhī*	果汁	n	6
furniture	*jiājù*	家具	n	26
geography	*dìlǐ*	地理	n	17
German person/people	*Déguórén*	德国人	n	1
Germany	*Déguó*	德国	n	1
get married	*jiéhūn*	结婚	v.o	25
get out of class	*xià kè*	下课	v.o	23
get off work	*xiàbān*	下班	v.o	23
girl	*gūniang*	姑娘	n	8
give	*gěi*	给	v	21
give as a gift	*sòng*	送	v	21
glass; cup	*bēi*	杯	n/m.w	12
glove; mitten	*shǒutào[fù/zhī]*	手套[副/只]	n	10
go	*qù*	去	v	14
go online	*shàngwǎng*	上网	v.o	5
go to school	*shàngxué*	上学	v.o	5
go to work	*shàngbān*	上班	v.o	5
golf	*gāoěrfūqiú*	高尔夫球	n	24
good; fine; well	*hǎo*	好	adj	11
graduation; to graduate	*bìyè*	毕业	n/v	25
grammar	*yǔfǎ*	语法	n	19
grandfather (paternal)	*yéye*	爷爷	n	2
grandmother (paternal)	*nǎinai*	奶奶	n	2
grape	*pútao*	葡萄	n	3
grape wine	*pútao jiǔ*	葡萄酒	n	6
grapefruit	*yòuzi*	柚子	n	3
grass	*cǎo*	草	n	30
gray; ash	*huī*	灰	adj/n	15
Great Britain; England	*Yīngguó*	英国	n	1
green	*lǜ*	绿	adj	15
gymnasium	*tǐyùguǎn*	体育馆	n	14
hair	*tóufa*	头发	n	20
half	*bàn*	半	n	8
hamburger	*hànbǎobāo*	汉堡包	n	4
hand	*shǒu*	手	n	20
happy	*kuàilè*	快乐	adj	12
hat; cap	*màozi[dǐng]*	帽子[顶]	n	10
have	*yǒu*	有	v	2
have to	*děi*	得	aux.v	28
he; him	*tā*	他	pron	1

English	Pinyin	Chinese	Part of speech	Lesson
head	*tóu*	头	n	20
health; body	*shēntǐ*	身体	n	11
height	*gèzi*	个子	n	20
help	*bāngzhù*	帮助	v	21
history	*lìshǐ*	历史	n	17
home; house; family	*jiā*	家	n	16
honeydew	*xiāngguā*	香瓜	n	3
hospital	*yīyuàn*	医院	n	22
hot	*rè*	热	adj	28
hot; spicy	*là*	辣	adj	12
house	*fángzi*	房子	n	25
how many; how much	*duōshao*	多少	pron	7
how many; how much	*jǐ*	几	pron	7
how old	*duōdà*	多大	ph	8
how; how is it going?	*zěnmeyàng*	怎么样	pron	11
hundred	*bǎi*	百	n.w	7
hurt; to be in pain	*téng*	疼	n	20
husband; sir; gentleman; Mr.	*xiānsheng*	先生	n	2
I; me	*wǒ*	我	pron	1
ice hockey	*bīngqiú*	冰球	n	24
if	*yàoshi*	要是	conj	18
in one's childhood	*xiǎoshíhou*	小时候	ph	21
in progress of	*zhèng(zài)*	正(在)	ad	30
in; inside	*lǐ*	里	n	16
in; on; upon	*shàng*	上	n	27
India	*Yìndù*	印度	n	1
Indian person/people	*Yìndùrén*	印度人	n	1
inexpensive; cheap	*piányi*	便宜	adj	11
inside	*lǐbian*	里边	n	17
inside	*lǐmiàn*	里面	n	17
intend; to plan	*dǎsuàn*	打算	v	25
introduce	*jièshào*	介绍	v	18
invite; please	*qǐng*	请	v	21
Italy	*Yìdàlì*	意大利	n	4
jacket	*shàngyī[jiàn]*	上衣[件]	n	10
Japan	*Rìběn*	日本	n	1
Japanese person/people	*Rìběnrén*	日本人	n	1
juice	*zhī*	汁	n	6
just now	*gāngcái*	刚才	ad	27
kick; to play (soccer)	*tī*	踢	v	24
kilogram	*gōngjīn*	公斤	n	29
kilometer	*gōnglǐ*	公里	n	29
know how to	*huì*	会	aux.v	24
laboratory	*shíyànshì*	实验室	n	14
lamp; light	*dēng[zhǎn]*	灯[盏]	n	16

English	Pinyin	Chinese	Part of speech	Lesson
last	*shàngge*	上个	pron	9
last year	*qùnián*	去年	n	9
lawyer; attorney	*lǜshī*	律师	n	13
leather belt	*pídài[tiáo]*	皮带[条]	n	15
leather shoe	*píxié[shuāng/zhī]*	皮鞋[双/只]	n	10
left	*zuǒ*	左	n	17
left	*zuǒbian*	左边	n	17
left	*zuǒmian*	左面	n	17
leg	*tuǐ*	腿	n	20
lemon	*níngméng*	柠檬	n	3
let	*ràng*	让	v	21
liberal arts	*rénwén*	人文	n	17
library	*túshūguǎn*	图书馆	n	14
like	*xǐhuan*	喜欢	v	3
listen	*tīng*	听	v	18
little; few	*shǎo*	少	adj	19
little; small; young	*xiǎo*	小	a	8
live; to reside	*zhù*	住	v	29
London	*Lúndūn*	伦敦	n	28
long	*cháng*	长	adj	11
look for	*zhǎo*	找	v	25
Los Angeles	*Luòshānjī*	洛杉矶	n	28
lunch	*wǔfàn*	午饭	n	5
m.w (measure word) for a pair of shoes and socks	*shuāng*	双	m.w	10
m.w for a single one (shoe, sock, glove, mitten)	*zhī*	只	m.w	10
m.w for buildings	*dòng*	栋	m.w	27
m.w for chunk-like objects	*kuài*	块	m.w	16
m.w for classes; period	*jié*	节	m.w	16
m.w for doors and windows	*shàn*	扇	m.w	16
m.w for gloves or mittens	*fù*	副	m.w	10
m.w for lamps and lights	*zhǎn*	盏	m.w	16
m.w for long and thin objects (pants, skirts, tie)	*tiáo*	条	m.w	10
m.w for movies	*chǎng*	场	m.w	27
m.w for objects that sit on a platform	*tái*	台	m.w	16
m.w for objects with a flat surface	*zhāng*	张	m.w	16
m.w for objects with a handle	*bǎ*	把	m.w	16
m.w for pens and writing brushes	*zhī*	枝	m.w	16
m.w for printed and bound things	*běn*	本	m.w	16
m.w for rooms	*jiān*	间	m.w	27
m.w for songs, poems	*shǒu*	首	m.w	27

English	Pinyin	Chinese	Part of speech	Lesson
m.w for things with a top (hats, caps)	*dǐng*	顶	m.w	10
m.w for upper body clothing (jackets, shirts)	*jiàn*	件	m.w	10
m.w for general use (most frequenly used)	*gè*	个	m.w	10
m.w; bottle	*píng*	瓶	m.w	27
m.w; some; a few	*yìxiē*	一些	m.w	27
magazine	*zázhì*	杂志	n	26
make; to do	*zuò*	做	v	4
male; man	*nán*	男	adj	23
manager	*jīnglǐ*	经理	n	13
many; much	*duō*	多	adj	19
map	*dìtú[zhāng]*	地图［张］	n	16
mathematics	*shùxué*	数学	n	17
May I ask?	*qǐngwèn*	请问	ph	8
may; can	*kěyǐ*	可以	aux.v	24
meet; to know	*rènshi*	认识	v	27
meter	*gōngchǐ*	公尺	n	29
midnight	*bànyè*	半夜	n	8
milk	*niúnǎi*	牛奶	n	6
mineral water	*kuàngquánshuǐ*	矿泉水	n	6
minute	*fēn*	分	n	8
Monday	*Xīngqīyī*	星期一	n	9
money	*qián*	钱	n	26
month	*yuè*	月	n	9
more than; to compare	*bǐ*	比	prep/v	29
morning	*zǎoshang*	早上	n	5
morning; early	*zǎo*	早	n/adj	11
most	*zuì*	最	ad	20
mother; mom	*māma*	妈妈	n	2
move (house)	*bān(jiā)*	搬（家）	v	30
movie; film	*diànyǐng*	电影	n	21
multiply; times	*chéng*	乘	v	7
museum	*bówùguǎn*	博物馆	n	22
music	*yīnyuè*	音乐	n	13
musician	*yīnyuèjiā*	音乐家	n	13
must	*bìxū*	必须	aux.v	28
must; to want; to need	*yào*	要	aux.v/v	24
neck	*bózi*	脖子	n	20
need not	*búyòng*	不用	aux.v	28
nervous	*jǐnzhāng*	紧张	adj	12
new	*xīn*	新	adj	14
new word; vocabulary	*shēngcí*	生词	n	19
New York City	*Niǔyuē*	纽约	n	28
next	*xiàge*	下个	pron	9
next year	*míngnián*	明年	n	9

English	Pinyin	Chinese	Part of speech	Lesson
nice and cool	*liángkuai*	凉快	adj	28
nice and warm	*nuǎnhuo*	暖和	adj	28
nine	*jiǔ*	九	n.w	7
no, not	*bù*	不	ad	1
noodles	*miàntiáo*	面条	n	4
noon	*zhōngwǔ*	中午	n	5
nose	*bízi*	鼻子	n	20
not have	*méi yǒu*	没有	v	2
now	*xiànzài*	现在	n	8
nurse	*hùshi*	护士	n	13
o'clock	*diǎn*	点	n	8
office	*bàngōngshì*	办公室	n	14
often	*cháng*	常	ad	5
old (things)	*jiù*	旧	adj	29
old (age)	*lǎo*	老	a	8
older brother	*gēge*	哥哥	n	2
older sister	*jiějie*	姐姐	n	2
one	*yī*	一	n.w	7
opera	*gējù*	歌剧	n	21
opera house; theater	*jùchǎng*	剧场	n	22
opposite to; facing	*duìmiàn*	对面	n	17
orange	*júzi*	桔子	n	3
orange (color)	*júhuáng*	桔黄	n	15
outside	*wài*	外	n	17
outside	*wàibian*	外边	n	17
outside	*wàimian*	外面	n	17
paint (house or wall)	*shuā*	刷	v	30
paint; to draw	*huà*	画	v	30
painting; picture	*huàr*	画儿	n	30
pajamas	*shuìyī[jiàn]*	睡衣[件]	n	15
paly (ball)	*dǎ(qiú)*	打(球)	v	24
paper	*zhǐ*	纸	n	26
Paris	*Bālí*	巴黎	n	28
particle	*ne*	呢	part	11
particle (complement marker)	*de*	得	part	19
particle (for yes-no questions)	*ma*	吗	part	3
particle (perfective)	*le*	了	a.p	25
particle (used to indicate supposition or doubt)	*ba*	吧	part	15
pay	*fù*	付	v	26
peach	*táozi*	桃子	n	3
pear	*lí*	梨	n	3
pen; writing brush	*bǐ[zhī]*	笔[枝]	n	16
pencil	*qiānbǐ*	铅笔	n	26

English	Pinyin	Chinese	Part of speech	Lesson
physics	*wùlǐ*	物理	n	17
piano	*gāngqín*	钢琴	n	30
pineapple	*bōluó*	菠萝	n	3
pink	*fěnhóng*	粉红	adj	15
ping-pong	*pīngpāngqiú*	乒乓球	n	24
pizza	*pīsàbǐng*	披萨饼	n	4
plan; to plan	*jìhuà*	计划	n/v	25
plant; to grow	*zhòng*	种	v	30
play (the piano)	*tán*	弹	v	30
play games	*zuò yóuxì*	做游戏	v.o	21
play Go	*xià wéiqí*	下围棋	v.o	21
play mahjong	*dǎ májiàng*	打麻将	v.o	21
poker	*pūkè*	扑克	n	24
police officer	*jǐngchá*	警察	n	13
political science; politics	*zhèngzhì*	政治	n	17
post office	*yóujú*	邮局	n	22
preparation; to prepare; to be going to	*zhǔnbèi*	准备	n/v	19
pretty	*piàoliang*	漂亮	adj	11
price	*jià/jiàgé*	价/价格	n	26
professor	*jiàoshòu*	教授	n	14
purple	*zǐ*	紫	adj	15
put in order	*zhěnglǐ*	整理	v	18
put on; wear (clothing, shoes, socks)	*chuān*	穿	v	10
put on; wear (hat, tie, gloves)	*dài*	戴	v	10
question; problem	*wèntí*	问题	n	19
rain	*xiàyǔ*	下雨	v.o	28
rain	*yǔ*	雨	n	28
raincoat	*yǔyī[jiàn]*	雨衣[件]	n	15
read aloud	*niàn*	念	v	19
reading room	*yuèlǎnshì*	阅览室	n	14
recently; these days	*zuìjìn*	最近	ad/adj	11
recording; to record	*lùyīn*	录音	n/v.o	19
red	*hóng*	红	adj	15
reduce	*jiǎn*	减	v	26
rent	*zū*	租	m.w	27
repair	*xiūlǐ*	修理	v	30
rest; to rest	*xiūxī*	休息	v/n	18
restaurant	*cānguǎn*	餐馆	n	22
restroom; toilet	*cèsuǒ*	厕所	n	17
return	*huán*	还	v	21
return (to a place)	*huí*	回	v	23
review; to review	*fùxí*	复习	n/v	19
rice (cooked)	*mǐfàn*	米饭	n	4
rice noodles	*mǐfěn*	米粉	n	4

English	Pinyin	Chinese	Part of speech	Lesson
right (direction)	*yòu*	右	n	17
right side	*yòubian*	右边	n	17
right	*yòumian*	右面	n	17
river	*hé*	河	n	29
road	*lù*	路	n	23
room	*wūzi*	屋子	n	18
run	*pǎobù*	跑步	v.o	18
Russia	*Éguó*	俄国	n	1
Russian person/people	*Éguórén*	俄国人	n	1
sad	*nánguò*	难过	adj	12
salty	*xián*	咸	adj	12
same as, the	*gēn…yíyàng*	跟……一样	ph	29
sandwich	*sānmíngzhì*	三明治	n	4
satisfied	*mǎnyì*	满意	adj	12
Saturday	*Xīngqīliù*	星期六	n	9
scarf	*wéijīn[tiáo]*	围巾[条]	n	15
school	*xuéxiào*	学校	n	14
school work; homework	*gōngkè*	功课	n	19
science and engineering	*lǐgōng*	理工	n	17
sesame cake	*shāobing*	烧饼	n	4
seven	*qī*	七	n.w	7
shave	*guā*	刮	v	23
she; her	*tā*	她	pron	1
shirt; blouse	*chènshān[jiàn]*	衬衫[件]	n	10
shop; store	*shāngdiàn*	商店	n	22
shopping mall	*shāngchǎng*	商场	n	22
short (height)	*ǎi*	矮	adj	11
short (length)	*duǎn*	短	adj	11
shorts	*duǎnkù[tiáo]*	短裤[条]	n	15
should; ought to	*yīnggāi*	应该	aux.v	28
shoulder	*jiānbǎng*	肩膀	n	20
sing	*chànggē*	唱歌	v.o	18
sit	*zuò*	坐	v	23
six	*liù*	六	n.w	7
skate	*huábīng*	滑冰	n	24
ski	*huáxuě*	滑雪	n	24
skirt	*qúnzi[tiáo]*	裙子[条]	n	10
slender; thin	*xì*	细	adj	20
sleep	*shuìjiào*	睡觉	v.o	5
slippers	*tuōxié[shuāng/zhī]*	拖鞋[双/只]	n	15
slow	*màn*	慢	adj	19
snow	*xiàxuě*	下雪	v.o	28
snow	*xuě*	雪	n	28
so; like that	*nàme*	那么	pron	29
so; like this	*zhème*	这么	pron	29
soccer; football	*zúqiú*	足球	n	24
sock	*wàzi[shuāng/zhī]*	袜子[双/只]	n	10
soda	*kělè*	可乐	n	6

English	Pinyin	Chinese	Part of speech	Lesson
soldier	*jūnrén*	军人	n	13
some; more than one	*xiē*	些	m.w	12
son	*érzi*	儿子	n	2
sour	*suān*	酸	adj	12
soybean milk	*dòujiāng*	豆浆	n	6
speak; to say	*shuō*	说	v	19
spring	*chūntiān*	春天	n	25
stadium	*tǐyùchǎng*	体育场	n	14
stationery	*wénjù*	文具	n	26
steamed bread	*mántou*	馒头	n	4
steamed stuffed bun	*bāozi*	包子	n	4
still; yet; even	*hái*	还	ad	11
stop; to cease	*tíng*	停	v	28
store; shop	*diàn*	店	n	26
strawberry	*cǎoméi*	草莓	n	3
stroll around	*guàng*	逛	v	26
structural particle	*de*	的	s.p	14
student	*xuésheng*	学生	n	13
study; to learn	*xué/xuéxí*	学/学习	v/n	18
subtract; minus	*jiǎn*	减	v	7
suit	*xīzhuāng[jiàn]*	西装[件]	n	15
summer	*xiàtiān*	夏天	n	25
sun, the	*tàiyáng*	太阳	n	28
Sunday	*Xīngqītiān/rì*	星期天/日	n	9
supermarket	*chāoshì*	超市	n	22
supper; dinner	*wǎnfàn*	晚饭	n	5
sweater	*máoyī[jiàn]*	毛衣[件]	n	10
sweep	*sǎo*	扫	v	18
sweet	*tián*	甜	adj	12
swim	*yóuyǒng*	游泳	v.o	18
table; desk	*zhuōzi[zhāng]*	桌子[张]	n	16
talk; to chat	*tánhuà*	谈话	v.o	30
tall; high	*gāo*	高	adj	11
tea	*chá*	茶	n	6
teach	*jiāo*	教	v	19
teacher	*lǎoshī*	老师	n	13
teaching building	*jiàoxué lóu*	教学楼	n	14
television; TV	*diànshì*	电视	n	5
tell	*gàosu*	告诉	v	21
temperature	*wēndù*	温度	n	28
ten	*shí*	十	n.w	7
tennis	*wǎngqiú*	网球	n	24
tennis shoes	*qiúxié[shuāng/zhī]*	球鞋[双/只]	n	15
test; to take a test	*kǎoshì*	考试	n/v	19
text	*kèwén*	课文	n	19
that; those	*nà*	那	pron	10
thermometer	*wēndùjì*	温度计	n	28

English	Pinyin	Chinese	Part of speech	Lesson
these	*zhèxiē*	这些	pron	12
they; them (*fam.*)	*tāmen*	她们	pron	1
they; them (*mas.*)	*tāmen*	他们	pron	1
thick; wide (diameter)	*cū*	粗	adj	20
thin	*shòu*	瘦	adj	11
thing; stuff	*dōngxi*	东西	n	26
this; these	*zhè*	这	pron	10
this (one)	*zhège*	这个	pron	9
this year	*jīnnián*	今年	n	8
those	*nàxiē*	那些	pron	12
three	*sān*	三	n.w	7
Thursday	*Xīngqīsì*	星期四	n	9
ticket	*piào*	票	n	21
tidy; orderly	*zhěngqí*	整齐	adj	20
tidy up	*shōushi*	收拾	v	18
tie	*lǐngdài[tiáo]*	领带［条］	n	10
time (a point in)	*shíhou*	时候	n	18
time (the concept of)	*shíjiān*	时间	n	18
tired	*lèi*	累	adj	11
to	*dào*	到	prep	22
today	*jīntiān*	今天	n	5
together	*yìqǐ*	一起	ad	24
tomorrow	*míngtiān*	明天	n	5
too	*tài*	太	ad	11
tooth	*yá/yáchǐ*	牙/牙齿	n	23
topcoat; overcoat	*dàyī[jiàn]*	大衣［件］	n	10
travel; to travel	*lǚyóu*	旅游	n/v	25
tree	*shù*	树	n	30
trousers; pants	*kùzi[tiáo]*	裤子［条］	n	10
T-shirt	*tīxùshān[jiàn]*	T-恤衫［件］	n	10
Tuesday	*Xīngqī'èr*	星期二	n	9
two	*èr*	二	n.w	7
two (usually with a measure word)	*liǎng*	两	n.w	8
ugly	*nánkàn*	难看	adj	11
underwear	*nèiyī[jiàn]*	内衣［件］	n	15
up (direction)	*shàng*	上	n	17
up (side)	*shàngbian*	上边	n	17
up top	*shàngmian*	上面	n	17
USA	*Měiguó*	美国	n	1
use	*yòng*	用	v	18
vacuum; to suck	*xī*	吸	v	18
vacuum cleaner	*xīchénqì*	吸尘器	n	18
very	*hěn*	很	ad	11
video recording; to record video	*lùxiàng*	录像	n/v.o	19

English	Pinyin	Chinese	Part of speech	Lesson
visit	*fǎngwèn*	访问	v	30
visit (a place)	*cānguān*	参观	v	30
volleyball	*páiqiú*	排球	n	24
waist; lower back	*yāo*	腰	n	20
waiter	*fúwùyuán*	服务员	n	13
walk; to leave	*zǒu*	走	v	23
want	*xiǎng*	想	v/aux.v	13
wash	*xǐ*	洗	v	18
watch; to look	*kàn*	看	v	5
water	*shuǐ*	水	n	6
watermelon	*xīguā*	西瓜	n	3
we; us	*wǒmen*	我们	pron	1
weather	*tiānqì*	天气	n	28
Wednesday	*Xīngqīsān*	星期三	n	9
week	*xīngqī*	星期	n	9
weekend	*zhōumò*	周末	n	25
welcome	*huānyíng*	欢迎	v	30
what	*shénme*	什么	pron	6
which	*nǎ*	哪	pron	6
white	*bái*	白	adj	15
who; whom	*shéi/shuí*	谁	pron	6
wife; Mrs.; madam	*tàitai*	太太	n	2
will (proably)	*huì*	会	aux.v	28
wind	*fēng*	风	n	28
window	*chuānghu[shàn]*	窗户[扇]	n	16
wine	*jiǔ*	酒	n	6
winter	*dōngtiān*	冬天	n	25
wipe	*cā*	擦	v	18
with	*gēn*	跟	prep	24
work; job	*gōngzuò*	工作	n/v	23
work out	*yùndòng*	运动	v	5
worker	*gōngrén*	工人	n	13
worried	*fánnǎo*	烦恼	adj	12
write	*xiě*	写	v	19
writer	*zuòjiā*	作家	n	13
year	*nián*	年	n	9
year (of age)	*suì*	岁	n	8
yellow	*huáng*	黄	adj	15
yesterday	*zuótiān*	昨天	n	9
you (*pl.*)	*nǐmen*	你们	pron	1
you (*polite*)	*nín*	您	pron	8
you (*sing.*)	*nǐ*	你	pron	1
younger brother	*dìdi*	弟弟	n	2
younger sister	*mèimei*	妹妹	n	2
zero	*líng*	零	n.w	7

Chinese (Pinyin)–English glossary

Pinyin	Chinese	English	Part of speech	Lesson
ǎi	矮	short (height)	adj	11
bā	八	eight	n.w	7
Bālí	巴黎	Paris	n	28
bǎ	把	m.w for objects with a handle	m.w	16
bàba	爸爸	father; dad	n	2
ba	吧	particle (used to indicate supposition or doubt)	part	15
bái	白	white	adj	15
báitiān	白天	daytime	n	5
bǎi	百	hundred	n.w	7
bān(jiā)	搬(家)	move (house)	v	30
bàn	半	half	n	8
bàngōngshì	办公室	office	n	14
bànyè	半夜	midnight	n	8
bāngzhù	帮助	help	v	21
bāozi	包子	steamed stuffed bun	n	4
bēi	杯	glass; cup	n/m.w	12
Běijīng	北京	Beijing	n	25
běn	本	m.w for printed and bound things	m.w	16
bízi	鼻子	nose	n	20
bǐ	比	more than; to compare	prep/v	29
bǐ [zhī]	笔[枝]	pen; writing brush	n	16
bìxū	必须	must	aux.v	28
bìyè	毕业	graduation; to graduate	n/v	25
bīngqiú	冰球	ice hockey	n	24
bōluó	菠萝	pineapple	n	3
bówùguǎn	博物馆	museum	n	22
bózi	脖子	neck	n	20
búyòng	不用	need not	aux.v	28
bù	不	no, not	ad	1

Pinyin	Chinese	English	Part of speech	Lesson
cā	擦	wipe	v	18
cài	菜	dish (of Chinese food)	n	12
cān	餐	food; meal	n	4
cānguān	参观	visit (a place)	v	30
cānguǎn	餐馆	restaurant	n	22
cānjiā	参加	attend; to join	v	27
cǎo	草	grass	n	30
cǎoméi	草莓	strawberry	n	3
cèsuǒ	厕所	restroom; toilet	n	17
chá	茶	tea	n	6
cháng	常	often	ad	5
cháng	长	long	adj	11
chǎng	场	m.w for movies	m.w	27
chànggē	唱歌	sing	v.o	18
chāoshì	超市	supermarket	n	22
chènshān[jiàn]	衬衫［件］	shirt; blouse	n	10
chéng	乘	multiply; times	v	7
chī	吃	eat	v	3
chuān	穿	put on; wear (clothing, shoes, socks)	v	10
chuán	船	boat	n	23
chuānghu[shàn]	窗户［扇］	window	n	16
chuáng	床	bed	n	23
chūntiān	春天	spring	n	25
cóng	从	from	prep	22
cū	粗	thick; wide (diameter)	adj	20
dǎgōng	打工	do manual work	v.o	30
dǎ májiàng	打麻将	play mahjong	v.o	21
dǎ(qiú)	打（球）	play (ball)	v	24
dǎsuàn	打算	intend; to plan	v	25
dà	大	big; large	adj	11
dàyī[jiàn]	大衣［件］	topcoat; overcaot	n	10
dài	戴	put on; wear (hat, tie, gloves)	v	10
dāng	当	become; act as	v	13
dào	到	to	prep	22
dào	到	arrive; to reach	v	25
de	的	structural particle	s.p	14
de	得	particle (complement marker)	part	19
Déguó	德国	Germany	n	1
Déguórén	德国人	German person/people	n	1
děi	得	have to	aux.v	28
dēng[zhǎn]	灯［盏］	lamp; light	n	16
děngyú	等于	equal	v	7
dì	地	floor; ground	n	18
dìdi	弟弟	younger brother	n	2

Pinyin	Chinese	English	Part of speech	Lesson
dìlǐ	地理	geography	n	17
dìtú[zhāng]	地图［张］	map	n	16
diǎn	点	o'clock	n	8
diàn	店	store; shop	n	26
diànnǎo[tái]	电脑［台］	computer	n	16
diànnǎoshì	电脑室	computer room	n	14
diànqì	电器	electrical appliance	n	26
diànshì	电视	television; TV	n	5
diànyǐng	电影	movie; film	n	21
diànyǐngyuàn	电影院	cinema; movie theater	n	22
dǐng	顶	m.w for things with a top (hats, caps)	m.w	10
dōngtiān	冬天	winter	n	25
dōngxi	东西	thing; stuff	n	26
dòng	栋	m.w for buildings	m.w	27
dōu	都	both; all	ad	4
dòujiāng	豆浆	soybean milk	n	6
dùzi	肚子	belly; stomach	n	20
duǎn	短	short (length)	adj	11
duǎnkù[tiáo]	短裤［条］	shorts	n	15
duìmiàn	对面	opposite to; facing	n	17
duō	多	many; much	adj	19
duōdà	多大	how old	ph	8
duōshao	多少	how many; how much	pron	7
Éguó	俄国	Russia	n	1
Éguórén	俄国人	Russian person/people	n	1
érzi	儿子	son	n	2
ěrduo	耳朵	ear	n	20
èr	二	two	n.w	7
Fǎguó	法国	France	n	1
Fǎguórén	法国人	French person/people	n	1
fánnǎo	烦恼	worried	adj	12
fángzi	房子	house	n	25
fǎngwèn	访问	visit	v	30
fēijī	飞机	airplane	n	23
fēn	分	minute	n	8
fěnhóng	粉红	pink	adj	15
fēng	风	wind	n	28
fúwùyuán	服务员	waiter	n	13
fù	副	m.w for gloves or mittens	m.w	10
fù	付	pay	v	26
fùxí	复习	review; to review	n/v	19
gānjìng	干净	clean	adj	20
gāngcái	刚才	just now	ad	27

Pinyin	Chinese	English	Part of speech	Lesson
gāngqín	钢琴	piano	n	30
gāo	高	tall; high	adj	11
gāoěrfūqiú	高尔夫球	golf	n	24
gāoxìng	高兴	delighted	adj	12
gàosu	告诉	tell	v	21
gēbo	胳膊	arm	n	20
gēge	哥哥	older brother	n	2
gējù	歌剧	opera	n	21
gè	个	m.w for general use (most frequently used)	m.w	10
gèzi	个子	height	n	20
gěi	给	give	v	21
gěi	给	for; to; to give	prep/v	27
gēn	跟	with	prep	24
gēn...yíyàng	跟......一样	the same as	ph	29
gōngchéng	工程	engineering	n	17
gōngchéngshī	工程师	engineer	n	13
gōngchǐ	公尺	meter	n	29
gōngfēn	公分	centimeter	n	29
gōnggòngqìchē	公共汽车	bus	n	23
gōngjīn	公斤	kilogram	n	29
gōngkè	功课	school work; homework	n	19
gōnglǐ	公里	kilometer	n	29
gōngrén	工人	worker	n	13
gōngsī	公司	company; firm	n	23
gōngzuò	工作	work; job	n/v	23
gūniang	姑娘	girl	n	8
gùkè	顾客	customer	n	26
guā	刮	shave	v	23
guāfēng	刮风	be windy	v.o	28
guàng	逛	stroll around	v	26
guì	贵	expensive	adj	11
guǒzhī	果汁	fruit juice	n	6
hái	还	still; yet; even	ad	11
hǎitān	海滩	beach	n	25
hànbǎobāo	汉堡包	hamburger	n	4
Hànyǔ	汉语	Chinese language	n	19
Hànzì	汉字	Chinese character	n	19
hǎo	好	good; fine; well	adj	11
hào	号	date (*informal*)	n	9
hē	喝	drink	v	6
hé	和	and	conj	4
hé	河	river	n	29
hēi	黑	black; dark	adj	15
hēibǎn[kuài]	黑板 [块]	blackboard	n	16
hēibǎncā	黑板擦	blackboard eraser	n	16
hěn	很	very	ad	11

Pinyin	Chinese	English	Part of speech	Lesson
hóng	红	red	adj	15
hòu	后	back	n	17
hòubian	后边	back	n	17
hòumian	后面	back	n	17
húzi	胡子	beard; mustache	n	23
hùshi	护士	nurse	n	13
huábīng	滑冰	skate	n	24
huáxuě	滑雪	ski	n	24
huà	画	paint; to draw	v	30
huàr	画儿	painting; picture	n	30
huàxué	化学	chemistry	n	17
huàzhuāng	化妆	apply make-up	v.o	23
huānyíng	欢迎	welcome	v	30
huán	还	return	v	21
huáng	黄	yellow	adj	15
huī	灰	gray; ash	adj/n	15
huí	回	return (to a place)	v	23
huídá	回答	answer; to reply	v	19
huì	会	know how to	aux.v	24
huì	会	will (proably)	aux.v	28
jīdòng	激动	excited	adj	12
jǐ	几	how many; how much	pron	7
jìhuà	计划	plan; to plan	n/v	25
jiā	加	add; plus	v	7
jiā	家	home; house; family	n	16
jiājù	家具	furniture	n	26
jiālǐ rén	家里人	family members	n	6
jià/jiàgé	价/价格	price	n	26
jiān	间	m.w for rooms	m.w	27
jiānbǎng	肩膀	shoulder	n	20
jiǎn	减	subtract; minus	v	7
jiǎn	减	reduce	v	26
jiàn	件	m.w for upper body clothing (jackets, shirts)	m.w	10
jiǎng	讲	explain; to speak	v	19
jiāo	教	teach	v	19
jiǎo	脚	foot	n	20
jiǎozi	饺子	dumpling	n	4
jiào	叫	ask	v	21
jiàoshì	教室	classroom	n	14
jiàoshòu	教授	professor	n	14
jiàoxué lóu	教学楼	teaching building	n	14
jiàoyù	教育	education	n	17
jié	节	m.w for classes; period	m.w	16
jiéhūn	结婚	get married	v.o	25
jiějie	姐姐	older sister	n	2
jiè	借	borrow	v	27

Pinyin	Chinese	English	Part of speech	Lesson
jièshào	介绍	introduce	v	18
jǐngchá	警察	policeman	n	13
jīnnián	今年	this year	n	8
jīntiān	今天	today	n	5
jǐnzhāng	紧张	nervous	adj	12
jīnglǐ	经理	manager	n	13
jiǔ	九	nine	n.w	7
jiǔ	酒	wine	n	6
jiǔba	酒吧	bar; tavern	n	22
jiù	就	exactly; precisely	ad	17
jiù	旧	old (things)	adj	29
júhuáng	桔黄	orange (color)	n	15
júzi	桔子	orange	n	3
jùchǎng	剧场	opera house; theater	n	22
jūnrén	军人	soldier	n	13
kāfēi	咖啡	coffee	n	6
kāi(chē)	开(车)	drive (auto)	v	23
kāihuì	开会	attend a meeting; to hold a meeting	v.o	25
kāishǐ	开始	begin; to start	v	25
kàn	看	watch; to look	v	5
kǎoshì	考试	test; to take a test	n/v	19
kělè	可乐	soda	n	6
kěnéng	可能	be probable	aux.v	28
kěshì	可是	but; however	conj	11
kěyǐ	可以	may; can	aux.v	24
kè	刻	a quarter (of an hour)	n	8
kèwén	课文	text	n	19
kōngtiáojī[tái]	空调机[台]	air-conditioner	n	16
kǔ	苦	bitter	adj	12
kùzi[tiáo]	裤子[条]	trousers; pants	n	10
kuài	块	m.w for chunk-like objects	m.w	16
kuài	快	fast; quick	adj	19
kuàilè	快乐	happy	adj	12
kuān	宽	broad; wide (width and breadth)	adj	20
kuàngquánshuǐ	矿泉水	mineral water	n	6
là	辣	hot; spicy	adj	12
lán	蓝	blue	adj	15
lánqiú	篮球	basketball	n	24
lǎo	老	old	a	8
lǎoshī	老师	teacher	n	13
le	了	particle (perfective)	a.p	25
lèi	累	tired	adj	11
lěng	冷	cold	adj	28

Pinyin	Chinese	English	Part of speech	Lesson
lí	梨	pear	n	3
lǐ	里	in; inside	n	16
lǐbian	里边	inside	n	17
lǐgōng	理工	science and engineering	n	17
lǐmiàn	里面	inside	n	17
lǐtáng	礼堂	auditorium	n	14
lìshǐ	历史	history	n	17
liǎn	脸	face	n	23
liànxí	练习	exercise; to practice	n/v	19
liángkuai	凉快	nice and cool	adj	28
liǎng	两	two (usually goes with a measure word)	n.w	8
líng	零	zero	n.w	7
lǐngdài[tiáo]	领带[条]	tie	n	10
liúlì	流利	fluent	adj	19
liù	六	six	n.w	7
lóu	楼	building	n	14
lù	路	road	n	23
lùxiàng	录像	video recording; to record video	n/v.o	19
lùyīn	绿 录音	recording; to record	n/v.o	19
lǚyóu	旅游	travel; to travel	n/v	25
lǜ	绿	green	adj	15
lǜshī	律师	lawyer; attorney	n	13
Lúndūn	伦敦	London	n	28
Luòshānjī	洛杉矶	Los Angeles	n	28
māma	妈妈	mother; mom	n	2
ma	吗	particle (for yes-no questions)	part	3
mǎi	买	buy	v	4
mántou	馒头	steamed bread	n	4
mǎnyì	满意	satisfied	adj	12
màn	慢	slow	adj	19
máng	忙	busy	adj	11
máoyī[jiàn]	毛衣[件]	sweater	n	10
màozi[dǐng]	帽子[顶]	hat; cap	n	10
méi yǒu	没有	not have	v	2
Měiguó	美国	USA	n	1
Měiguórén	美国人	American person/people	n	1
mèimei	妹妹	younger sister	n	2
mén[shàn]	门[扇]	door	n	16
mǐfàn	米饭	(cooked) rice	n	4
mǐfěn	米粉	rice noodles	n	4
miànbāo	面包	bread	n	4
miànjī	面积	area	n	29
miàntiáo	面条	noodles	n	4
míngnián	明年	next year	n	9
míngtiān	明天	tomorrow	n	5

Pinyin	Chinese	English	Part of speech	Lesson
nǎ	哪	which	pron	6
nà	那	that; those	pron	10
nàme	那么	so; like that	pron	29
nàxiē	那些	those	pron	12
nǎilào	奶酪	cheese	n	4
nǎinai	奶奶	grandmother (paternal)	n	2
nán	男	male; man	adj	23
nánguò	难过	sad	adj	12
nánkàn	难看	ugly	adj	11
ne	呢	particle	part	11
nèiyī[jiàn]	内衣[件]	underwear	n	15
néng	能	can; to be able to	aux.v	24
nǐ	你	you (*sing.*)	pron	1
nián	年	year	n	9
niàn	念	read aloud	v	19
nǐmen	你们	you (*pl.*)	pron	1
nín	您	you (*polite*)	pron	8
níngméng	柠檬	lemon	n	3
niúnǎi	牛奶	milk	n	6
Niǔyuē	纽约	New York	n	28
nóngmín	农民	farmer	n	13
nǚ	女	female; woman	adj	23
nǚ'ér	女儿	daughter	n	2
nuǎnhuo	暖和	nice and warm	adj	28
páiqiú	排球	volleyball	n	24
pángbiān	旁边	beside; next to	n	17
pàng	胖	fat (people)	adj	11
pǎobù	跑步	run	v.o	18
péngyou	朋友	friend	n	8
pīsàbǐng	披萨饼	pizza	n	4
pídài[tiáo]	皮带[条]	leather belt	n	15
píjiǔ	啤酒	beer	n	6
píxié[shuāng/zhī]	皮鞋[双/只]	leather shoe	n	10
piányi	便宜	inexpensive; cheap	adj	11
piào	票	ticket	n	21
piàoliang	漂亮	pretty	adj	11
pīngpāngqiú	乒乓球	ping-pong	n	24
píng	瓶	m.w; bottle	m.w	27
píngguǒ	苹果	apple	n	3
pūkè	扑克	poker	n	24
pútao	葡萄	grape	n	3
pútao jiǔ	葡萄酒	grape wine	n	6
qī	七	seven	n.w	7
qiānbǐ	铅笔	pencil	n	26
qián	钱	money	n	26
qián	前	front	n	17
qiánbian	前边	front	n	17

Pinyin	Chinese	English	Part of speech	Lesson
qiánmian	前面	front	n	17
qīngchu	清楚	clear	adj	19
qíng	晴	fine; clear; sunny	adj	28
qǐng	请	invite; please	v	21
qǐngwèn	请问	May I ask?	ph	8
qiūtiān	秋天	autumn; fall	n	25
qiúxié[shuāng/zhī]	球鞋［双／只］	tennis shoes	n	15
qù	去	go	v	14
qùnián	去年	last year	n	9
qúnzi[tiáo]	裙子［条］	skirt	n	10
ràng	让	let	v	21
rè	热	hot	adj	28
rénwén	人文	liberal arts	n	17
rènshi	认识	meet; to know	v	27
rènzhēn	认真	conscientious	adj	19
rì	日	date	n	9
Rìběn	日本	Japan	n	1
Rìběnrén	日本人	Japanese person/people	n	1
sān	三	three	n.w	7
sānmíngzhì	三明治	sandwich	n	4
sǎo	扫	sweep	v	18
shàn	扇	m.w for doors and windows	m.w	16
shāngchǎng	商场	shopping mall	n	22
shāngdiàn	商店	shop; store	n	22
shāngrén	商人	businessman	n	13
shàng	上	up	n	17
shàng	上	in; on; upon	n	27
shàng kè	上课	attend class	v.o	23
shàngbān	上班	go to work	v.o	5
shàngbian	上边	up	n	17
shàngge	上个	last	pron	9
shàngmian	上面	up	n	17
shàngwǎng	上网	go online	v.o	5
shàngxué	上学	go to school	v.o	5
shàngyī[jiàn]	上衣［件］	jacket	n	10
shāobing	烧饼	sesame cake	n	4
shǎo	少	little; few	adj	19
shéi/shuí	谁	who; whom	pron	6
shēntǐ	身体	health; body	n	11
shénme	什么	what	pron	6
shēngcí	生词	new word; vocabulary	n	19
shēngqì	生气	angry	adj	12
shēngri	生日	birthday	n	9
shēngwù	生物	biology	n	17
shīwàng	失望	disappointed	adj	12

Pinyin	Chinese	English	Part of speech	Lesson
shí	十	ten	n.w	7
shíhou	时候	time (a point in)	n	18
shíjiān	时间	time (the concept of)	n	18
shítáng	食堂	cafeteria	n	14
shíyànshì	实验室	laboratory	n	14
shì	是	be (am, is, are)	v	1
shōushi	收拾	tidy up	v	18
shǒu	手	hand	n	20
shǒu	首	m.w for songs, poems	m.w	27
shǒutào[fù/zhī]	手套[副/只]	glove; mitten	n	10
shòu	瘦	thin	adj	11
shū[běn]	书[本]	book	n	14
shūdiàn	书店	bookstore	n	14
shù	树	tree	n	30
shùxué	数学	mathematics	n	17
shuā	刷	brush; to brush	n/v	23
shuā	刷	paint (house or wall)	v	30
shuāng	双	m.w for a pair of shoes and socks	m.w	10
shuǐ	水	water	n	6
shuìjiào	睡觉	sleep	v.o	5
shuìyī[jiàn]	睡衣[件]	pajamas	n	15
shuō	说	speak; to say	v	19
sì	四	four	n.w	7
sòng	送	give as a gift	v	21
sùshè	宿舍	dormitory	n	14
suān	酸	sour	adj	12
suì	岁	year (of age)	n	8
suìshu	岁数	age; years	n	8
tā	他	he; him	pron	1
tā	她	she; her	pron	1
tāmen	他们	they; them (*mas.*)	pron	1
tāmen	她们	they; them (*fam.*)	pron	1
tái	台	m.w for objects that sit on a platform	m.w	16
tài	太	too	ad	11
tàitai	太太	wife; Mrs.; madam	n	2
tàiyáng	太阳	the sun	n	28
tán	弹	play (the piano)	v	30
tánhuà	谈话	talk; to chat	v.o	30
táozi	桃子	peach	n	3
téng	疼	hurt; to be in pain	n	20
tī	踢	kick; to play (soccer)	v	24
tīxùshān[jiàn]	T-恤衫[件]	T-shirt	n	10
tǐyùchǎng	体育场	stadium	n	14
tǐyùguǎn	体育馆	gymnasium	n	14
tiānqì	天气	weather	n	28

Pinyin	Chinese	English	Part of speech	Lesson
tián	甜	sweet	adj	12
tiáo	条	m.w for long and thin objects (pants, skirts, tie)	m.w	10
tiàowǔ	跳舞	dance	v.o	18
tīng	听	listen	v	18
tíng	停	stop; to cease	v	28
tóu	头	head	n	20
tóufa	头发	hair	n	20
túshūguǎn	图书馆	library	n	14
tuǐ	腿	leg	n	20
tuōxié[shuāng/zhī]	拖鞋［双／只］	slippers	n	15
wàzi[shuāng/zhī]]	袜子［双／只］	sock	n	10
wài	外	outside	n	17
wàibian	外边	outside	n	17
wàimian	外面	outside	n	17
wàiyǔ	外语	foreign language	n	17
wǎn	碗	m.w; bowl	n/m.w	18
wǎnfàn	晚饭	supper; dinner	n	5
wǎnhuì	晚会	evening party	n	21
wǎnshang	晚上	evening	n	5
wǎngqiú	网球	tennis	n	24
wéijīn[tiáo]	围巾［条］	scarf	n	15
wēndù	温度	temperature	n	28
wēndùjì	温度计	thermometer	n	28
wénjù	文具	stationery	n	26
wèntí	问题	question; problem	n	19
wǒ	我	I; me	pron	1
wǒmen	我们	we; us	pron	1
wūzi	屋子	room	n	18
wǔ	五	five	n.w	7
wǔfàn	午饭	lunch	n	5
wǔhuì	舞会	dance party; ball	n	21
wù	雾	fog	n	28
wùlǐ	物理	physics	n	17
xī	吸	vaccum; to suck	v	18
xīchénqì	吸尘器	vaccum cleaner	n	18
xīguā	西瓜	watermelon	n	3
xīzhuāng[jiàn]	西装［件］	suit	n	15
xǐ	洗	wash	v	18
xǐhuan	喜欢	like	v	3
xǐzǎo	洗澡	bathe; to take a shower	v.o	23
xì	细	slender; thin	adj	20
xià	下	down	n	17
xià kè	下课	get out of class	v.o	23
xià wéiqí	下围棋	play Go	v.o	21

Pinyin	Chinese	English	Part of speech	Lesson
xiàbān	下班	get off work	v.o	23
xiàbian	下边	down	n	17
xiàge	下个	next	pron	9
xiàmian	下面	down	n	17
xiàtiān	夏天	summer	n	25
xiàwǔ	下午	afternoon	n	5
xiàwù	下雾	be foggy	v.o	28
xiàxuě	下雪	snow	v.o	28
xiàyǔ	下雨	rain	v.o	28
xiānsheng	先生	husband; sir; gentleman; Mr.	n	2
xián	咸	salty	adj	12
xiànzài	现在	now	n	8
xiāngguā	香瓜	honeydew	n	3
xiāngjiāo	香蕉	banana	n	3
xiǎng	想	want	v/aux.v	13
xiàngqí	象棋	chess	n	24
xiǎo	小	little; small; young	a	8
xiǎoshíhou	小时候	in one's childhood	ph	21
xiē	些	some; more than one	m.w	12
xiě	写	write	v	19
xīn	新	new	adj	14
xīngqī	星期	week	n	9
Xīngqī'èr	星期二	Tuesday	n	9
Xīngqīliù	星期六	Saturday	n	9
Xīngqīsān	星期三	Wednesday	n	9
Xīngqīsì	星期四	Thursday	n	9
Xīngqītiān/rì	星期天/日	Sunday	n	9
Xīngqīwǔ	星期五	Friday	n	9
Xīngqīyī	星期一	Monday	n	9
xíngzhèng	行政	administration	n	17
xiūlǐ	修理	repair	v	30
xiūxī	休息	rest; to rest	v/n	18
xuésheng	学生	student	n	13
xué/xuéxí	学/学习	study; to learn	v/n	18
xuéxiào	学校	school	n	14
xuě	雪	snow	n	28
yá/yáchǐ	牙/牙齿	tooth	n	23
yǎnjing	眼睛	eye	n	20
yánsè/sè	颜色/色	color	n	15
yǎnyuán	演员	actor	n	13
yāo	腰	waist; lower back	n	20
yào	要	must; want; to need	aux.v/v	24
yàoshi	要是	if	conj	18
yéye	爷爷	grandfather (paternal)	n	2
yě	也	also; too	ad	4
yī	一	one	n.w	7
yīfu[jiàn]	衣服[件]	clothes	n	10

Pinyin	Chinese	English	Part of speech	Lesson
yīshēng	医生	doctor	n	13
yīyuàn	医院	hospital	n	22
yíxiàr	一下儿	for a little while; briefly	ad	18
yǐjīng	已经	already	ad	27
yǐzi[bǎ]	椅子[把]	chair	n	16
Yìdàlì	意大利	Italy	n	4
yìdiǎnr	一点儿	a little bit	n	29
yìqǐ	一起	together	ad	24
yìxiē	一些	m.w; some; a few	m.w	27
yīn	阴	cloudy; overcast	adj	28
yīnyuè	音乐	music	n	13
yīnyuèhuì	音乐会	concert	n	21
yīnyuèjiā	音乐家	musician	n	13
yínháng	银行	bank	n	22
yǐnliào	饮料	beverages	n	6
Yìndù	印度	India	n	1
Yìndùrén	印度人	Indian person/people	n	1
yīngchǐ	英尺	English foot	n	29
yīngcùn	英寸	English inch	n	29
yīnggāi	应该	should; ought to	aux.v	28
Yīngguó	英国	Great Britain; England	n	1
Yīngguórén	英国人	English person/people	n	1
yīnglǐ	英里	English mile	n	29
yòng	用	use	v	18
yòngpǐn	用品	articles for use	n	26
yóujú	邮局	post office	n	22
yóuyǒng	游泳	swim	v.o	18
yǒu	有	have	v	2
yǒudiǎnr	有点儿	a little bit	ph	11
yòu	右	right	n	17
yòubian	右边	right	n	17
yòumian	右面	right	n	17
yòuzi	柚子	grapefruit	n	3
yǔ	雨	rain	n	28
yǔfǎ	语法	grammar	n	19
yǔyī[jiàn]	雨衣[件]	raincoat	n	15
yuè	月	month	n	9
yuèlǎnshì	阅览室	reading room	n	14
yùndòng	运动	work out	v	5
yùndòngyuán	运动员	athlete	n	13
zázhì	杂志	magazine	n	26
zài	在	be in/at/on/upon; in; at; on; upon	v/prep	17
		in progress of	a.p	30
zāng	脏	dirty	adj	18
zǎo	早	morning; early	n/adj	11
zǎofàn	早饭	breakfast	n	5
zǎoshang	早上	morning	n	5

Pinyin	Chinese	English	Part of speech	Lesson
zěnmeyàng	怎么样	how; how is it going?	pron	11
zhǎn	盏	m.w for lamps and lights	m.w	16
zhāng	张	m.w for objects with a flat surface	m.w	16
zháojí	着急	anxious	adj	12
zhǎo	找	look for	v	25
zhè	这	this; these	pron	10
zhège	这个	this (one)	pron	9
zhème	这么	so; like this	pron	29
zhèxiē	这些	these	pron	12
zhěnglǐ	整理	put in order	v	18
zhěngqí	整齐	tidy; orderly	adj	20
zhèng(zài)	正(在)	in progress of	ad	30
zhèngzhì	政治	political science; politics	n	17
zhī	汁	juice	n	6
zhī	只	m.w for a single one (shoe, sock, glove, mitten)	m.w	10
zhī	枝	m.w for pens and writing brushes	m.w	16
zhíyuán	职员	clerk	n	13
zhǐ	纸	paper	n	26
zhōng	钟	time; clock; bell	n	8
Zhōngguó	中国	China	n	1
Zhōngguórén	中国人	Chinese person/people	n	1
zhōngjiān	中间	between	n	17
Zhōngwén	中文	Chinese (language)	n	14
zhōngwǔ	中午	noon	n	5
zhòng	种	plant; to grow	v	30
zhōumò	周末	weekend	n	25
zhù	住	live; to reside	v	29
zhǔnbèi	准备	preparation; to prepare; to be going to	n/v	19
zhuōzi[zhāng]	桌子[张]	table; desk	n	16
zǐ	紫	purple	adj	15
zǒngshì	总是	always	ad	20
zǒu	走	walk; to leave	v	23
zū	租	rent	m.w	27
zúqiú	足球	soccer; football	n	24
zuì	最	most	ad	20
zuìjìn	最近	recently; these days	ad/adj	11
zuótiān	昨天	yesterday	n	9
zuǒ	左	left	n	17
zuǒbian	左边	left	n	17
zuǒmian	左面	left	n	17
zuò	坐	sit	v	23
zuò	做	make; to do	v	4
zuòjiā	作家	writer	n	13
zuò yóuxì	做游戏	play games	v.o	21

Answer key

I

1·1   1. c   2. g   3. i   4. a   5. d   6. f   7. e   8. b   9. j   10. h

1·2   1. f   2. g   3. a   4. c   5. b   6. e   7. h   8. d

1·3   1. He is Japanese.
2. They are not French.
3. We are Chinese.
4. You are not British.
5. He is American.
6. You are not Russian.
7. I'm Indian.
8. They are not German.

1·4   1. 我是美国人。*Wǒ shì Měiguórén.*
2. 他们不是俄国人。*Tāmen bú shì Éguórén.*
3. 我们不是日本人。*Wǒmen bú shì Rìběn rén.*
4. 你是法国人。*Nǐ shì Fǎguórén.*
5. 他是中国人。*Tā shì Zhōngguórén.*
6. 你们不是英国人。*Nǐmen bú shì Yīngguórén.*
7. 他们是德国人。*Tāmen shì Déguórén.*
8. 她不是印度人。*Tā bú shì Yìndùrén.*

2·1   1. f   2. e   3. a   4. b   5. c   6. d   7. i   8. l   9. k   10. g   11. h   12. j

2·2   1. 他不是爷爷。*Tā bú shì yéye.*
2. 你不是姐姐。*Nǐ bú shì jiějie.*
3. 她不是妹妹。*Tā bú shì mèimei.*
4. 他不是哥哥。*Tā bú shì gēge.*
5. 你不是妈妈。*Nǐ bú shì māma.*
6. 我没有先生。*Wǒ méi yǒu xiānsheng.*
7. 他们没有儿子。*Tāmen méi yǒu érzi.*
8. 她们没有奶奶。*Tāmen méi yǒu nǎinai.*
9. 我们没有弟弟。*Wǒmen méi yǒu dìdi.*
10. 我没有太太。*Wǒ méi yǒu tàitai.*
11. 他们没有女儿。*Tāmen méi yǒu nǚ'ér.*
12. 她没有爸爸。*Tā méi yǒu bàba.*

2·3   1. 你有哥哥。*Nǐ yǒu gēge.*
2. 你们没有妹妹。*Nǐmen méi yǒu mèimei.*
3. 他们有儿子。*Tāmen yǒu érzi.*
4. 我们没有女儿。*Wǒmen méi yǒu nǚ'ér.*
5. 她有先生。*Tā yǒu xiānsheng.*
6. 他没有太太。*Tā méi yǒu tàitai.*
7. 奶奶有哥哥。*Nǎinai yǒu gēge.*
8. 你没有爷爷。*Nǐ méi yǒu yéye.*
9. 妈妈有弟弟。*Māma yǒu dìdi.*
10. 他们没有奶奶。*Tāmen méi yǒu nǎinai.*
11. 她没有弟弟。*Tā méi yǒu dìdi.*
12. 爸爸有姐姐。*Bàba yǒu jiějie.*

13. 他没有爸爸。 *Tā méi yǒu bàba.*
14. 爷爷有妹妹。 *Yéye yǒu mèimei.*
15. 我没有妈妈。 *Wǒ méi yǒu māma.*

3·1 1. d 2. f 3. b 4. a 5. c 6. e 7. j 8. g 9. k 10. h 11. l 12. i

3·2 The following are sample answers.

1. 有，我有妈妈。 *Yǒu, wǒ yǒu māma.*
2. 没有，我没有哥哥。 *Méiyǒu, wǒ méiyǒu gēge.*
3. 没有，我没有妹妹。 *Méiyǒu, wǒ méiyǒu mèimei.*
4. 有，我有先生。 *Yǒu, wǒ yǒu xiānshēng.*
5. 没有，我没有女儿。 *Méiyǒu, wǒ méiyǒu nǚ'ér.*
6. 吃，我吃香蕉。 *Chī, wǒ chī xiāngjiāo.*
7. 吃，他吃西瓜。 *Chī, tā chī xīguā.*
8. 不，他不吃柠檬。 *Bù, tā bù chī níngméng.*
9. 不，他不吃柚子。 *Bù, tā bù chī yòuzi.*
10. 吃，他吃桔子。 *Chī, tā chī júzi.*

3·3 1. 我弟弟吃菠萝吗? *Wǒ dìdi chī bōluó ma?*
2. 你姐姐吃香蕉吗? *Nǐ jiějie chī xiāngjiāo ma?*
3. 她妹妹吃西瓜吗? *Tā mèimei chī xīguā ma?*
4. 他哥哥吃苹果吗? *Tā gēge chī píngguǒ ma?*
5. 我先生吃香瓜吗? *Wǒ xiānsheng chī xiāngguā ma?*
6. 他们儿子吃梨吗? *Tāmen érzi chī lí ma?*
7. 我们爷爷喜欢柠檬吗? *Wǒmen yéye xǐhuan níngméng ma?*
8. 她们奶奶喜欢草莓吗? *Tāmen nǎinai xǐhuan cǎoméi ma?*
9. 我太太喜欢吃桃子吗? *Wǒ tàitài xǐhuan chī táozi ma?*
10. 你妈妈喜欢吃桔子吗? *Nǐ māma xǐhuan chī júzi ma?*
11. 他们女儿喜欢吃柚子吗? *Tāmen nǚ'ér xǐhuan chī yòuzi ma?*
12. 你们爸爸喜欢吃葡萄吗? *Nǐmen bàba xǐhuan chī pútao ma?*

3·4 1. 我喜欢吃香蕉。 *Wǒ xǐhuan chī xiāngjiāo.*
2. 你吃梨吗? *Nǐ chī lí ma?*
3. 我爸爸不喜欢吃柠檬。 *Wǒ bàba bù xǐhuan chī níngméng.*
4. 他妈妈喜欢吃草莓吗? *Tā māma xǐhuan chī cǎoméi ma?*
5. 她哥哥不吃葡萄。 *Tā gēge bù chī pútao.*
6. 你妹妹喜欢桔子吗? *Nǐ mèimei xǐhuan júzi ma?*
7. 你奶奶喜欢西瓜。 *Nǐ nǎinai xǐhuan xīguā.*
8. 她先生吃柚子吗? *Tā xiānsheng chī yòuzi ma?*
9. 他们妈妈喜欢吃香瓜。 *Tāmen māma xǐhuan chī xiāngguā.*
10. 他爷爷喜欢桃子吗? *Tā yéye xǐhuan táozi ma?*
11. 我们儿子不喜欢吃苹果。 *Wǒmen érzi bù xǐhuan chī píngguǒ.*
12. 他太太吃菠萝吗? *Tā tàitai chī bōluó ma?*

4·1 1. c 2. e 3. f 4. b 5. a 6. d 7. l 8. k 9. j 10. g 11. h 12. i

4·2 1. …也喜欢吃…。 *…yě xǐhuan chī….* 2. …也喜欢吃…。 *…yě xǐhuan chī….*
3. …也喜欢吃…。 *…yě xǐhuan chī….* 4. …也喜欢吃…。 *…yě xǐhuan chī….*
5. …都喜欢吃…。 *…dōu xǐhuan chī….* 6. …都喜欢吃…。 *… dōu xǐhuan chī….*
7. …都喜欢吃…。 *… dōu xǐhuan chī….* 8. …都喜欢吃…。 *… dōu xǐhuan chī….*

4·3 1. 都 *dōu*; His older brother and older sister both like eating rice noodles.
2. 也 *yě*; Her grandfather also likes eating cheese pizzas.
3. 都不 *dōu bù*; None of his younger brothers and younger sisters likes eating noodles.
4. 也不 *yě bù*; They do not like to make steamed bread and sesame cakes, either.
5. 都 *dōu*; Both your husband and my wife like eating rice.
6. 也 *yě*; Our grandmother also likes to make dumplings and steamed stuffed buns.
7. 也不 *yě bù*; My parents do not like to buy bread either.
8. 都 *dōu*; They all like to make sandwiches and hamburgers.

4·4 1. 我先生也喜欢吃米饭。 *Wǒ xiānsheng yě xǐhuan chī mǐfàn.*
2. 我太太也不喜欢意大利披萨饼。 *Wǒ tàitai yě bù xǐhuan Yìdàlì pīsàbǐng.*
3. 你们都喜欢做饺子吗? *Nǐmen dōu xǐhuan zuò jiǎozi ma?*
4. 我女儿都不买汉堡包。 *Wǒ nǚ'ér dōu bù mǎi hànbǎobāo.*
5. 你们都喜欢吃法国奶酪。 *Nǐmen dōu xǐhuan chī Fǎguó nǎilào.*
6. 我儿子也不喜欢做米粉。 *Wǒ érzi yě bù xǐhuan zuò mǐfěn.*

7. 她哥哥和弟弟也喜欢买包子。*Tā gēge hé dìdi yě xǐhuan mǎi bāozi.*
8. 我们都喜欢吃烧饼。*Wǒmen dōu xǐhuan chī shāobing.*
9. 日本人也喜欢做面条吗? *Rìběnrén yě xǐhuan zuò miàntiáo ma?*
10. 德国人都喜欢汉堡包。*Déguórén dōu xǐhuan hànbǎobāo.*
11. 印度人也做三明治吗? *Yìndùrén yě zuò sānmíngzhì ma?*
12. 俄国人也买馒头吗? *Éguórén yě mǎi mántou ma?*

5·1 1. c 2. i 3. h 4. f 5. g 6. d 7. e 8. a 9. b 10. n 11. o 12. p 13. J
14. r 15. q 16. l 17. k 18. m

5·2 1. d 2. h 3. a 4. g 5. i 6. b 7. j 8. f 9. c 10. e

5·3 The following are sample answers.

1. 是, 我常看电视。*Shì, wǒ cháng kàn diànshì.*
2. 喜欢, 我喜欢晚上运动。*xǐhuan, wǒ xǐhuan wǎnshang yùndòng.*
3. 不, 我晚上不常上网。*Bù, wǒ wǎnshang bù cháng shàngwǎng.*
4. 我今天也不上班。*Wǒ jīntiān yě bú shàngbān.*
5. 是, 他喜欢白天睡觉。*Shì, tā xǐhuan báitiān shuìjiào.*
6. 我也不上学。*Wǒ yě bú shàngxué.*

5·4 1. 我哥哥常不吃早饭。*Wǒ gēge cháng bù chī zǎofàn.*
2. 她爸爸和妈妈晚上都上班。*Tā bàba hé māma wǎnshang dōu shàngbān.*
3. 他太太晚上上网吗? *Tā tàitai wǎnshang shàngwǎng ma?*
4. 我们奶奶下午常运动。*Wǒmen nǎinai xiàwǔ cháng yùndòng.*
5. 我姐姐和妹妹明天都上学。*Wǒ jiějie hé mèimei míngtiān dōu shàngxué.*
6. 你先生白天常睡觉吗? *Nǐ xiānsheng báitiān cháng shuìjiào ma?*
7. 他爷爷早上看电视。*Tā yéye zǎoshang kàn diànshì.*
8. 晚饭你常吃意大利面包和法国奶酪吗? *Wǎnfàn nǐ cháng chī Yìdàlì miànbāo hé Fǎguó nǎilào ma?*
9. 我儿子和女儿都不常上网。*Wǒ érzi hé nǚ'ér dōu bù cháng shàngwǎng.*
10. 中国人晚上常看电视。*Zhōngguórén wǎnshang cháng kàn diànshì.*
11. 美国人早上常运动。*Měiguórén zǎoshang cháng yùndòng.*
12. 我妹妹白天上班, 我姐姐晚上上班。*Wǒ mèimei báitiān shàngbān, wǒ jiějie wǎnshang shàngbān.*

R1·1 The following are sample answers.

你是 _____ 吗?
Nǐ shì _____ ma?

	是 *shì*	不是 *bú shì*			是 *shì*	不是 *bú shì*
1. 英国人 *Yīngguórén*		x		6. 美国人 *Měiguórén*	x	
2. 日本人 *Rìběnrén*		x		7. 法国人 *Fǎguórén*		x
3. 印度人 *Yìndùrén*		x		8. 中国人 *Zhōngguórén*		x
4. 俄国人 *Éguórén*		x		9. 德国人 *Déguórén*		x
5. 意大利人 *Yìdàlìrén*		x				

你有 _____ 吗?
Nǐ yǒu _____ ma?

	有 *yǒu*	没有 *méi yǒu*			有 *yǒu*	没有 *méi yǒu*
10. 奶奶 *nǎinai*		x		12. 妈妈 *māma*	x	
11. 爷爷 *yéye*		x		13. 爸爸 *bàba*	x	

		喜欢吃	不喜欢吃			喜欢吃	不喜欢吃
14.	太太 *tàitai*		x	18.	弟弟 *dìdi*	x	
15.	先生 *xiānsheng*	x		19.	哥哥 *gēge*	x	
16.	姐姐 *jiějie*		x	20.	女儿 *nǚ'ér*		x
17.	妹妹 *mèimei*	x		21.	儿子 *érzi*	x	

你喜欢吃 ＿＿＿＿＿ 吗?
Nǐ xǐhuan chī ___ ma?

		喜欢吃 *xǐhuan chī*	**不喜欢吃** *bù xǐhuan chī*			**喜欢吃** *xǐhuan chī*	**不喜欢吃** *bù xǐhuan chī*
22.	香瓜 *xiāngguā*	x		30.	汉堡包 *hànbǎobāo*		x
23.	菠萝 *bōluó*	x		31.	面条 *miàntiáo*	x	
24.	草莓 *cǎoméi*	x		32.	披萨饼 *pīsàbǐng*	x	
25.	桔子 *júzi*	x		33.	面包 *miànbāo*	x	
26.	苹果 *píngguǒ*	x		34.	饺子 *jiǎozi*	x	
27.	葡萄 *pútao*	x		35.	中国餐 *Zhōngguó cān*	x	
28.	馒头 *mántou*	x		36.	美国餐 *Měiguó cān*	x	
29.	奶酪 *nǎilào*	x		37.	印度餐 *Yìndù cān*		x

R1·2 1. 都 *dōu* 2. 也 *yě* 3. 不 *bù* 4. 常 *cháng* 5. 都不 *dōu bù* 6. 也不 *yě bù* 7. 都 *dōu*

R1·3 The following are sample answers.

		上班 *shàngbān*	上学 *shàngxué*	上网 *shàngwǎng*	运动 *yùndòng*	睡觉 *shuìjiào*	看电视 *kàn diànshì*
1.	上午 *shàngwǔ*		x				
2.	中午 *zhōngwǔ*				x		
3.	下午 *xiàwǔ*			x			
4.	白天 *báitiān*		x		x		
5.	晚上 *wǎnshang*					x	x

R1·4
1. 我不是英国人; 我是美国人。*Wǒ bú shì Yīngguórén; wǒ shì Měiguórén.*
2. 她是中国人, 他先生也是中国人。*Tā shì Zhōngguórén, tā xiānsheng yě shì Zhōngguórén.*
3. 她没有哥哥, 也没有姐姐。*Tā méi yǒu gēge, yě méi yǒu jiějie.*
4. 你有爷爷和奶奶吗? *Nǐ yǒu yéye hé nǎinai ma?*
5. 他儿子和女儿都喜欢吃中国米粉吗? *Tā érzi hé nǚ'ér dōu xǐhuan chī Zhōngguó mǐfěn ma?*

6. 早饭她爸爸和妈妈常买馒头和烧饼。*Zǎofàn tā bàba hé māma cháng mǎi mántou hé shāobing.*
7. 晚饭中国人常吃米饭和面条。*Wǎnfàn Zhōngguórén cháng chī mǐfàn hé miàntiáo.*
8. 午饭德国人常做汉堡包吗? *Wǔfàn Déguórén cháng zuò hànbǎobāo ma?*
9. 我白天睡觉，晚上上班。*Wǒ báitiān shuìjiào, wǎnshang shàngbān.*
10. 我太太常中午上网，下午运动。*Wǒ tàitai cháng zhōngwǔ shàngwǎng, xiàwǔ yùndòng.*
11. 他女儿都不喜欢看电视。*Tā nǚ'ér dōu bù xǐhuan kàn diànshì.*
12. 她妈妈不常吃香瓜和西瓜。*Tā māma bù cháng chī xiāngguā hé xīguā.*

R1·5 1. T 2. F 3. T 4. F 5. F 6. F 7. F 8. T

II

6·1 The following are sample answers.

	喜欢喝 *xǐhuan hē*	不喜欢喝 *bù xǐhuan hē*
1. 茶 *chá*	x	
2. 水 *shuǐ*	x	
3. 酒 *jiǔ*	x	
4. 果汁 *guǒzhī*	x	
5. 牛奶 *niúnǎi*	x	
6. 咖啡 *kāfēi*		x
7. 豆浆 *dòujiāng*	x	
8. 可乐 *kělè*		x
9. 啤酒 *píjiǔ*	x	
10. 葡萄酒 *pútaojiǔ*	x	
11. 桔子汁 *júzi zhī*	x	
12. 苹果汁 *píngguǒzhī*	x	
13. 葡萄汁 *pútaozhī*	x	
14. 菠萝汁 *bōluózhī*		x
15. 矿泉水 *kuàngquánshuǐ*		x

6·2
1. 你妈妈今天喝什么? *Nǐ māma jīntiān hē shénme?*
2. 谁明天喝中国茶? *Shéi míngtiān hē Zhōngguó chá?*
3. 她先生中午喝什么酒? *Tā xiānsheng zhōngwǔ hē shénme jiǔ?*
4. 他太太晚上喝什么酒? *Tā tàitai wǎnshang hē shénme jiǔ?*
5. 谁早上喝豆浆? *Shéi zǎoshang hē dòujiāng?*
6. 我女儿上午喝什么? *Wǒ nǚ'ér shàngwǔ hē shénme?*
7. 她哥哥下午常喝什么酒? *Tā gēge xiàwǔ cháng hē shénme jiǔ?*
8. 谁常喝饮料? *Shéi cháng hē yǐnliào?*
9. 爷爷也喜欢喝什么? *Yéye yě xǐhuan hē shénme?*
10. 谁不喝菠萝汁? *Shéi bù hē bōluó zhī?*
11. 他姐姐和妹妹都喜欢喝什么? *Tā jiějie hé mèimei dōu xǐhuan hē shénme?*
12. 她弟弟都不喝什么汁? *Tā dìdi dōu bù hē shénme zhī?*

6·3 The following are sample answers.

1. 德国人, 日本人, 英国人, 和中国人都喜欢喝啤酒。
   Déguórén Rìběnrén Yīngguórén hē Zhōngguórén dōu xǐhuan hē píjiǔ.
2. 中国人和日本人喜欢喝茶。*Zhōngguórén hé Rìběnrén xǐhuan hē chá.*
3. 美国人喜欢喝可乐。*Měiguórén xǐhuan hē kělè.*
4. 美国人喜欢喝牛奶。*Měiguórén xǐhuan hē niúnǎi.*
5. 中国人喜欢喝豆浆。*Zhōngguórén xǐhuan hē dòujiāng.*
6. 法国人喜欢喝葡萄酒。*Fǎguórén xǐhuan hē pútao jiǔ.*
7. 意大利人喜欢喝咖啡。*Yìdàlìrén xǐhuan hē kāfēi.*

6·4 The following are sample answers.

1. 我早上常吃面包, 喝牛奶。*Wǒ zǎoshang cháng chī miànbāo, hē niúnǎi.*
2. 午饭我常吃美国餐, 喝果汁。*Wǔfàn wǒ cháng chī Měiguó cān, hē guǒzhī.*
3. 晚饭我常吃美国餐, 喝水。*Wǎnfàn wǒ cháng chī Měiguó cān, hē shuǐ.*
4. 我妈妈喜欢喝咖啡。*Wǒ māma xǐhuan hē kāfēi.*
5. 我喜欢葡萄酒。*Wǒ xǐhuan pútáojiǔ.*
6. 没有人喜欢喝可乐。*Méiyǒu rén xǐhuan hē kělè.*

7. 我爸爸喜欢喝茶。*Wǒ bàba xǐhuan hē chá.*
8. 我姐姐喜欢喝矿泉水。*Wǒ jiějie xǐhuan hē kuàngquán shuǐ.*
9. 我喜欢喝果汁。*Wǒ xǐhuan hē guǒzhī.*
10. 我爷爷喜欢喝豆浆。*Wǒ yéye xǐhuan hē dòujiāng.*
11. 我喜欢喝牛奶。*Wǒ xǐhuan hē niúnǎi.*
12. 我哥哥喜欢喝啤酒。*Wǒ gēge xǐhuan hē píjiǔ.*

6·5
1. 先生，你喝什么? *Xiānsheng, nǐ hē shénme?*
2. 妈妈，你喝什么果汁? *Māma, nǐ hē shénme guǒzhī?*
3. 他哥哥下午常喝什么饮料? *Tā gēge xiàwǔ cháng hē shénme yǐnliào?*
4. 你家里人，谁不喜欢喝牛奶? *Nǐ jiālǐrén, shéi bù xǐhuan hē niúnǎi?*
5. 晚饭你爸爸喜欢吃什么，喝什么? *Wǎnfàn nǐ bàba xǐhuan chī shénme, hē shénme?*
6. 哪国人喜欢白天喝咖啡? *Nǎ guó rén xǐhuan báitiān hē kāfēi?*
7. 你家里人，谁喜欢德国啤酒? *Nǐ jiālǐrén, shéi xǐhuan Déguó píjiǔ?*
8. 午饭哪国人喜欢喝葡萄酒? *Wǔfàn nǎ guó rén xǐhuan hē pútao jiǔ?*
9. 你奶奶晚上喜欢喝什么酒? *Nǐ nǎinai wǎnshang xǐhuan hē shénme jiǔ?*
10. 早饭中国人常喜欢喝什么? *Zǎofàn Zhōngguórén cháng xǐhuan hē shénme?*

7·1
1. 六加二等于八 *Liù jiā èr děngyú bā*   2. 四加十等于十四 *Sì jiā shí děngyú shísì*   3. 九加一等于十 *Jiǔ jiā yi děngyú shí*   4. 二加七等于九 *Èr jiā qī děngyú jiǔ*   5. 八十六加四等于九十 *Bāshíliù jiā sì děngyú jiǔshí*   6. 二十加三十五等于五十五 *Èrshí jiā sānshíwǔ děngyú wǔshíwǔ*

7·2
1. 八减六等于二 *Bā jiǎn liù děngyú èr*   2. 十减三等于七 *Shí jiǎn sān děngyú qī*   3. 七减二等于五 *Qī jiǎn èr děngyú wǔ*   4. 九减五等于四 *Jiǔ jiǎn wǔ děngyú sì*   5. 三十四减二十一等于十三 *Sānshísì jiǎn èrshíyī děngyú shísān*   6. 九十八减十八等于八十 *Jiǔshíbā jiǎn shíbā děngyú bāshí*

7·3
1. 二乘四等于八 *Èr chéng sì děngyú bā*   2. 三乘三等于九 *Sān chéng sān děngyú jiǔ*   3. 七乘一等于七 *Qī chéng yī děngyú qī*   4. 五乘二等于十 *Wǔ chéng èr děngyú shí*   5. 六乘九等于五十四 *Liù chéng jiǔ děngyú wǔshísì*   6. 四十乘七等于两/二百八十 *Sìshí chéng qī děngyú liǎng/èrbǎi bāshí*

7·4
1. 三加四等于几? *Sān jiā sì děngyú jǐ?*
2. 十五加二十七等于四十二。*Shíwǔ jiā èrshíqī děngyú sìshí'èr.*
3. 七十加二十等于九十。*Qīshí jiā èrshí děngyú jiǔshí.*
4. 六十加四十等于一百。*Liùshí jiā sìshí děngyú yī bǎi.*
5. 九减八等于一。*Jiǔ jiǎn bā děngyú yī.*
6. 三十六减四等于多少? *Sānshíliù jiǎn sì děngyú duōshao?*
7. 十减一等于九。*Shí jiǎn yī děngyú jiǔ.*
8. 三十一减二十三等于八。*Sānshíyī jiǎn èrshísān děngyú bā.*
9. 二乘四等于几? *Èr chéng sì děngyú jǐ?*
10. 十乘四等于四十。*Shí chéng sì děngyú sìshí.*
11. 九乘八等于七十二。*Jiǔ chéng bā děngyú qīshí'èr.*
12. 二十乘三等于多少? *Èrshí chéng sān děngyú duōshao?*

8·1   1. f   2. e   3. d   4. b   5. a   6. c

8·2   The following are sample answers.
1. 我今年三十一岁。*Wǒ jīnnián sānshíyī suì.*
2. 我爷爷七十九岁，我奶奶七十七岁。*Wǒ yéye qīshíjiǔ suì, wǒ nǎinai qīshíqī suì.*
3. 我爸爸今年五十五岁，妈妈五十四岁。*Wǒ bàba jīnnián wǔshíwǔ suì, māma wǔshísì suì.*
4. 我太太今年三十岁。*Wǒ tàitai jīnnián sānshí suì.*
5. 我哥哥今年三十二岁。*Wǒ gēge jīnnián sānshí'èr suì.*
6. 我妹妹今年二十六岁。*Wǒ mèimei jīnnián èrshíliù suì.*
7. 我儿子今年一岁。*Wǒ érzi jīnnián yí suì.*

8·3   1. b   2. f   3. a   4. c   5. d   6. e   7. l   8. k   9. g   10. h   11. i   12. j

8·4
1. 现在一点钟。*Xiànzài yī diǎn zhōng.*
2. 现在三点半。*Xiànzài sāndiǎn bàn.*
3. 现在两点一刻。*Xiànzài liǎng diǎn yí kè.*
4. 现在十点三十五分。*Xiànzài shí diǎn sānshíwǔ fēn.*
5. 现在六点五十五分。*Xiànzài liù diǎn wǔshíwǔ fēn.*
6. 现在十二点钟。*Xiànzài shí'èr diǎn zhōng.*
7. 现在五点三分。*Xiànzài wǔ diǎn sān fēn.*
8. 现在两点二十分。*Xiànzài liǎng diǎn èrshí fēn.*

8·5
1. 我二十岁。*Wǒ èrshí suì.*
2. 请问，您爷爷今年多大岁数? *Qǐngwèn, nín yéye jīnnián duōdà suìshu?*

3. 你好, 小姑娘! 你今年几岁? *Nǐ hǎo, xiǎo gūniang! Nǐ jīnnián jǐ suì?*
4. 我妹妹今年十八岁。*Wǒ mèimei jīnnián shíbā suì.*
5. 现在九点。*Xiànzài jiǔdiǎn.*
6. 现在半夜十二点。*Xiànzài bànyè shí'èr diǎn.*
7. 现在八点一刻。*Xiànzài bā diǎn yíkè.*
8. 现在几点? *Xiànzài jǐ diǎn?*

9·1

昨天 *zuótiān* yesterday	今天 *jīntiān* today	明天 *míngtiān* tomorrow
去年 *qùnián* last year	今年 *jīnnián* this year	明年 *míngnián* next year
上个月 *shàngge yuè* last month	这个月 *zhège yuè* this month	下个月 *xiàge yuè* next month
上个星期 *shàngge xīngqī* last week	这个星期 *zhège xīngqī* this week	下个星期 *xiàge xīngqī* next week

9·2 The following are sample answers.
2. 昨天一号, 今天二号, 明天三号。*Zuótiān yī hào, jīntiān èr hào, míngtiān sān hào.*
3. 昨天星期二, 今天星期三, 明天星期四。*Zuótiān xīngqī'èr, jīntiān xīngqīsān, míngtiān xīngqīsì.*
4. 星期三。*Xīngqīsān.*
5. 三月十号。*Sānyuè shí hào.*
6. 星期五。*Xīngqīwǔ.*
7. 四月二日。*Sìyuè èr rì.*
8. 三月八号。*Sānyuè bā hào.*

9·3 The following are sample answers.
1. 我的生日是三月五号。*Wǒ de shēngrì shì Sānyuè wǔ hào.*
2. 我爷爷的生日是七月十八号。*Wǒ yéye de shēngrì shì Qīyuè shíbā hào.*
3. 我妈妈的生日是六月九号。*Wǒ māma de shēngrì shì Liùyuè jiǔ hào.*
4. 你朋友的生日是八月二十号。*Nǐ péngyǒu de shēngrì shì Bāyuè èrshí hào.*
5. 你哥哥的生日是十二月一号。*Nǐ gēge de shēngrì shì Shí'èryuè yī hào.*
6. 我没有弟弟。*Wǒ méiyǒu dìdi.*
7. 我没有姐姐。*Wǒ méiyǒu jiějie.*
8. 我妹妹的生日是八月二号。*Wǒ mèimei de shēngrì shì Bāyuè èr hào.*
9. 我没有儿子。*Wǒ méiyǒu érzi.*
10. 我没有女儿。*Wǒ méiyǒu nǚ'ér.*

9·4
1. 今天几月几号? *Jīntiān jǐ yuè jǐ hào?*
2. 今天星期几? *Jīntiān Xīngqī jǐ?*
3. 昨天二月十二日, 星期天。*Zuótiān Èryuè shí'èr rì, Xīngqītiān.*
4. 今天二月十三日, 星期一。*Jīntiān Èryuè shísān rì, Xīngqīyī.*
5. 明天二月十四日, 星期二。*Míngtiān Èryuè shísì rì, Xīngqī'èr.*
6. 你妈妈的生日几月几日? *Nǐ māma de shēngri jǐ yuè jǐ rì?*
7. 今年哪一年? *Jīnnián nǎ yì nián?*

9·5
1. 今天五月七号。*Jīntiān Wǔyuè qī hào.*
2. 今天八月三十一号。*Jīntiān Bāyuè sānshíyī hào.*
3. 今天十月十九号。*Jīntiān Shíyuè shíjiǔ hào.*
4. 今天六月二十七号。*Jīntiān Liùyuè èrshíqī hào.*
5. 今天四月一号。*Jīntiān Sìyuè yī hào.*
6. 今天三月二十二号。*Jīntiān Sānyuè èrshí'èr hào.*
7. 今天一月十二号。*Jīntiān Yīyuè shí'èr hào.*
8. 今天七月十七号。*Jīntiān Qīyuè shíqī hào.*

10·1 1. c 2. e 3. f 4. a 5. b 6. d 7. k 8. g 9. j 10. l 11. h 12. i

10·2 1. c 2. f 3. a 4. b 5. g 6. d 7. h 8. e

10·3 The following are sample answers.

1. 我有一个哥哥，没有弟弟。*Wǒ yǒu yí ge gēge, méiyǒu dìdi.*
2. 我有两个妹妹，没有姐姐。*Wǒ yǒu liǎng ge mèimei, méiyǒu jiějie.*
3. 我没有儿子，也没有女儿。*Wǒ méiyǒu érzi, yě méiyǒu nǚ'ér.*
4. 我有很多顶帽子。*Wǔ yǒu hěnduō dǐng màozi.*
5. 我没有手套。*Wǒ méiyǒu shǒutào.*
6. 我有三条领带。*Wǒ yǒu sān tiáo lǐngdài.*
7. 我有两件毛衣，五件衬衫，六件T-恤衫。*Wǒ yǒu liǎng jiàn máoyī, wǔ jiàn chènshān, liù jiàn T-xùshān.*
8. 我有一双皮鞋，很多双袜子。*Wǒ yǒu yì shuāng píxié, hěnduō shuāng wàzi.*
9. 我有两条裤子，一条裙子。*Wǒ yǒu liǎng tiáo kùzi, yì tiáo qúnzi.*
10. 我有一件上衣，一件大衣。*Wǒ yǒu yí jiàn shàngyī, yí jiàn dàyī.*

10·4 The following are sample answers.

1. 我这个星期不穿T-恤衫。*Wǒ zhè ge xīngqī bù chuān T-xùshān.*
2. 我这个月常穿毛衣。*Wǒ zhè ge yuè cháng chuān máoyī.*
3. 我今天不穿皮鞋。*Wǒ jīntiān bù chuān píxié.*
4. 我喜欢戴帽子。*Wǒ xǐhuan dài màozi.*
5. 我不喜欢戴领带。*Wǒ bù xǐhuan dài lǐngdài.*
6. 星期六和星期天喜欢穿T-恤衫。*Xīngqīliù hé xīngqītiān xǐhuan chuān T-xùshān.*
7. 我白天穿衬衫。*Wǒ báitiān chuān chènshān.*
8. 我晚上穿T-恤衫。*Wǒ wǎnshàng chuān T-xùshān.*
9. 我爸爸喜欢穿衬衫。*Wǒ bàba xǐhuan chuān chènshān.*
10. 我朋友喜欢穿T-恤衫。*Wǒ péngyǒu xǐhuan chuān T-xùshān.*

10·5

1. 我姐姐有两条裙子和三件毛衣。*Wǒ jiějie yǒu liǎng tiáo qúnzi hé sān jiàn máoyī.*
2. 他们现在有多少件印度上衣？—他们有五十件印度上衣。*Tāmen xiànzài yǒu duōshao jiàn Yìndù shàngyī?—Tāmen yǒu wǔshí jiàn Yìndù shàngyī.*
3. 我儿子今天穿一件法国衬衫和一双意大利皮鞋。*Wǒ érzi jīntiān chuān yí jiàn Fǎguó chènshān hé yì shuāng Yìdàlì píxié.*
4. 你今天买多少件大衣？—我买两百件大衣。*Nǐ jīntiān mǎi duōshao jiàn dàyī?—Wǒ mǎi liǎng bǎi jiàn dàyī.*
5. 她朋友有两条中国领带。*Tā péngyou yǒu liǎng tiáo Zhōngguó lǐngdài.*
6. 我不喜欢那双日本袜子。*Wǒ bù xǐhuan nà shuāng Rìběn wàzi.*
7. 他爸爸今天戴一顶英国帽子。*Tā bàba jīntiān dài yì dǐng Yīngguó màozi.*
8. 那个美国人喜欢哪件T-恤衫？—他喜欢这件德国T-恤衫。*Nà ge Měiguórén xǐhuan nǎ jiàn T-xùshàn?—Tā xǐhuan zhè jiàn Déguó T-xùshàn.*
9. 你妈妈下个星期做几副手套？*Nǐ māma xià ge xīngqī zuò jǐ fù shǒutào?*

R2·1 The following are sample answers.

你现在常喝什么饮料？ *Nǐ xiànzài cháng hē shénme yǐnliào?*	常 喝 *cháng hē*	不常 喝 *bù cháng hē*
1. 水 *shuǐ*	X	_____
2. 茶 *chá*	X	_____
3. 牛奶 *niúnǎi*	X	_____
4. 果汁 *guǒzhī*	X	_____
5. 可乐 *kělè*	_____	X
6. 啤酒 *píjiǔ*	_____	X
7. 豆浆 *dòujiāng*	_____	X
8. 桔子汁 *júzi zhī*	X	_____
9. 矿泉水 *kuàngquánshuǐ*	_____	X
10. 葡萄汁 *pútao zhī*	_____	X

R2·2

1. 他爸爸喜欢喝**什么**？*Tā bàba xǐhuan hē **shénme**?*
2. **谁**早上常喝牛奶？*Shéi zǎoshang cháng hē niúnǎi?*
3. 你妈妈喜欢喝**什么**咖啡？*Nǐ māma xǐhuan hē **shénme** kāfēi?*
4. 哪国人中午喜欢喝葡萄酒？*Nǎ guórén zhōngwǔ xǐhuan hē pútao jiǔ?*
5. 四加三等于**几**？*Sì jiā sān děngyú **jǐ**?*
6. 五乘九等于**多少**？*Wǔ chéng jiǔ děngyú **duōshao**?*
7. 他奶奶今年**多大岁数**？*Tā nǎinai jīnnián **duōdà suìshu**?*
8. 她儿子去年**几岁**？*Tā érzi qùnián **jǐ suì**?*

9. 他朋友明年**多大**? *Tā péngyou míngnián duōdà?*
10. 明天**几月几号**, 星期几? *Míngtiān jǐ yuè jǐ hào, xīngqī jǐ?*
11. 现在晚上**几点**? *Xiànzài wǎnshang jǐ diǎn?*
12. 他太太有**多少**双袜子? *Tā tàitai yǒu duōshao shuāng wàzi?*
13. 他们有**几件**衬衫? *Tāmen yǒu jǐ jiàn chènshān?*
14. 你女儿有**几条**裙子? *Nǐ nǚ'ér yǒu jǐ tiáo qúnzi?*

R2·3
1. 条 *tiáo*, 条 *tiáo*; His younger sister has 12 skirts and 32 pairs of pants.
2. 个 *gè*, 件 *jiàn*, 顶 *dǐng*; Does that Chinese guy like this shirt and this hat?
3. 件 *jiàn*, 双 *shuāng*, 双 *shuāng*; His wife buys these two jackets, those three pairs of leather shoes and those six pairs of socks.
4. 件 *jiàn*, 件 *jiàn*; My younger brother wears a sweater and a overcoat today.
5. 条 *tiáo*, 副 *fù*; Will your friend wear that tie and that pair of gloves tomorrow?

R2·4 The following are sample answers.
1. 我喜欢喝桔子汁。*Wǒ xǐhuan hē júzi zhī.*
2. 我早上常吃面包。*Wǒ zǎoshang cháng chī miànbāo.*
3. 中国人喜欢喝豆浆。*Zhōngguó rén xǐhuan hē dòujiāng.*
4. 我哥哥喜欢喝茶。*Wǒ gēge xǐhuan hē chá.*
5. 十五减七等于八。*Shíwǔ jiǎn qī děngyú bā.*
6. 八乘九十等于七百二十。*Bā chéng jiǔshí děngyú qībǎi èrshí.*
7. 现在八点十分。*Xiànzài bā diǎn shí fēn.*
8. 我明天八点上班。*Wǒ míngtiān bā diǎn shàngbān.*
9. 我今年二十岁。*Wǒ jīnnián èrshí suì.*
10. 我爷爷七十九岁, 我奶奶七十七岁。*Wǒ yéye qīshíjiǔ suì, wǒ nǎinai qīshíqī suì.*
11. 我的生日是 1980 年, 三月一号。*Wǒ de shēngrì shì yījiǔbālíng nián, Sānyuè yī hào.*
12. 上个星期天一月九号。*Shàng ge Xīngqītiān Yīyuè jiǔ hào.*
13. 我没有弟弟。*Wǒ méiyǒu dìdi.*
14. 我有五件衬衫。*Wǒ yǒu wǔ jiàn chènshān.*
15. 我明天穿衬衫。*Wǒ míngtiān chuān chènshān.*

R2·5
1. 你家里人, 谁喜欢喝咖啡? —我爸爸喜欢喝咖啡。*Nǐ jiālǐrén, shéi xǐhuan hē kāfēi? —Wǒ bàba xǐhuan hē kāfēi.*
2. 你今天吃什么, 喝什么? —我吃汉堡包, 喝可乐。*Nǐ jīntiān chī shénme, hē shénme? —Wǒ chī hànbǎobāo, hē kělè.*
3. 你是哪国人? — 我是中国人。*Nǐ shì nǎ guó rén? — Wǒ shì Zhōngguórén.*
4. 五加四等于几? —五加四等于九。*Wǔ jiā sì děngyú jǐ? — Wǔ jiā sì děngyú jiǔ.*
5. 四百减三百等于多少? — 四百减三百等于一百。*Sì bǎi jiǎn sān bǎi děngyú duōshao? — Sì bǎi jiǎn sān bǎi děngyú yì bǎi.*
6. 你奶奶去年多大岁数? — 她去年九十二岁。*Nǐ nǎinai qùnián duōdà suìshu? — Tā qùnián jiǔshí'èr suì.*
7. 你朋友今年多大? — 他今年二十五岁。*Nǐ péngyou jīnnián duōdà? — Tā jīnnián èrshíwǔ suì.*
8. 你女儿明年几岁? — 她明年五岁。*Nǐ nǚ'ér míngnián jǐ suì? — Tā míngnián wǔ suì.*
9. 现在几点? —现在两点半。*Xiànzài jǐ diǎn? — Xiànzài liǎng diǎn bàn.*
10. 今天几月几号? 星期几? —今天二月二十三日, 星期四。*Jīntiān jǐ yuè jǐ hào? Xīngqī jǐ? — Jīntiān Èryuè èrshísān rì, Xīngqīsì.*
11. 她昨天穿什么? —她穿一件T-恤衫。*Tā zuótiān chuān shénme? — Tā chuān yíjiàn tīxùshān.*
12. 明天你穿什么? —我穿那件法国衬衫。*Míngtiān nǐ chuān shénme? — Wǒ chuān nà jiàn Fǎguó chènshān.*

R2·6 1. F 2. F 3. F 4. T 5. F 6. T 7. T 8. F 9. T

III

11·1 1. c 2. f 3. a 4. i 5. g 6. e 7. d 8. j 9. b 10. h

11·2 The following are sample answers.
1. 我很好, 你呢? *Wǒ hěn hǎo. Nǐ ne?*
2. 我不忙, 你呢? *Wǒ bù máng. Nǐ ne?*
3. 还好, 你呢? *Hái hǎo. Nǐ ne?*
4. 您早! *Nín zǎo!*
5. 我有点儿累。*Wǒ yǒu diǎnr lèi.*
6. 她很好。*Tā hěn hǎo.*

7. 他很好。*Tā hěn hǎo.*
8. 他很忙。*Tā hěn máng.*

11·3
1. 不，我妈妈很高。*Bù, wǒ māma hěn gāo.*
2. 不，我家很小。*Bù, wǒ jiā hěn xiǎo.*
3. 不，我爸爸很胖。*Bù, wǒ bàba hěn pàng.*
4. 不，美国水果很便宜。*Bù, Měiguó shuǐguǒ hěn piányi.*
5. 不，现在白天很短。*Bù, xiànzài báitiān hěn duǎn.*
6. 不，我朋友很漂亮。*Bù, wǒ péngyou hěn piàoliang.*

11·4 The following are sample answers.
1. 我爸爸身体也很好。*Wǒ bàba shēntǐ yě hěn hǎo.*
2. 我也是美国人。*Wǒ yě shì Měiguó rén.*
3. 我有两个哥哥，一个弟弟。*Wǒ yǒu liǎng ge gēge, yí ge dìdi.*
4. 我也喜欢吃水果。*Wǒ yě xǐhuan chī shuǐguǒ.*
5. 中国人喜欢喝茶。*Zhōngguó rén xǐhuan hē chá.*
6. 德国人喜欢吃汉堡包。*Déguó rén xǐhuan chī hànbǎobāo.*
7. 我今年二十岁。*Wǒ jīnnián èrshí suì.*
8. 我的生日是七月十二日。*Wǒ de shēngrì shì Qīyuè shí'èr rì.*
9. 我喜欢穿黑裤子和红衬衫。*Wǒ xǐhuan chuān hēi kùzi hé hóng chènshān.*
10. 我家里有四把椅子。*Wǒ jiā li yǒu sì bǎ yǐzi.*

11·5
1. "你先生最近怎么样？"—"他还好。" *"Nǐ xiānsheng zuìjìn zěnmeyàng?" – "Tā hái hǎo".*
2. "你们最近怎么样？"—"我们都很好。" *"Nǐmen zuìjìn zěnmeyàng?" – "Wǒmen dōu hěn hǎo".*
3. "您早！您好吗？"—"不太好，今天我有点儿累。" *"Nín zǎo! Nín hǎo ma?" – "Bú tài hǎo, jīntiān wǒ yǒu diǎnr lèi".*
4. "您爷爷最近身体怎么样？"—"他身体不太好。" *"Nín yéye zuìjìn shēntǐ zěnmeyàng?" – "Tā shēntǐ bú tài hǎo".*
5. "您忙吗？"—"我很忙。您呢？" *"Nín máng ma?" – "Wǒ hěn máng. Nín ne?"*
6. 我奶奶很好。您奶奶呢？*Wǒ nǎinai hěn hǎo. Nín nǎinai ne?*
7. 他爸爸很胖，可是他妈妈很瘦。*Tā bàba hěn pàng, kěshì tā māma hěn shòu.*
8. "那顶帽子太大吗？"—"不，那顶帽子太小！" *"Nà dǐng màozi tài dà ma?" –"Bù, nà dǐng màozi tài xiǎo!"*
9. 这件衬衫很贵，可是那件衬衫很便宜。*Zhè jiàn chènshān hěn guì, kěshì nà jiàn chènshān hěn piányi.*
10. 我哥哥很矮，可是我弟弟很高。*Wǒ gēge hěn ǎi, kěshì wǒ dìdi hěn gāo.*
11. 这条短领带很难看。*Zhè tiáo duǎn lǐngdài hěn nánkàn.*
12. 那条长裙子很漂亮。*Nà tiáo cháng qúnzi hěn piàoliang.*

12·1
1. 你有没有弟弟和哥哥？*Nǐ yǒu méiyǒu dìdi hé gēge?*
2. 他有没有姐姐和妹妹？*Tā yǒu méiyǒu jiějie hé mèimei?*
3. 你弟弟高不高？*Nǐ dìdi gāo bu gāo?*
4. 你儿子今天穿不穿毛衣？*Nǐ érzi jīntiān chuān bu chuān máoyī?*
5. 你是不是美国人？*Nǐ shì bu shì Měiguórén?*
6. 你爷爷最近忙不忙？*Nǐ yéye zuìjìn máng bu máng?*
7. 你爸爸看不看电视？*Nǐ bàba kàn bu kàn diànshì?*
8. 你今天累不累？*Nǐ jīntiān lèi bu lèi?*
9. 你朋友喝不喝茶？*Nǐ péngyou hē bu hē chá?*
10. 你奶奶吃不吃披萨饼？*Nǐ nǎinai chī bu chī pīsàbǐng?*

12·2
1. 你奶奶今天高兴吗？*Nǐ nǎinai jīntiān gāoxìng ma?*
2. 她朋友昨天难过吗？*Tā péngyou zuótiān nánguò ma?*
3. 英国人现在紧张吗？*Yīngguórén xiànzài jǐnzhāng ma?*
4. 他妈妈上个星期一着急吗？*Tā māma shàng ge Xīngqīyī zháojí ma?*
5. 你哥哥昨天激动吗？*Nǐ gēge zuótiān jīdòng ma?*
6. 他儿子现在烦恼吗？*Tā érzi xiànzài fánnǎo ma?*
7. 你太太今年快乐吗？*Nǐ tàitai jīnnián kuàilè ma?*
8. 她先生最近满意吗？*Tā xiānsheng zuìjìn mǎnyì ma?*
9. 你爷爷失望吗？*Nǐ yéye shīwàng ma?*
10. 她姐姐生气吗？*Tā jiějie shēngqì ma?*

12·3
1. 那杯果汁酸不酸？*Nà bēi guǒzhī suān bu suān?*
2. 这些西瓜甜不甜？*Zhè xiē xīguā tián bu tián?*
3. 那些柠檬酸不酸？*Nà xiē níngméng suān bu suān?*

4. 这个菜辣不辣? *Zhè ge cài là bu là?*
5. 那杯咖啡苦不苦? *Nà bēi kāfēi kǔ bu kǔ?*
6. 这些饺子咸不咸? *Zhè xiē jiǎozi xián bu xián?*
7. 这杯葡萄酒甜不甜? *Zhè bēi pútáo jiǔ tián bu tián?*

12·4
1. 他太太现在满意不满意? *Tā tàitai xiànzài mǎnyì bu mǎnyì?*
2. 这些桔子甜不甜? *Zhè xiē júzi tián bu tián?*
3. 他女儿现在快乐不快乐? *Tā nǚ'ér xiànzài kuàilè bu kuàilè?*
4. 那个中国人昨天难过不难过? *Nà ge Zhōngguórén zuótiān nánguò bu nánguò?*
5. 这个葡萄酒苦不苦? *Zhè ge pútao jiǔ kǔ bu kǔ?*
6. 你们是不是俄国人? *Nǐmen shì bu shì Éguórén?*
7. 你这个星期忙不忙? *Nǐ zhè ge xīngqī máng bu máng?*
8. 你吃不吃汉堡包? *Nǐ chī bu chī hànbǎobāo?*
9. 你有没有中国朋友? *Nǐ yǒu méiyǒu Zhōngguó péngyou?*
10. 你们喝不喝咖啡? *Nǐmen hē bu hē kāfēi?*

13·1
1. e   2. h   3. f   4. b   5. g   6. c   7. a   8. d   9. l   10. p   11. i   12. n   13. o
14. k   15. j   16. m

13·2
1. 学生 *xuésheng*   2. 演员 *yǎnyuán*   3. 工程师 *gōngchéngshī*   4. 商人 *shāngrén*   5. 医生
yīshēng   6. 军人 *jūnrén*   7. 运动员 *yùndòngyuán*   8. 音乐家 *yīnyuèjiā*   9. 作家 *zuòjiā*

13·3
The following are sample answers.

我想当 _____ 。
Wǒ xiǎng dāng _____.

1. 律师 *lùshī*
2. 作家 *zuòjiā*
3. 职员 *zhíyuán*
4. 医生 *yīshēng*
5. 商人 *shāngrén*
6. 警察 *jǐngchá*
7. 运动员 *yùndòngyuán*
8. 农民 *nóngmín*
9. 工程师 *gōngchéngshī*

13·4
The following are sample answers.

他/她是 *tā shì* …   都不是 *dōu bú shì*

1. 作家 *zuòjiā*
2. 老师 *lǎoshī*
3.   √
4.   √
5. 医生 *yīshēng*
6.   √

13·5
1. 你是医生还是护士? *Nǐ shì yīshēng háishì hùshi?*
2. Tom Hanks 是演员还是运动员? Tom Hanks *shì yǎnyuán háishì yùndòngyuán?*
3. 你爸爸是工程师还是经理? *Nǐ bàba shì gōngchéngshī háishì jīnglǐ?*
4. 你想当工人还是商人? *Nǐ xiǎng dāng gōngrén háishì shāngrén?*
5. 他太太是律师还是音乐家? *Tā tàitai shì lùshī háishì yīnyuèjiā?*
6. 他儿子想当警察还是军人? *Tā érzi xiǎng dāng jǐngchá háishì jūnrén?*
7. 你先生是作家还是老师? *Nǐ xiānsheng shì zuòjiā háishì lǎoshī?*
8. 你女儿想当职员还是农民? *Nǐ nǚ'ér xiǎng dāng zhíyuán háishì nóngmín?*
9. 你妈妈是经理还是服务员? *Nǐ māma shì jīnglǐ háishì fúwùyuán?*

14·1
1. b   2. d   3. a   4. c   5. h   6. i   7. j   8. e   9. g   10. f

14·2
1. 很小的教室 *hěn xiǎo de jiàoshì*
2. 漂亮的图书馆 *piàoliang de túshūguǎn*
3. 我们(的)老师 *wǒmen (de) lǎoshī* (the "的 *de*" is optional)
4. 新(的)体育馆 *xīn (de) tǐyùguǎn* (the "的 *de*" is optional)
5. 便宜的食堂 *piányi de shítáng*
6. 学生的实验室 *xuésheng de shíyànshì*
7. 他们学校的礼堂 *tāmen xuéxiào de lǐtáng*

8. 我朋友的书店 *wǒ péngyou de shūdiàn*
9. 学校的电脑室 *xuéxiào de diànnǎoshì*
10. 很新的阅览室 *hěn xīn de yuèlǎnshì*

14·3   The following are sample answers.

1. 我们学校的图书馆很漂亮。*Wǒmen xuéxiào de túshūguǎn hěn piàoliang.*
2. 我很喜欢我们学校的食堂。*Wǒ hěn xǐhuan wǒmen xuéxiào de shítáng.*
3. 我不常去学校的体育馆运动。*Wǒ bù cháng qù xuéxiào de tǐyùguǎn yùndòng.*
4. 我很喜欢我们的中文教授。*Wǒ hěn xǐhuan wǒmen de Zhōngwén jiàoshòu.*
5. 我常去教授的办公室。*Wǒ cháng qù jiàoshòu de bàngōngshì.*
6. 我们的宿舍不小。*Wǒmen de sùshè bù xiǎo.*
7. 教学楼的教室不新。*Jiàoxué lóu de jiàoshì bù xīn.*
8. 我常去阅览室看书。*Wǒ cháng qù yuèlǎnshì kàn shū.*
9. 学校的礼堂很漂亮。*Xuéxiào de lǐtáng hěn piàoliang.*
10. 我常去学校的书店买书。*Wǒ cháng qù xuéxiào de shūdiàn mǎi shū.*
11. 学校的实验室不大。*Xuéxiào de shíyànshì bú dà.*
12. 我常去电脑室上网。*Wǒ cháng qù diànnǎoshì shàng wǎng.*

14·4
1. 那个新的教室很大吗? *Nà ge xīnde jiàoshì hěn dà ma?*
2. 学生都喜欢那个漂亮的食堂。*Xuésheng dōu xǐhuan nà ge piàoliang de shítáng.*
3. 我常去我爸爸的办公室看书。*Wǒ cháng qù wǒ bàba de bàngōngshì kàn shū.*
4. 学生们不喜欢那个很小的体育场。*Xuéshengmen bù xǐhuan nà ge hěn xiǎo de tǐyùchǎng.*
5. 我们的教室很大, 可是我们的阅览室很小。*Wǒmen de jiàoshì hěn dà, kěshì wǒmen de yuèlǎnshì hěn xiǎo.*
6. 那个书店的书很便宜吗? *Nà ge shūdiàn de shū hěn piányi ma?*
7. 他们学校的礼堂很高。*Tāmen xuéxiào de lǐtáng hěn gāo.*
8. 我妈妈喜欢我们的宿舍。*Wǒ māma xǐhuan wǒmen de sùshè.*
9. 我朋友常去学校的体育馆运动。*Wǒ péngyou cháng qù xuéxiào de tǐyùguǎn yùndòng.*

15·1   1. b   2. d   3. a   4. e   5. c   6. g   7. i   8. j   9. f   10. h

15·2   1. c   2. f   3. b   4. a   5. g   6. d   7. i   8. j   9. e   10. h

15·3   The following are sample answers.

1. 对, 我喜欢穿蓝裤子。*Duì, wǒ xǐhuan chuān lán kùzi.*
2. 对, 他喜欢穿黑色的西装。*Duì, tā xǐhuan chuān hēisè de xīzhuāng.*
3. 不, 她不喜欢戴粉红色的围巾。*Bù, tā bù xǐhuan dài fěnhóngsè de wéijīn.*
4. 不, 她不喜欢穿绿睡衣。*Bù, tā bù xǐhuan chuān lǜ shuìyī.*
5. 对, 他喜欢穿灰色的拖鞋。*Duì, tā xǐhuan chuān huīsè de tuōxié.*
6. 对, 他喜欢黄球鞋。*Duì, tā xǐhuan huáng qiúxié.*
7. 不, 我不喜欢桔黄色的雨衣。*Bù, wǒ bù xǐhuan jú huángsè de yǔyī.*
8. 对, 他喜欢穿白短裤。*Duì, tā xǐhuan chuān bái duǎnkù.*
9. 不, 她不喜欢买紫色的内衣。*Bù, tā bù xǐhuan mǎi zǐsè de nèiyī.*
10. 对, 我们都喜欢黑皮带。*Duì, wǒmen dōu xǐhuan hēi pídài.*

15·4
1. 这双白球鞋是她的。*Zhè shuāng bái qiúxié shì tā de.*
2. 你喜欢红颜色吧? *Nǐ xǐhuan hóng yánsè ba?*
3. 那件绿雨衣是我们老师的。*Nà jiàn lǜ yǔyī shì wǒmen lǎoshī de.*
4. 这条短裤不是我儿子的。*Zhè tiáo duǎnkù bú shì wǒ érzi de.*
5. 这两条粉红色的围巾是我的。*Zhè liǎng tiáo fěnhóngsè de wéijīn shì wǒ de.*
6. 你的新皮鞋是紫色的吧? *Nǐ de xīn píxié shì zǐsè de ba?*
7. 这双桔黄色的拖鞋是那个演员的。*Zhè shuāng júhuángsè de tuōxié shì nà ge yǎnyuán de.*
8. 那件蓝睡衣是你的吧? *Nà jiàn lán shuìyī shì nǐ de ba?*

R3·1   The following are sample answers.

1. 我很好, 我朋友也很好。*Wǒ hěn hǎo; wǒ péngyǒu yě hěn hǎo.*
2. 我爸爸, 妈妈身体都很好, 爷爷, 奶奶也都很好。*Wǒ bàba, māma shēntǐ dōu hěn hǎo; yéye, nǎinai yě dōu hěn hǎo.*
3. 我现在不忙, 我哥哥也不忙。*Wǒ xiànzài bù máng; wǒ gēge yě bù máng.*
4. 我不累, 我的朋友们也不累。*Wǒ bú lèi, wǒ de péngyǒumen yě búlèi.*
5. 我很高, 我弟弟也很高。*Wǒ hěn gāo, wǒ dìdi yě hěn gāo.*
6. 我没有姐姐, 也没有妹妹。*Wǒ méiyǒu jiějie, yě méiyǒu mèimei.*
7. 今天我很高兴。*Jīntiān wǒ hěn gāoxìng.*
8. 香蕉不酸, 柠檬很酸。*Xiāngjiāo bù suān, níngméng hěn suān.*

9. 我很喜欢学校的图书馆。*Wǒ hěn xǐhuan xuéxiào de túshūguǎn.*
10. 学生宿舍很漂亮。*Xuéshēng sùshè hěn piàoliang.*
11. 我是学生。*Wǒ shì xuésheng.*
12. 他都不是。*Tā dōu bú shì.*
13. 他是演员。*Tā shì yǎnyuán.*
14. 我想当工程师。*Wǒ xiǎng dāng gōngchéngshī.*
15. 我想喝咖啡。*Wǒ xiǎng hē kāfēi.*
16. 对，我不是警察。*Duì, wǒ bú shì jǐngchá.*
17. 对，我喜欢穿白衬衫和蓝裤子。*Duì, wǒ xǐhuan chuān bái chènshān hé lán kùzi.*
18. 对，现在意大利皮鞋很贵。*Duì, xiànzài Yìdàlì píxié hěn guì.*

R3·2 1. 条 *tiáo*, 件 *jiàn*   2. 个 *gè*, 双 *shuāng*, 双 *shuāng*   3. 件 *jiàn*, 条 *tiáo*   4. 条 *tiáo*, 条 *tiáo*
5. 件 *jiàn*, 件 *jiàn*   6. 副 *fù*, 顶 *dǐng*

R3·3 1. 老师**的**好朋友 *lǎoshī **de** hǎo péngyou*
2. 他爸爸和妈妈 *tā bàba hé māma* ("的 *de*" is optional.)
3. 医生**的**办公室 *yīshēng **de** bàngōngshì*
4. 漂亮**的**体育馆 *piàoliang **de** tǐyùguǎn*
5. 今天**的**早饭 *jīntiān **de** zǎofàn*
6. 很大**的**电脑室 *hěn dà **de** diànnǎoshì*
7. 学校**的**教室 *xuéxiào **de** jiàoshì*
8. 很小**的**体育场 *hěn xiǎo **de** tǐyùchǎng*
9. 工程师**的**实验室 *gōngchéngshī **de** shíyànshì*
10. 图书馆**的**阅览室 *túshūguǎn **de** yuèlǎnshì*

R3·4 1. Lemon is sour, but banana is sweet.
2. Coffee is bitter, so is tea.
3. This is our Chinese teacher's new office.
4. I have a black belt and a white belt, but I like the black one.
5. Are these two pairs of yellow sneakers hers?
6. This green scarf and that gray suit are both my friend's.
7. This pair of red shorts is his younger brother's.
8. That pair of blue slippers is not yours, right?

R3·5 1. 你爷爷身体怎么样？你奶奶呢？*Nǐ yéye shēntǐ zěnmeyàng? Nǐ nǎinai ne?*
2. 您最近忙不忙？*Nín zuìjìn máng bu máng?*
3. 我很累。你呢？*Wǒ hěn lèi. Nǐ ne?*
4. 你是不是美国人？你爸爸、妈妈呢？*Nǐ sì bu shì Měiguórén? Nǐ bàba, māma ne?*
5. 他爷爷很瘦，可是他奶奶很胖。*Tā yéye hěn shòu, kěshì tā nǎinai hěn pàng.*
6. 这些菜都很咸，很辣！*Zhè xiē cài dōu hěn xián, hěn là!*
7. 他是音乐家还是律师？*Tā shì yīnyuèjiā háishì lǜshī?*
8. 我妹妹喜欢这双拖鞋。*Wǒ mèi mei xǐhuan zhè shuāng tuōxié.*
9. 这两条灰皮带都是他的。*Zhè liǎng tiáo huī pídài dōu shì tā de.*
10. 你喜欢穿白球鞋吧？*Nǐ xǐhuan chuān bái qiúxié ba?*

R3·6 1. T   2. F   3. F   4. F   5. T   6. F   7. T   8. F   9. F   10. T

IV

16·1 1. 扇 *shàn*, 2 windows   2. 把 *bǎ*, 5 chairs   3. 个 *gè*, 1 clock   4. 张 *zhāng*, 30 tables   5. 张 *zhāng*, 3 maps   6. 盏 *zhǎn*, 100 lights   7. 本 *běn*, 200 books   8. 扇 *shàn*, 4 doors   9. 块 *kuài*, 5 blackboards   10. 枝 *zhī*, 90 pens   11. 台 *tái*, 10 air conditioners   12. 块 *kuài*, 6 blackboard erasers

16·2 The following are sample answers.
1. 有，我们教室里有二十把椅子。*Yǒu, wǒmen jiàoshì lǐ yǒu èrshí bǎ yǐzi.*
2. 我们教室里有十张桌子。*Wǒmen jiàoshì lǐ yǒu shí zhāng zhuōzi.*
3. 没有，我们教室里没有空调机。*Méiyǒu, wǒmen jiàoshì lǐ méiyǒu kōngtiáojī.*
4. 我们教室里没有书。*Wǒmen jiàoshì lǐ méiyǒu shū.*
5. 我们教室里有一个门和三扇窗户。*Wǒmen jiàoshì lǐ yǒu yī ge mén hé sān shàn chuānghu.*
6. 我们教室里有一块黑板和一块黑板擦。*Wǒmen jiàoshì lǐ yǒu yí kuài hēibǎn hé yí kuài hēibǎncā.*
7. 有，我们教室里有一张地图。*Yǒu, wǒmen jiàoshì lǐ yǒu yī zhāng dìtú.*
8. 没有，我今天没有中文课。*Méiyǒu, wǒ jīntiān méiyǒu Zhōngwén kè.*
9. 有，明天有三节课。*Yǒu, míngtiān yǒu sān jié kè.*
10. 晚上有一节英文课。*Wǎnshàng yǒu yì jié Yīngwén kè.*

16·3 1. 我们教室里有三十六把椅子。*Wǒmen jiàoshì lǐ yǒu sānshíliù bǎ yǐzi.*
2. 他们教室里有两块黑板。*Tāmen jiàoshì lǐ yǒu liǎng kuài hēibǎn.*
3. 我家里有十扇窗户和三扇门。*Wǒ jiā lǐ yǒu shí shàn chuānghu hé sān shàn mén.*
4. 她家里有五百本书。*Tā jiā lǐ yǒu wǔ bǎi běn shū.*
5. 你爷爷家里有钟吗? *Nǐ yéye jiā lǐ yǒu zhōng ma?*
6. 我朋友家里没有空调机。*Wǒ péngyou jiā lǐ méi yǒu kōngtiáojī.*
7. 他家里有一张中国地图。*Tā jiālǐ yǒu yì zhāng Zhōngguó dìtú.*
8. 这个星期有法文课吗? *Zhè gè xīngqī yǒu Fǎwén kè ma?*
9. 下个星期没有中文课。*Xià gè xīngqī méi yǒu Zhōngwén kè.*
10. 你家里有几台电脑? *Nǐ jiālǐ yǒu jǐ tái diànnǎo?*

17·1 1. e 2. f 3. i 4. h 5. d 6. c 7. k 8. j 9. b 10. a 11. g

17·2 1. At home 2. Inside the gym 3. Beside the dorm 4. Outside the school 5. On the left of the cafeteria 6. On the table 7. On the right of the library 8. Between the bookstore and the auditorium 9. Inside the office 10. Opposite the teaching building 11. In front of the classroom 12. On the sports field

17·3 1. There is a bookstore between the administrative building and the political science building.
2. Is the engineering building opposite the math building?
3. There is a student cafeteria on the left of the education building.
4. Precisely to the right of the foreign language building is the geography building.
5. Is the biology building behind the history building?
6. In front of the liberal arts building is the science and engineering building.
7. The chemistry building is beside the physics building.
8. Is there a restroom outside the gymnasium?
9. The reading rooms are inside the library.
10. Right above the lab is the computer room.
11. There is a lab below the computer room.

17·4 1. 数学楼旁边有一个小书店。*Shùxué lóu pángbiān yǒu yí ge xiǎo shūdiàn.*
2. 物理楼就在化学楼左边。*Wùlǐ lóu jiù zài huàxué lóu zuǒbian.*
3. 生物楼和历史楼中间是地理楼。*Shēngwù lóu hé lìshǐ lóu zhōngjiān shì dìlǐ lóu.*
4. 外语楼里(边)有一个电脑室吗? *Wàiyǔ lóu lǐ(bian) yǒu yí ge diànnǎoshì ma?*
5. 教育楼在工程楼对面。*Jiàoyù lóu zài gōngchéng lóu duìmiàn.*
6. 中文楼右边就是图书馆。*Zhōngwén lóu yòubian jiù shì túshūguǎn.*
7. 人文楼在行政楼后面吗? *Rénwén lóu zài xíngzhèng lóu hòumian ma?*
8. 实验室上边有一个厕所。*Shíyànshì shàngbian yǒu yí ge cèsuǒ.*
9. 理工楼前边是政治楼? *Lǐgōng lóu qiánbian shì zhèngzhì lóu ma?*
10. 学校外边有一个书店。*Xuéxiào wàibian yǒu yí ge shūdiàn.*
11. 我的办公室就在新阅览室下边。*Wǒ de bàngōngshì jiù zài xīn yuèlǎnshì xiàbian.*

18·1 1. 吃吃 *chīchi* 2. 跑跑步 *pǎopaobù* 3. 想想 *xiǎngxiang* 4. 游游泳 *yóuyouyǒng* 5. 喝喝 *hēhe* 6. 唱唱歌 *chàngchanggē* 7. 问问 *wènwen* 8. 跳跳舞 *tiàotiaowǔ* 9. 穿穿 *chuānchuan* 10. 介绍介绍 *jièshàojièshào* 11. 洗洗 *xǐxi* 12. 休息休息 *xiūxixiūxi* 13. 擦擦 *cāca* 14. 运动运动 *yùndòngyùndòng* 15. 扫扫 *sǎosao* 16. 学习学习 *xuéxíxuéxí* 17. 吸吸 *xīxi* 18. 收拾收拾 *shōushishōushi* 19. 用用 *yòngyong* 20. 整理整理 *zhěnglǐzhěnglǐ*

18·2 1. 想想 *xiǎngxiang* 2. 学习学习 *xuéxíxuéxí* 3. 看看 *kànkan* 4. 唱唱歌 *chàngchanggē* 5. 休息休息 *xiūxixiūxi* 6. 收拾收拾 *shōushishōushi* 7. 用用 *yòngyong* 8. 跑跑步 *pǎopaobù* 9. 游游泳 *yóuyouyǒng* 10. 跳跳舞 *tiàotiaowǔ* 11. 整理整理 *zhěnglǐzhěnglǐ* 12. 扫扫 *sǎosao* 13. 介绍介绍 *jièshàojièshào* 14. 听听 *tīngting* 15. 擦擦 *cāca* 16. 洗洗 *xǐxi*

18·3 1. You wash those dirty socks this afternoon, OK?
2. Shall we use the new vacuum cleaner to vacuum the floor now?
3. You guys tidy up your rooms in the morning, OK?
4. You wash these dirty bowls when you have time, OK?
5. Now we have some free time, shall we have a break?
6. Shall we put these books in good order?
7. You guys wipe the windows if you have time, OK?
8. You will sweep the floor tomorrow morning, OK?
9. Shall we wipe those tables and chairs?
10. You wash these dirty shirts and pants, OK?

18·4 1. 你们洗洗这些脏衣服, 好吗? *Nǐmen xǐxi zhèxiē zāng yīfu, hǎo ma?*
2. 我们现在扫扫地, 好不好? *Wǒmen xiànzài sǎosao dì, hǎo bu hǎo?*

3. 你整理整理那些中文书，好吗? *Nǐ zhěnglǐzhěnglǐ nàxiē Zhōngwén shū, hǎo ma?*
4. 你用新吸尘器吸吸地，好不好? *Nǐ yòng xīn xīchénqì xīxi dì, hǎo bu hǎo?*
5. 我们现在休息休息，好吗? *Wǒmen xiànzài xiūxixiūxi, hǎo ma?*
6. 你们明天收拾收拾你们的屋子，好不好? *Nǐmen míngtiān shōushishōushi nǐmen de wūzi, hǎo bu hǎo?*
7. 要是有时间，你擦擦那些桌子，好吗? *Yàoshì yǒu shíjiān, nǐ cāca nàxiē zhuōzi, hǎo ma?*
8. 要是有时间，我们跳跳舞，好不好? *Yàoshì yǒu shíjiān, wǒmen tiàotiaowǔ, hǎo bu hǎo?*
9. 你洗洗这些脏碗，好吗? *Nǐ xǐxi zhèxiē zāng wǎn, hǎo ma?*
10. 你看看这件新衬衫，好不好? *Nǐ kànkan zhe jiàn xīn chènshān, hǎo bu hǎo?*
11. 现在有时间，我们学习学习中文，好吗? *Xiànzài yǒu shíjiān, wǒmen xuéxíxuéxí Zhōngwén, hǎo ma?*
12. 你们听听这个新音乐CD，好不好? *Nǐmen tīngting zhè ge xīn yīnyuè CD, hǎo bu hǎo?*
13. 你介绍介绍你的新朋友，好吗? *Nǐ jièshàojièshào nǐ de xīn péngyou, hǎo ma?*
14. 我们唱唱歌，好不好? *Wǒmen chàngchanggē, hǎo bu hǎo?*
15. 你想想，好吗? *Nǐ xiǎngxiang, hǎo ma?*

19·1
1. 学生们学语法学得很好。*Xuéshengmen xué yǔfǎ xué de hěn hǎo.*
2. 学生问问题问得很多吗? *Xuésheng wèn wèntí wèn de hěn duō ma?*
3. 这些学生回答问题回答得很快。*Zhèxiē xuésheng huídá wèntí huídá de hěn kuài.*
4. 他们做语法练习做得很慢。*Tāmen zuò yǔfǎ liànxí zuò de hěn màn.*
5. 你们准备考试准备得很认真吗? *Nǐmen zhǔnbèi kǎoshì zhǔnbèi de hěn rènzhēn ma?*
6. 那些学生念新课文念得很流利。*Nàxiē xuésheng niàn xīn kèwén niàn de hěn liúlì.*
7. 黄老师说汉语说得很快吗? *Huáng lǎoshī shuō Hànyǔ shuō de hěn kuài ma?*
8. 法国学生听录音听得很少。*Fǎguó xuésheng tīng lùyīn tīng de hěn shǎo.*

19·2
1. 日本学生汉语考试都考得不好。*Rìběn xuésheng Hànyǔ kǎoshì dōu kǎo de bù hǎo.*
2. 那个学生生词念得不清楚。*Nà ge xuésheng shēngcí niàn de bù qīngchu.*
3. 俄国学生学汉语学得不慢。*Éguó xuésheng xué Hànyǔ xué de bù màn.*
4. 他们汉语功课复习得不认真。*Tāmen Hànyǔ gōngkè fùxí de bù rènzhēn.*
5. 这些美国学生汉语说得不流利。*Zhèxiē Měiguó xuésheng Hànyǔ shuō de bù liúlì.*
6. 黄老师汉语语法教得不少。*Huáng lǎoshī Hànyǔ yǔfǎ jiāo de bù shǎo.*
7. 他们看录像看得不多。*Tāmen kàn lùxiàng kàn de bù duō.*
8. 你们汉字写得不快。*Nǐmen Hànzì xiě de bú kuài.*

19·3
1. 学生们考试准备得认真不认真? *Xuéshengmen kǎoshì zhǔnbèi de rènzhen bu rènzhēn?*
2. 黄教授汉语说得快不快? *Huáng jiàoshòu Hànyǔ shuō de kuài bu kuài?*
3. 法国学生汉语考试考得好不好? *Fǎguó xuésheng Hànyǔ kǎoshì kǎo de hǎo bu hǎo?*
4. 这些日本学生汉语说得流利不流利? *Zhèxiē Rìběn xuésheng Hànyǔ shuō de liúlì bu liúlì?*
5. 新学生语法学得好不好? *Xīn xuésheng yǔfǎ xué de hǎo bu hǎo?*
6. 学生录音听得多不多? *Xuésheng lùyīn tīng de duō bu duō?*
7. 这个学生生词念得清楚不清楚? *Zhè ge xuésheng shēngcí niàn de qīngchu bu qīngchu?*
8. 那些学生问题回答得慢不慢? *Nàxiē xuésheng wèntí huídá de màn bu màn?*
9. 学生们看录像看得多不多? *Xuéshengmen kàn lùxiàng kàn de duō bu duō?*

19·4
1. 他语法问题问得很多。*Tā yǔfǎ wèntí wèn de hěn duō.*
2. 这个美国学生课文念得很流利。*Zhè ge Měiguó xuésheng kèwén niàn de hěn liúlì.*
3. 新学生看录像看得很少吗? *Xīn xuésheng kàn lùxiàng kàn de hěn shǎo ma?*
4. 这些学生听录音听得很多。*Zhèxiē xuésheng tīng lùyīn tīng de hěn duō.*
5. 你们功课复习得快不快? *Nǐmen gōngkè fùxí de kuài bu kuài?*
6. 那些俄国学生汉语考试准备得很认真。*Nàxiē Éguó xuésheng Hànyǔ kǎoshì zhǔnbèi de hěn rènzhēn.*
7. 他们念生词念得很好。*Tāmen niàn shēngcí niàn de hěn hǎo.*
8. 你现在说汉语说得流利不流利? *Nǐ xiànzài shuō Hànyǔ shuō de liúlì bu liúlì?*
9. 这些日本学生汉字写得很快。*Zhèxiē Rìběn xuésheng Hànzì xiě de hěn kuài.*
10. 我做语法练习做得很多。*Wǒ zuò yǔfǎ liànxí zuò de hěn duō.*
11. 那个中国学生问题回答得很快吗? *Nà ge Zhōngguó xuésheng wèntí huídá de hěn kuài ma?*
12. 白教授今天的语法讲得很清楚。*Bái jiàoshòu jīntiān de yǔfǎ jiǎng de hěn qīngchu.*

20·1
1. g 2. k 3. f 4. e 5. a 6. c 7. j 8. l 9. b 10. h 11. i 12. d
13. n 14. m

20·2 The following are sample answers.
1. 我姐姐眼睛最漂亮。*Wǒ jiějie yǎnjing zuì piàoliang.*
2. 我弟弟耳朵最大。*Wǒ dìdi ěrduo zuì dà.*
3. 我哥哥个子最高。*Wǒ gēge gèzi zuì gāo.*

4. 我妹妹头发最长。*Wǒ mèimei tóufa zuì cháng.*
5. 我弟弟鼻子最小。*Wǒ dìdi bízi zuì xiǎo.*
6. 我哥哥肩膀最宽。*Wǒ gēge jiānbǎng zuì kuān.*
7. 我爸爸肚子最胖。*Wǒ bàba dùzi zuì pàng.*
8. 我哥哥胳膊最粗。*Wǒ gēge gēbo zuì cū.*
9. 我弟弟脚最大。*Wǒ dìdi jiǎo zuì dà.*
10. 我哥哥手最长。*Wǒ gēge shǒu zuì cháng.*
11. 现在我头不疼。*Xiànzài wǒ tóu bù téng.*
12. 昨天我腰不疼。*Zuótiān wǒ yāo bù téng.*

20·3　1. 长长 *chángcháng*　　2. 漂漂亮亮 *piàopiàoliàngliàng*　　3. 短短 *duǎnduǎn*　　4. 高高兴兴 *gāogāoxìngxìng*　　5. 早早 *zǎozǎo*　　6. 宽宽 *kuānkuān*　　7. 高高 *gāogāo*　　8. 清清楚楚 *qīngqīngchǔchǔ*　　9. 矮矮 *ǎiǎi*　　10. 整整齐齐 *zhěngzhěngqíqí*　　11. 慢慢 *mànmàn*　　12. 干干净净 *gāngānjìngjìng*　　13. 瘦瘦 *shòushòu*　　14. 胖胖 *pàngpàng*　　15. 红红 *hónghóng*　　16. 白白 *báibái*　　17. 蓝蓝 *lánlán*　　18. 绿绿 *lǜlǜ*　　19. 粗粗 *cūcū*　　20. 细细 *xìxì*

20·4　1. 大大的 *dàdà de*; We all like the largish eyes of hers.
2. 漂漂亮亮的 *piàopiàoliàngliàng de*; His younger <u>sister</u> is prettily dressed tonight.
3. 长长的 *chángcháng de*; Is that long-haired girl your friend?
4. 红红的 *hónghóng de*; Whose bright reddish sweater is this?
5. 宽宽的 *kuānkuān de*; This broad-shouldered gentleman is his younger brother.
6. 细细的 *xìxì de*; They all like the actress with a slenderish waist.
7. 短短的 *duǎnduǎn de*; Is the man with shortish legs a writer?
8. 清清楚楚的 *qīngqīngchǔchǔ de*; Professor Bai explained today's grammar very clearly.
9. 瘦瘦小小的 *shòushòuxiǎoxiǎo de*; His father is thinish and smallish.

20·5　1. 那个个子高高的工程师是我哥哥。*Nà ge gèzi gāogāo de gōngchéngshī shì wǒ gēge.*
2. 这个脖子细细的姑娘现在头疼吗？*Zhè ge bózi xìxì de gūniang xiànzài tóu téng ma?*
3. 你家里人，谁眼睛最漂亮？*Nǐ jiālǐrén, shéi yǎnjing zuì piàoliang?*
4. 她喜欢那个肩膀宽宽的运动员吗？*Tā xǐhuan nà ge jiānbǎng kuānkuān de yùndòngyuán ma?*
5. 那个警察嘴巴大大的。*Nà ge jǐngchá zuǐbā dàdà de.*
6. 她的医生手长长的。*Tā de yīshēng shǒu chángcháng de.*
7. 现在我肚子不疼，可是我腰疼。*Xiànzài wǒ dùzi bù téng, kěshì wǒ yāo téng.*
8. 那个女服务员的毛衣黄黄的，我不喜欢。*Nà ge nǚ fúwùyuán de máoyī huánghuáng de, wǒ bù xǐhuan.*
9. 这些干干净净的衣服是我妹妹的。*Zhèxiē gāngānjìngjìng de yīfú shì wǒ mèimei de.*
10. 我的屋子总是收拾得整整齐齐的。*Wǒ de wūzi zǒngshì shōushi de zhěngzhěngqíqí de.*
11. 那个胖胖的经理是你爸爸的朋友吗？*Nà ge pàngpàng de jīnglǐ shì nǐ bàba de péngyou ma?*

R4·1　1. 块 *kuài*, 个 *gè*　　2. 扇 *shàn*, 扇 *shàn*　　3. 盏 *zhǎn*　　4. 张 *zhāng*, 把 *bǎ*　　5. 本 *běn*　　6. 张 *zhāng*　　7. 枝 *zhī*　　8. 个 *gè*　　9. 台 *tái*　　10. 台 *tái*

R4·2　1. 整整齐齐 *zhěngzhěngqíqí*　　2. 胖胖 *pàngpàng*　　3. 干干净净 *gāngānjìngjìng*　　4. 说说 *shuōshuo*　　5. 清清楚楚 *qīngqīngchǔchǔ*　　6. 写写 *xiěxie*　　7. 高高兴兴 *gāogāoxìngxìng*　　8. 休息休息 *xiūxixiūxi*　　9. 粗粗 *cūcū*　　10. 跑跑步 *pǎopaobù*　　11. 宽宽 *kuānkuān*　　12. 游游泳 *yǒuyouyǒng*　　13. 慢慢 *mànmàn*　　14. 跳跳舞 *tiàotiaowǔ*　　15. 整理整理 *zhěnglǐzhěnglǐ*　　16. 练习练习 *liànxíliànxí*　　17. 大大 *dàdà*　　18. 介绍介绍 *jièshàojièshào*　　19. 高高 *gāogāo*　　20. 唱唱歌 *chàngchanggē*

R4·3　1. The administrative building is between the library and the stadium.
2. Beside the foreign language building is the gym.
3. There is an auditorium opposite the geography building.
4. The political science building is on the left of the biology building.
5. In front of the chemistry building is the history building.
6. There's a cafeteria on the right of the physics building.
7. The teachers' offices are above the bathroom.
8. Behind the liberal arts building is the science and engineering building.
9. There is a bookstore outside the school.
10. There are two air conditioners in our classroom.
11. The lab is below the computer room.
12. On the left of the math building is the engineering building.

R4·4　The following are sample answers.
1. 现在我汉语学得很好。*Xiànzài wǒ Hànyǔ xué de hěn hǎo.*
2. 老师语法讲得很清楚。*Lǎoshī yǔfǎ jiǎng de hěn qīngchu.*

3. 现在我说汉语说得不流利。*Xiànzài wǒ shuō Hànyǔ shuō de bù liúlì.*
4. 我们语法练习做得很多。*Wǒmen yǔfǎ liànxí zuò de hěn duō.*
5. 我汉语考试考得不好。*Wǒ Hànyǔ kǎoshì kǎo de bù hǎo.*
6. 我看录像看得很少。*Wǒ kàn lùxiàng kàn de hěn shǎo.*
7. 我们汉语课文念得很流利。*Wǒmen Hànyǔ kèwén niàn de hěn liúlì.*
8. 他学习得很认真。*Tā xuéxí de hěn rènzhēn.*
9. 我看得很清楚。*Wǒ kàn de hěn qīngchu.*
10. 我弟弟个子最高。*Wǒ dìdi gèzi zuì gāo.*
11. 我弟弟眼睛最漂亮。*Wǒ dìdi yǎnjing zuì piàoliang.*
12. 我哥哥肩膀最宽。*Wǒ gēge jiānbǎng zuì kuān.*
13. 我哥哥腿最长。*Wǒ gēge tuǐ zuì cháng.*
14. 我弟弟胳膊最粗。*Wǒ dìdi gēbo zuì cū.*
15. 我现在肚子,腰,脖子都不疼。*Wǒ xiànzài dùzi, yāo, bózi dōu bù téng.*

R4·5
1. 我们宿舍里有两百本书和三十枝笔。*Wǒmen sùshè lǐ yǒu liǎng bǎi běn shū hé sānshí zhī bǐ.*
2. 他们教室里有两台空调机和二十盏灯。*Tāmen jiàoshì lǐ yǒu liǎng tái kōngtiáojī hé èrshí zhǎn dēng.*
3. 下个星期没有汉语课。*Xià ge xīngqī méi yǒu Hànyǔ kè.*
4. 你们教室里有十五张桌子和十六把椅子吗? *Nǐmen jiàoshì lǐ yǒu shíwǔ zhāng zhuōzi hé shíliù bǎ yǐzi ma?*
5. 化学楼右边有一个厕所。*Huàxué lóu yòubian yǒu yí ge cèsuǒ.*
6. 人文楼在理工楼后边吗? *Rénwén lóu zài lǐgōng lóu hòubian ma?*
7. 数学楼前边就是物理楼。*Shùxué lóu qiánbian jiù shì wùlǐ lóu.*
8. 现在我们去体育场跑跑步, 好吗? *Xiànzài wǒmen qù tǐyùchǎng pǎopaobù, hǎo ma?*
9. 你们明天擦擦这些门和窗户, 好吗? *Nǐmen míngtiān cāca zhèxiē mén hé chuānghu, hǎo ma?*
10. 你洗洗这些脏碗, 好吗? *Nǐ xǐxi zhèxiè zāng wǎn, hǎo ma?*
11. 我们现在休息休息, 好吗? *Wǒmen xiànzài xiūxixiūxi, hǎo ma?*
12. 学生们回答老师的问题回答得很快。*Xuéshengmen huídá lǎoshī de wèntí huídá de hěn kuài.*
13. 你朋友汉语说得很流利吗? *Nǐ péngyou Hànyǔ shuō de hěn liúlì ma?*
14. 黄教授今天的语法讲得清清楚楚的! *Huáng jiàoshòu jīntiān de yǔfǎ jiǎng de qīngqīngchǔchǔ de!*
15. 那个头发长长的先生是你爸爸吗? *Nà ge tóufa chángcháng de xiānsheng shì nǐ bàba ma?*
16. 我们老师今天晚上穿得整整齐齐的。*Wǒmen lǎoshī jīntiān wǎnshang chuān de zhěngzhěngqíqí de.*

R4·6 1. F   2. T   3. T   4. F   5. T   6. T   7. T   8. F   9. T   10. T   11. F   12. T   13. T
14. F   15. T   16. F   17. T   18. F

V

21·1
1. 请 *qǐng*; Next week whom will he invite to eat dumplings?
2. 教 *jiāo*; The teacher teaches the students how to dance every day.
3. 让 *rang*; Does her father let her drink beer?
4. 教 *jiāo*; My grandfather is teaching me how to play Go.
5. 请 *qǐng*; Her girlfriend invited him to her home to play mahjong.
6. 让 *rang*; Mom does not let me listen to French music.
7. 请 *qǐng*; That pretty actress invited me to dance.
8. 帮助 *bāngzhù*; The teacher helps the students play the games.
9. 请 *qǐng*; Tomorrow won't you invite your friends over for a drink?
10. 叫 *jiào*; That musician asked her to go to the auditorium to sing.

21·2 The following are sample answers.
1. 爸爸教我唱歌。*Bàba jiāo wǒ chànggē.*
2. 小时候, 爷爷教我跳舞。*Xiǎoshíhou, yéye jiāo wǒ tiàowǔ.*
3. 老师常教我们做游戏。*Lǎoshī cháng jiāo wǒmen zuò yóuxì.*
4. 爸爸不让我喝酒。*Bàba bú ràng wǒ hē jiǔ.*
5. 爸爸常让我看电视。*Bàba cháng ràng wǒ kàn diànshì.*
6. 小时候, 妈妈常让我上网。*Xiǎoshíhou, māma cháng ràng wǒ shàng wǎng.*
7. 小时候, 妈妈常让我听音乐。*Xiǎoshíhou, māma cháng ràng wǒ tīng yīnyuè.*
8. 最近我朋友常请我去打麻将。*Zuìjìn wǒ péngyou cháng qǐng wǒ qù dǎ májiàng.*
9. 星期天我朋友常请我去下围棋。*Xīngqītiān wǒ péngyou cháng qǐng wǒ qù xià wéiqí.*
10. 现在我常请朋友去喝酒。*Xiànzài wǒ cháng qǐng péngyou qù hē jiǔ.*
11. 中文老师常请学生吃饭。*Zhōngwén lǎoshī cháng qǐng xuésheng chī fàn.*
12. 我常帮助妈妈做饭。*Wǒ cháng bāngzhù māma zuò fàn.*

21·3
1. 给 *gěi*; I gave him two tickets for the ball.
2. 告诉 *gàosu*; The writer told us the name of the opera.
3. 还 *huán*; He'll return the Chinese books to Professor Huang tomorrow.
4. 送 *sòng*; My dad is giving me a concert ticket as a gift.
5. 问 *wèn*; The students often ask the music teacher questions.
6. 告诉 *gàosu*; I won't tell you the name of that movie.
7. 给 *gěi*; What kind of tickets does the lawyer want to give you?
8. 问 *wèn*; The police officer is asking the actor a few questions.
9. 送 *sòng*; My older sister gave me a ticket for the evening party as a gift.
10. 还 *huán*; Will you return the mahjong to my younger brother next week?

21·4
1. 这些演员今天请那些美国军人跳舞吗? *Zhèxiē yǎnyuán jīntiān qǐng nàxiē Měiguó jūnrén tiàowǔ ma?*
2. 我哥哥给我一张舞会票。 *Wǒ gēge gěi wǒ yì zhāng wǔhuì piào.*
3. 老师常教学生们唱中国歌。 *Lǎoshī cháng jiāo xuéshēngmen chàng Zhōngguó gē.*
4. 我妈妈不让我妹妹听法国音乐。 *Wǒ māma bú ràng wǒ mèimei tīng Fǎguó yīnyuè.*
5. 他的好朋友送他两张意大利歌剧票。 *Tā de hǎo péngyou sòng tā liǎng zhāng Yìdàlì gējù piào.*
6. 明天那个职员还我哥哥麻将吗? *Míngtiān nà ge zhíyuán huán wǒ gēge májiàng ma?*
7. 妈妈今天叫我们做游戏吗? *Māma jīntiān jiào wǒmen zuò yóuxì ma?*
8. 律师不告诉他们那个新电影的名字。 *Lǜshī bú gàosu tāmen nà ge xīn diànyǐng de míngzi.*
9. 他爸爸不教他下围棋。 *Tā bàba bù jiāo tā xià wéiqí.*
10. 音乐家问你那个音乐会的名字。 *Yīnyuèjiā wèn nǐ nà ge yīnyuèhuì de míngzi.*

22·1
1. 学生们现在从宿舍去银行。 *Xuéshengmen xiànzài cóng sùshè qù yínháng.*
2. 你朋友明天也到邮局去吗? *Nǐ péngyou míngtiān yě dào yóujú qù ma?*
3. 这些新医生都在那个医院上班。 *Zhèxiē xīn yīshēng dōu zài nà ge yīyuàn shàngbān.*
4. 那个演员常到那个小商店去。 *Nà ge yǎnyuán cháng dào nà ge xiǎo shāngdiàn qù.*
5. 这个老警察周末常在酒吧喝酒。 *Zhè ge lǎo jǐngchá zhōumò cháng zài jiǔbā hē jiǔ.*
6. 他们没从黄先生那儿来我们这儿。 *Tāmen méi cóng Huáng xiānsheng nàr lái wǒmen zhèr.*
7. 职员们今天从商场来。 *Zhíyuánmen jīntiān cóng shāngchǎng lái.*
8. 你们中午想到我这儿来吗? *Nǐmen zhōngwǔ xiǎng dào wǒ zhèr lái ma?*

22·2
1. 从 *cóng*; Today his older brother is not going from his home to the supermarket.
2. 到 *dào*; My younger sister will not go to the museum this afternoon.
3. 在 *zài*; Do all of them have dinner at Professor Bai's place?
4. 到 *dào*; Where are these workers going now?
5. 在 *zài*; The teachers often dine in that restaurant.
6. 从 *cóng*; Where did you guys come from?
7. 到 *dào*; Will your older brother also go to the cinema tomorrow?
8. 到 *dào*; I don't often go to that opera house.

22·3
1. 现在我爸爸在邮局上班。 *Xiànzài wǒ bàba zài yóujú shàngbān.*
2. 我明天从那个商店去中国银行。 *Wǒ míngtiān cóng nà ge shāngdiàn qù Zhōngguó yínháng.*
3. 律师们常在那个小酒吧喝啤酒。 *Lǜshīmen cháng zài nà ge xiǎo jiǔbā hē píjiǔ.*
4. 音乐家们晚上到剧场去吗? *Yīnyuèjiāmen wǎnshang dào jùchǎng qù ma?*
5. 这些军人现在不常到那个电影院去。 *Zhèxiē jūnrén xiànzài bù cháng dào nà ge diànyǐngyuàn qù.*
6. 那个老农民从你们那儿来吗? *Nà ge lǎo nóngmíng cóng nǐmen nàr lái ma?*
7. 这个作家常在餐馆吃饭。 *Zhè ge zuòjiā zài cānguǎn chīfàn.*
8. 那些服务员今天上午从超市去博物馆。 *Nàxiē fúwùyuán jīntiān shàngwǔ cóng chāoshì qù bówùguǎn.*
9. 那些护士都在那个医院上班吗? *Nàxiē hùshi dōu zài nà ge yīyuàn shàngbān ma?*
10. 这些工人下午不到商场去。 *Zhèxiē gōngrén xiàwǔ búdào shāngchǎng qù.*

23·1
1. When do you get up every morning? When do you go to school?
2. We'll attend class at 9:00 and get out of class at 10:30 today.
3. Those female nurses all eat lunch in the cafeteria.
4. Do these students take a bath every evening?
5. These old police officers are not drinking coffee this week.
6. These new doctors work conscientiously.
7. Her older brother is a businessperson, and her younger brother is also a businessperson.
8. My grandfather goes to bed early every evening.
9. That actor does not work now.
10. That female lawyer likes red ties the most.

23·2 The following are sample answers.

1. 对，我每天都刷牙，洗脸。*Duì, wǒ měitiān dōu shuā yá, xǐ liǎn.*
2. 对，我每天早上都刮胡子。*Duì, wǒ měitiān zǎoshang dōu guā húzi.*
3. 对，我每天都化妆。*Duì, wǒ měitiān dōu huàzhuāng.*
4. 我上午八点去学校上学。*Wǒ shàngwǔ bā diǎn qù xuéxiào shàngxué.*
5. 我坐公共汽车去。*Wǒ zuò gōnggòng qìchē qù.*
6. 我也常骑自行车去。*Wǒ yě cháng qí zìxíngchē qù.*
7. 我每天五点下班回家。*Wǒ měitiān wǔ diǎn xià bān huíjiā.*
8. 我坐车回家。*Wǒ zuò chē huíjiā.*
9. 对，我也常走路回家。*Duì, wǒ yě cháng zǒu lù huíjiā.*
10. 我常在家里吃晚饭。*Wǒ cháng zài jiā li chī wǎnfàn.*
11. 对，星期天我常去餐馆吃晚饭。*Duì, Xīngqītiān wǒ cháng qù cānguǎn chī wǎnfàn.*
12. 我晚上十点上床睡觉。*Wǒ wǎnshang shí diǎn shàng chuáng shuìjiào.*

23·3 The following are sample answers.

1. 上班 *shàng bān*
2. 吃饭 *chī fàn*
3. 上班 *shàng bān*
4. 看书 *kàn shū*
5. 休息 *xiūxi*
6. 睡觉 *shuìjiào*
7. 上学 *shàng xué*
8. 上班 *shàng bān*
9. 去医院 *qù yīyuàn*
10. 回家 *huíjiā*

23·4
1. 学生们上午从八点到十点在大教室上汉语课。*Xuéshengmen cóng shàngwǔ bā diǎn dào shí diǎn zài dà jiàoshì shàng Hànyǔ kè.*
2. 新经理明天开车来公司上班。*Xīn jīnglǐ míngtiān kāi chē lái gōngsī shàngbān.*
3. 你每天都洗脸、刷牙吗？*Nǐ měitiān dōu xǐ liǎn, shuā yá ma?*
4. 他爸爸坐公共汽车去上班还是骑自行车去上班？*Tā bàba zuò gōnggòng qìchē qù shàngbān háishì qí zìxíngchē qù shàngbān?*
5. 那个作家不常回家吃晚饭。*Nà ge zuòjiā bù cháng huí jiā chī wǎnfàn.*
6. 那些运动员每天都去体育馆运动吗？*Nàxiē yùndòngyuán měitiān dōu qù tǐyùguǎn yùndòng ma?*
7. 这个音乐家晚上十一点上床睡觉。*Zhè ge yīnyuèjiā wǎnshang shíyī diǎn shàng chuáng shuìjiào.*
8. 那个商人不坐船去法国，他坐飞机去。*Nà ge shāngrén bú zuò chuán qù Fǎguó, tā zuò fēijī qù.*
9. 这些农民现在没有汽车，他们常走路回家。*Zhèxiē nóngmín xiànzài méi yǒu qìchē, tāmen cháng zǒu lù huí jiā.*
10. 音乐家们星期六常去新剧场唱歌吗？*Yīnyuèjiāmen Xīngqīliù cháng qù xīn jùchǎng chàng gē ma?*

24·1 The following are sample answers.

1. 我今天不想去体育馆打冰球。*Wǒ jīntiān bù xiǎng qù tǐyùguǎn dǎ bīngqiú.*
2. 我下午要去体育场踢足球。*Wǒ xiàwǔ yào qù tǐyùchǎng tī zúqiú.*
3. 我爸爸会打篮球和排球。*Wǒ bàba huì dǎ lánqiú hé páiqiú.*
4. 我朋友明天可以打乒乓球。*Wǒ péngyou míngtiān kěyǐ dǎ pīngpāngqiú.*
5. 一个眼睛不好的人不能打网球。*Yí ge yǎnjing bù hǎo de rén bù néng dǎ wǎngqiú.*
6. 我明年要学打高尔夫。*Wǒ míngnián yào xué dǎ gāo'ěrfūqiú.*
7. 我妈妈不能教我滑冰。*Wǒ māma bù néng jiāo wǒ huábīng.*
8. 今年我不想学滑雪。*Jīnnián wǒ bù xiǎng xué huáxuě.*
9. 我朋友今天可以跟我一起去打球。*Wǒ péngyou jīntiān kěyǐ gēn wǒ yìqǐ qù dǎ qiú.*
10. 我爸爸，妈妈会打扑克。*Wǒ bàba, māma huì dǎ pūkè.*

24·2
1. 我晚上不想跟哥哥一起下象棋。*Wǒ wǎnshang **bù xiǎng** gēn gēge yìqǐ xià xiàngqí.* I don't want to play chess together with my older brother in the evening.
2. 他们下午不能去体育场踢足球。*Tāmen xiàwǔ **bù néng** qù tǐyùchǎng tī zúqiú.* They cannot go to the stadium to play soccer in the afternoon.
3. 他爸爸不会打高尔夫球。*Tā bàba bú huì dǎ gāo'ěrfūqiú.* His father does not know how to play golf.
4. 演员们明天不想去体育馆滑冰。*Yǎnyuánmen míngtiān bù xiǎng qù tǐyùguǎn huábīng.* The actors do not want to go to the gymnasium to skate tomorrow.
5. 那些律师星期天不能去打网球。*Nàxiē lǜshī Xīngqītiān bù néng qù dǎ wǎngqiú.* Those lawyers cannot go play tennis on Sundays.
6. 我们不想跟那些军人一起打篮球。*Wǒmen **bù xiǎng** gēn nàxiē jūnrén yìqǐ dǎ lánqiú.* We don't want to play basketball with the soldiers.

7. 白先生不想学打冰球。*Bái xiānsheng bù xiǎng xué dǎ bīngqiú.* Mr. Bai does not want to learn how to play ice hockey.
8. 我下个月不能教你们打排球。*Wǒ xià ge yuè bù néng jiāo nǐmen dǎ páiqiú.* I cannot teach you how to play volleyball next month.
9. 你不能跟我一起下围棋。*Nǐ **bù néng** gēn wǒ yìqǐ xià wéiqí.* You cannot play Go with me.
10. 在上班时间，护士们不可以打扑克。*Zài shàngbān shíjiān, hùshimen bù kěyǐ dǎ pūkè.* (prohibition) During their working hours, the nurses are not allowed to play poker.

24·3
1. 我不会下围棋，也不会下象棋。*Wǒ bú huì xià wéiqí, yě bú huì xià xiàngqí.*
2. 你们今天能/可以跟我们一起做游戏吗？*Nǐmen jīntiān néng/kěyǐ gēn wǒmen yìqǐ zuò yóuxì ma?*
3. 她想下个月学打麻将。*Tā xiǎng xià ge yuè xué dǎ májiàng.*
4. 我朋友下午要去体育馆打篮球。*Wǒ péngyou xiàwǔ yào qù tǐyùguǎn dǎ lánqiú.*
5. 我可以不可以跟你们一起打扑克？*Wǒ kěyǐ bu kěyǐ gēn nǐmen yìqǐ dǎ pūkè?*
6. 那个老作家会打排球和篮球。*Nà ge lǎo zuòjiā huì dǎ páiqiú hé lánqiú.*
7. 你们想不想跟老师们一起打冰球？*Nǐmen xiǎng bu xiǎng gēn lǎoshīmen yìqǐ dǎ bīngqiú?*
8. 这些运动员能/可以在我们学校的体育馆打网球和乒乓球。*Zhèxiē yùndòngyuán néng/kěyǐ zài wǒmen xuéxiào de tǐyùguǎn dǎ wǎngqiú hé pīngpāngqiú.*
9. 妈妈，我们这个星期天可以去滑雪吗？--不，你们不能去。*Māma, wǒmen zhè ge Xīngqītiān kěyǐ qù huáxuě ma?—Bù, nǐmen bù néng qù.*
10. 白教授下个星期要教那些律师打高尔夫球。*Bái jiàoshòu xià ge xīngqī yào jiāo nàxiē lǜshī dǎ gāo'ěrfūqiú.*

25·1 The following are sample answers.
1. 我明天会去体育馆打球。*Wǒ míngtiān huì qù tǐyùguǎn dǎqiú.*
2. 我晚上要跟我朋友一起打扑克。*Wǒ wǎnshang yào gēn wǒ péngyou yìqǐ dǎ pūkè.*
3. 我星期六打算去中国餐馆吃饭。*Wǒ Xīngqīliù dǎsuàn qù Zhōngguó cānguǎn chīfàn.*
4. 我周末准备收拾一下儿我的屋子。*Wǒ zhōumò zhǔnbèi shōushi yíxiàr wǒ de wūzi.*
5. 下个星期我打算去海滩游泳。*Xià ge xīngqī wǒ dǎsuàn qù hǎitān yóuyǒng.*
6. 我计划明年秋天买房子。*Wǒ jìhuà míngnián qiūtiān mǎi fángzi.*
7. 我准备明年找新工作。*Wǒ zhǔnbèi míngnián zhǎo xīn gōngzuò.*
8. 今年夏天我就要去意大利旅游了。*Jīnnián xiàtiān wǒ jiù yào qù Yìdàlì lǚyóu le.*
9. 我计划明年春天结婚。*Wǒ jìhuà míngnián chūntiān jiéhūn.*
10. 我快要去中国开会了。*Wǒ kuàiyào qù Zhōngguó kāihuì le.*

25·2
1. 他们快要到北京去工作了。*Tāmen kuài yào dào Běijīng qù gōngzuò le.*
2. 经理们快要开会了。*Jīnglǐmen kuài yào kāihuì le.*
3. 那些学生快要从大学毕业了。*Nàxiē xuésheng kuài yào cóng dàxué bìyè le.*
4. 爸爸和妈妈快要回家了。*Bàba hé māma kuài yào huíjiā le.*
5. 新护士快要上班了吗？*Xīn hùshi kuài yào shàngbān le ma?*
6. 音乐会两点半就要开始了。*Yīnyuèhuì liǎng diǎn bàn jiù yào kāishǐ le.*
7. 这些律师明年夏天就要去北京学习了。*Zhèxiē lǜshī míngnián xiàtiān jiù yào qù Běijīng xuéxí le.*
8. 这个星期六她就要跟他结婚了吗？*Zhè ge Xīngqīliù tā jiù yào gēn tā jiéhūn le ma?*
9. 老师们下个月就要去旅游了。*Lǎoshīmen xià ge yuè jiù yào qù lǚyóu le.*
10. 黄先生明年春天就要买房子了。*Huáng xiānsheng míngnián chūntiān jiù yào mǎi fángzi le.*

25·3
1. ...(还)不会... *...(hái) bú huì...*; These teachers won't have a meeting tomorrow (yet).
2. ...(还)不会... *...(hái) bú huì...*; That waiter won't go to work (yet).
3. ...(还)不会... *...(hái) bú huì...*; The bus will not come (yet).
4. ...(还)不会... *...(hái) bú huì...*; My older sister is not going to get married (yet).
5. ...(还)不会... *...(hái) bú huì...*; This Saturday my mother is not coming to see me (yet).
6. ...(还)不会... *...(hái) bú huì...*; That lawyer is not going to arrive in Beijing (yet).
7. ...(还)不会... *...(hái) bú huì...*; The ball is not going to start (yet).
8. ...(还)不会... *...(hái) bú huì...*; These athletes won't rest now (yet).
9. ...(还)不会... *...(hái) bú huì...*; My younger brother will not graduate (yet) this autumn.
10. ...不计划... *...bú jìhuà...*; Professor Bai does not plan to buy a new house next spring.
11. ...不想... *...bù xiǎng...*; Those clerks do not want to go to the beach to swim in the summer.
12. ...不打算... *...bù dǎsuàn...*; He does not intend to go to China to look for a job.
13. ...不准备... *...bù zhǔnbèi...*; My father is not going to Shanghai to attend a meeting next week.
14. ...不想... *...bù xiǎng...*; This winter we don't want to go to China for a tour.

25·4
1. 这些老师明年要去中国旅游。*Zhèxiē lǎoshī míngnián yào qù Zhōngguó lǚyóu.*
2. 音乐会快要开始了。*Yīnyuèhuì kuài yào kāishǐ le.*

3. 他妹妹快要毕业了。*Tā mèimei kuài yào bìyè le.*
4. 我弟弟下个月就要开始找新工作了。*Wǒ dìdi xià ge yuè jiù yào kāishǐ zhǎo xīn gōngzuò le.*
5. 黄教授计划明年秋天买新汽车吗? *Huáng jiàoshòu jìhuà míngnián qiūtiān mǎi xīn qìchē ma?*
6. 她今年冬天还不会跟我结婚。*Tā jīnnián dōngtiān hái bú huì gēn wǒ jiéhūn.*
7. 这些演员准备这个周末来海滩游泳吗? *Zhèxiē yǎnyuán zhǔnbèi zhè ge zhōumò lái hǎitān yóuyǒng ma?*
8. 你们打算今年夏天到中国去学习汉语吗? *Nǐmen dǎsuàn jīnnián xiàtiān dào Zhōngguó qù xuéxí Hànyǔ ma?*
9. 今年春天我朋友会在北京买房子。*Jīnnián chūntiān wǒ péngyou huì zài Běijīng mǎi fángzi.*
10. 教授们上午十点不会开会。*Jiàoshòumen shàngwǔ shídiǎn bú huì kāihuì.*

R5·1 1. d   2. e   3. b   4. j   5. a   6. g   7. c   8. f   9. k   10. o   11. n   12. h   13. q
14. i   15. m   16. s   17. v   18. u   19. l   20. y   21. p   22. r   23. t   24. z   25. w
26. x

R5·2 The following are sample answers.

1. 吃饭 *chī fàn*
2. 看录像 *kàn lùxiàng*
3. 去意大利旅游 *qù Yìdàlì lǚyóu*
4. 收拾屋子 *shōushi wūzi*
5. 打扑克 *dǎ pūkè*
6. 打网球 *dǎ wǎngqiú*
7. 化妆 *huàzhuāng*
8. 老师 *lǎoshī*
9. 一件事 *yí jiàn shì*
10. 爸爸 *bàba*
11. 我朋友 *wǒ péngyou*

R5·3 1. 跟 *gēn*; His friend did not go to the bar to drink with him.
2. 从 *cóng*; Tomorrow he will not go from his home to work.
3. 在 *zài*; All the students are having lunch here at my place now.
4. 到 *dào*; I don't want to go to the doctor's office today.
5. 从 *cóng*; Where do these farmers who are touring Beijing come from?
6. 在 *zài*; The lawyers often dine in this Chinese restaurant.
7. 跟 *gēn*; I don't usually go to the shop with him.
8. 到 *dào*; Will her younger sister also go to the post office this Saturday afternoon?

R5·4 1. They drive to the school to attend class every morning.
2. My mother will go home by bus at 5:00 p.m.
3. Do they have supper in the student cafeteria today?
4. You guys may walk to the gymnasium to play basketball every day.
5. These doctors won't go to the gymnasium to work out tomorrow.
6. After graduation she also would like to go to Beijing to look for a job.
7. All of the new nurses work very conscientiously.
8. Her older brother also often goes to work at the company by bike.
9. My father comes to the dormitory to see me very early every Sunday.
10. Can the actors apply their makeup in the opera house?
11. This female lawyer prefers to travel by boat.
12. He won't have time to shave his beard tomorrow morning.

R5·5 1. 我**不想**跟弟弟一起下中国象棋。*Wǒ **bù xiǎng** gēn dìdi yìqǐ xià Zhōngguó xiàngqí.*
2. 他们星期六**不能**去体育场踢足球。*Tāmen Xīngqīliù **bù néng** qù tǐyùchǎng tī zúqiú.*
3. 我们经理不会打高尔夫球。*Wǒmen jīnglǐ bú huì dǎ gāo'ěrfūqiú.*
4. 她妹妹明天不想去体育馆滑冰。*Tā mèimei míngtiān bù xiǎng qù tǐyùguǎn huábīng.*
5. 那些军人星期天不能去打篮球。*Nàxiē jūnrén Xīngqītiān bù néng qù dǎ lánqiú.*
6. 我们明天**不会**跟那些律师一起打网球。*Wǒmen míngtiān **bú huì** gēn nàxiē lǜshī yìqǐ dǎ wǎngqiú.*
7. 那些职员下午不会去体育馆打排球。*Nàxiē zhíyuán xiàwǔ bú huì qù tǐyùguǎn dǎ páiqiú.*
8. 下个月这些学生**还不会**毕业。*Xià ge yuè zhèxiē xuésheng **hái bú huì** bìyè.*
9. 学生们**还不会**去中国旅游。*Xuéshengmen **hái bú huì** qù Zhōngguó lǚyóu.*
10. 现在姑娘们还不会下班。*Xiànzài gūniangmen hái bú huì xiàbān.*
11. 那个警察**还不会**结婚。*Nà ge jǐngchá xiànzài **hái bú huì** jiéhūn.*
12. 我爸爸今年夏天不打算买新房子。*Wǒ bàba jīnnián xiàtiān bù dǎsuàn mǎi xīn fángzi.*

R5·6
1. 黄教授不让他的学生在教室里打扑克。*Huáng jiàoshòu bú ràng tā de xúsheng zài jiàoshì lǐ dǎ pūkè.*
2. 我可以叫他明年跟你一起去中国。*Wǒ kěyǐ jiào tā míngnián gēn nǐ yìqǐ qù Zhōngguó.*
3. 我姐姐明天要给我一张舞会票。*Wǒ jiějie míngtiān yào gěi wǒ yì zhāng wǔhuì piào.*
4. 你能不能告诉我那个歌剧的名字？*Nǐ néng bu néng gàosu wǒ nà ge gējù de míngzi?*
5. 那个女演员最近常到博物馆来吗？*Nà ge nǚ yǎnyuán zuìjìn cháng dào bówùguǎn lái ma?*
6. 这个老护士今天晚上会从她那儿去医院。*Zhè ge lǎo hùshi jīntiān wǎnshang huì cóng tā nàr qù yīyuàn.*
7. 工人们今天不会在食堂吃午饭。*Gōngrénmen jīntiān bú huì zài shítáng chī wǔfàn.*
8. 你妈妈要你在新公司认真地工作。*Nǐ māma yào nǐ zài xīn gōngsī rènzhēn de gōngzuò.*
9. 你们周末想到我这儿来打麻将吗？*Nǐmen zhōumò xiǎng dào wǒ zhèr lái dǎ májiàng ma?*
10. 你星期六可以跟她一起坐公共汽车去商场。*Nǐ Xīngqīliù kěyǐ gēn tā yìqǐ zuò gōnggòng qìchē qù shāngchǎng.*
11. 这个农民星期天就要坐飞机去法国旅游了。*Zhè ge nóngmín Xīngqītiān jiù yào zuò fēijī qù Fǎguó lǚyóu le.*
12. 你哥哥快要结婚了吗？—不，他还不会结婚。*Nǐ gēge kuài yào jiéhūn le ma?—Bù, tā hái bú huì jiéhūn.*
13. 我们经理不会下中国象棋。*Wǒmen jīnglǐ bú huì xià Zhōngguó xiàngqí.*
14. 你们要不要跟我们一起踢足球？—不，我们不想跟你们一起踢足球。*Nǐmen yào bu yào gēn wǒmen yìqǐ tī zúqiú?—Bù, Wǒmen bù xiǎng gēn nǐmen yìqǐ tī zúqiú.*
15. 妈妈，我今天下午可以去打网球吗？—不，你不能去打网球。*Māma, wǒ jīntiān xiàwǔ kěyǐ qù dǎ wǎngqiú ma?—Bù, nǐ bù néng qù dǎ wǎngqiú.*
16. 今年冬天白教授计划教学生们滑雪。*Jīnnián dōngtiān Bái jiàoshòu jìhuà jiāo xuéshengmen huáxuě.*

R5·7
1. T   2. F   3. F   4. F   5. T   6. T   7. F   8. T   9. F   10. F   11. T   12. F   13. F
14. T   15. F

VI

26·1
1. 我哥哥去电器店买吸尘器了。*Wǒ gēge qù diànqì diàn mǎi xīchénqì le.*
2. 姑娘们去逛商场了。*Gūniangmen qù guàng shāngchǎng le.*
3. 这些意大利皮鞋都减价了。*Zhèxiē Yìdàlì píxié dōu jiǎnjià le.*
4. 那些女顾客都付钱了。*Nàxiē nǚ gùkè dōu fù qián le.*
5. 他朋友去家具店买桌子和椅子了。*Tā péngyou qù jiājù diàn mǎi zhuōzi hé yǐzi le.*
6. 他们没(有)去体育用品店买篮球。*Tāmen méi(yǒu) qù tǐyù yòngpǐn diàn mǎi lánqiú.*
7. 那个律师没(有)去文具店买纸和铅笔。*Nà ge lǜshī méi(yǒu) qù wénjù diàn mǎi zhǐ hé qiānbǐ.*
8. 爸爸没(有)去水果店买香蕉和苹果。*Bàba méi(yǒu) qù shuǐguǒ diàn mǎi xiāngjiāo hé píngguǒ.*
9. 黄先生没(有)跟太太一起去逛商店。*Huáng Xiānsheng méi(yǒu) gēn tàitai yìqǐ qù guàng shāngdiàn.*
10. 白老师没(有)去书店买英文杂志。*Bái lǎoshī méi(yǒu) qù shūdiàn mǎi Yīngwén zázhì.*

26·2
1. 她昨天买电器了吗？*Tā zuótiān mǎi diànqì le ma?*
   她昨天没(有)买电器。*Tā zuótiān méi(yǒu) mǎi diànqì.*
2. 他们上个周末去逛商场了吗？*Tāmen shàng ge zhōumò qù guàng shāngchǎng le ma?*
   他们上个周末没(有)去逛商场。*Tāmen shàng ge zhōumò méi(yǒu) qù guàng shāngchǎng.*
3. 日本空调机减价了吗？*Rìběn kōngtiáojī jiǎn jià le ma?*
   日本空调机没(有)减价。*Rìběn kōngtiáojī méi(yǒu) jiǎn jià.*
4. 那个俄国顾客付钱了吗？*Nà ge Éguó gùkè fù qián le ma?*
   那个俄国顾客没(有)付钱。*Nà ge Éguó gùkè méi(yǒu) fù qián.*
5. 那个作家上午买杂志了吗？*Nà ge zuòjiā shàngwǔ mǎi zázhì le ma?*
   那个作家上午没(有)买杂志。*Nà ge zuòjiā shàngwǔ méi(yǒu) mǎi zázhì.*
6. 今天他去体育用品店买篮球了吗？*Jīntiān tā qù tǐyù yòngpǐn diàn mǎi lánqiú le ma?*
   今天他没(有)去体育用品店买篮球。*Jīntiān tā méi(yǒu) qù tǐyù yòngpǐn diàn mǎi lánqiú.*
7. 小白今天逛商店了吗？*Xiǎo Bái jīntiān guàng shāngdiàn le ma?*
   小白今天没(有)逛商店。*Xiǎo Bái jīntiān méi(yǒu) guàng shāngdiàn.*
8. 上个星期电器减价了吗？*Shàng ge xīngqī diànqì jiǎn jià le ma?*
   上个星期电器没(有)减价。*Shàng ge xīngqī diànqì méi(yǒu) jiǎn jià.*
9. 今天下午他弟弟去文具店了吗？*Jīntiān xiàwǔ tā dìdi qù wénjù diàn le ma?*
   今天下午他弟弟没(有)去文具店。*Jīntiān xiàwǔ tā dìdi méi(yǒu) qù wénjù diàn.*

26·3 The following are sample answers.

1. 上个周末我去超市买东西了。*Shàng ge zhōumò wǒ qù chāoshì mǎi dōngxi le.*
   我买牛奶了。*Wǒ mǎi niúnǎi le.*
2. 上个周末我没有去衣服店买衣服。*Shàng ge zhōumò wǒ méiyǒu qù yīfu diàn mǎi yīfu.*
3. 上个周末我去电器店买电器了。*Shàng ge zhōumò wǒ qù diànqì diàn mǎi diànqì le.*
   我没有买吸尘器。*Wǒ méiyǒu mǎi xīchénqì.*
4. 上个周末我没有去家具店买家具。*Shàng ge zhōumò wǒ méiyǒu qù jiājù diàn mǎi jiājù.*
5. 我昨天去体育用品店买东西了。*Wǒ zuótiān qù tǐyù yòngpǐn diàn mǎi dōngxi le.*
   我没买足球。*Wǒ méi mǎi zúqiú.*
6. 我昨天去文具店买文具了。*Wǒ zuótiān qù wénjù diàn mǎi wénjù le.*
   我买纸和铅笔了。*Wǒ mǎi zhǐ hé qiānbǐ le.*
7. 我昨天没有去书店买书。*Wǒ zuótiān méiyǒu qù shūdiàn mǎi shū.*
8. 我昨天去水果店买水果了。*Wǒ zuótiān qù shuǐguǒ diàn mǎi shuǐguǒ le.*
   我买苹果了。*Wǒ mǎi píngguǒ le.*

26·4
1. 妈妈昨天买水果了没有？*Māma zuótiān mǎi shuǐguǒ le méiyǒu?*
2. 那个男顾客没有付钱。*Nà ge nán gùkè méiyǒu fù qián.*
3. 这个作家下午去文具店买纸和铅笔了。*Zhè ge zuòjiā xiàwǔ qù wénjù diàn mǎi zhǐ hé qiānbǐ le.*
4. 今天上午他有没有去那个电器店买电脑？*Jīntiān shàngwǔ tā yǒuméiyǒu qù nà ge diànqì diàn mǎi diànnǎo?*
5. 上个周末你买没买中文杂志？*Shàng ge zhōumò nǐ mǎi mei mǎi Zhōngwén zázhì?*
6. 女学生昨天晚上都去逛商场了。*Nǚ xuésheng zuótiān wǎnshang dōu qù guàng shāngchǎng le.*
7. 那些运动员有没有在体育用品店买篮球？*Nàxiē yùndòngyuán yǒu méiyǒu zài tǐyù yòngpǐn diàn mǎi lánqiú?*
8. 上个星期天他们去商场买东西了吗？*Shàng ge Xīngqītiān tāmen qù shāngchǎng mǎi dōngxi le ma?*

27·1
1. 我姐姐上午洗了那些脏衣服。*Wǒ jiějie shàngwǔ xǐ le nàxiē zāng yīfu.* My older sister (has) washed those dirty clothes this morning.
2. 妈妈给我做了一条黑裤子。*Māma gěi wǒ zuò le yì tiáo hēi kùzi.* Mom (has) made a pair of black pants for me.
3. 她星期六戴了姐姐的红帽子。*Tā Xīngqīliù dài le jiějie de hóng màozi.* She wore her older sister's red hat on Saturday.
4. 他朋友今天看了两本中文杂志。*Tā péngyou jīntiān kàn le liǎng běn Zhōngwén zázhì.* His friend (has) read two Chinese magazines today.
5. 白教授给我们介绍了一些朋友。*Bái jiàoshòu gěi wǒmen jièshào le yìxiē péngyou.* Professor Bai (has) introduced some friends to us.
6. 这个学生买了几枝铅笔。*Zhè ge xuésheng mǎi le jǐ zhī qiānbǐ.* This student (has) bought a few pencils.
7. 我参加了她的生日晚会。*Wǒ cānjiā le tā de shēngrì wǎnhuì.* I went to her birthday party.
8. 这个周末我弟弟借了很多英文书。*Zhè ge zhōumò wǒ dìdi jiè le hěn duō Yīngwén shū.* This weekend my younger brother (has) borrowed a lot of English books.

27·2
1. 他们晚上没有看美国电影。*Tāmen wǎnshang méiyǒu kàn Měiguó diànyǐng.*
2. 爸爸刚才没有喝热茶。*Bàba gāngcái méiyǒu hē rè chá.*
3. 这个月他没有学很多英文生词。*Zhè ge yuè tā méiyǒu xué hěn duō Yīngwén shēngcí.*
4. 我没有在晚会上唱中国歌。*Wǒ méiyǒu zài wǎnhuì shang chàng Zhōngguó gē.*
5. 白教授上午没有上语法课。*Bái jiàoshòu shàngwǔ méiyǒu shàng yǔfǎ kè.*
6. 妹妹没有在医院外面租房子。*Mèimei méiyǒu zài yīyuàn wàimian zū fángzi.*
7. 他弟弟今天没有穿白衬衫。*Tā dìdi jīntiān méiyǒu chuān bái chènshān.*
8. 我们没有认识法国朋友。*Wǒmen méiyǒu rènshi Fǎguó péngyou.*

27·3
1. 我没有看你家的新家具。*Wǒ méiyǒu kàn nǐ jiā de xīn jiājù.*
2. 这个运动员没有吃那些馒头。*Zhè ge yùndòngyuán méiyǒu chī nàxiē mántou.*
3. 他今天没有逛这个商场。*Tā jīntiān méiyǒu guàng zhè ge shāngchǎng.*
4. 刚才服务员没有擦桌子。*Gāngcái fúwùyuán méiyǒu cā zhuōzi.*
5. 白老师没有去那个小商店。*Bái lǎoshī méiyǒu qù nà ge xiǎo shāngdiàn.*
6. 她喝了那杯咖啡。*Tā hē le nà bēi kāfēi.*
7. 我找了他们经理。*Wǒ zhǎo le tāmen jīnglǐ.*
8. 刚才她回答了老师的问题。*Gāngcái tā huídá le lǎoshī de wèntí.*
9. 我哥哥上午收拾了他的屋子。*Wǒ gēge shàngwǔ shōushi le tā de wūzi.*
10. 我租了那栋大房子。*Wǒ zū le nà dòng dà fángzi.*

27·4
1. 白小姐已经买了那双皮鞋了没有？*Bái xiǎojie yǐjīng mǎi le nà shuāng píxié le méiyǒu?*
2. 那个律师在图书馆借了三本英文杂志。*Nà ge lǜshī zài túshūguǎn jiè le sān běn Yīngwén zázhì.*
3. 他今天喝了几杯咖啡？*Tā jīntiān hē le jǐ bēi kāfēi?*
4. 上个周末他看没看那些新电器？*Shàng ge zhōumò tā kàn mei kàn nàxiē xīn diànqì?*
5. 现在我已经租了那栋小房子了。*Xiànzài wǒ yǐjīng zū le nà dòng xiǎo fángzi le.*
6. 刚才那些服务员都没有逛商场。*Gāngcái nàxiē fúwùyuán dōu méiyǒu guàng shāngchǎng.*
7. 妈妈给我们做了几件冬天的衣服。*Māma gěi wǒmen zuò le jǐ jiàn dōngtiān de yīfu.*
8. 昨天晚上他们看了一场中国电影。*Zuótiān wǎnshang tāmen kàn le yì chǎng Zhōngguó diànyǐng.*

28·1
1. 现在天气还没有冷呢。*Xiànzài tiānqì hái méiyǒu lěng ne.*
2. 现在天气没有凉快呢。*Xiànzài tiānqì hái méiyǒu liángkuai ne.*
3. 现在天气还没有暖和呢。*Xiànzài tiānqì hái méiyǒu nuǎnhuo ne.*
4. 现在巴黎还没有下雨呢。*Xiànzài Bālí hái méiyǒu xiàyǔ ne.*
5. 现在伦敦还没有下雾呢。*Xiànzài Lúndūn hái méiyǒu xiàwù ne.*
6. 现在纽约还没有下雪呢。*Xiànzài Niǔyuē hái méiyǒu xiàxuě ne.*
7. 现在洛杉矶还没有太阳呢。*Xiànzài Luòshānjī hái méiyǒu tàiyáng ne.*
8. 现在北京还没有刮风呢。*Xiànzài Běijīng hái méiyǒu guāfēng ne.*

28·2
1. Now it's not cold anymore.
2. Now it's not hot anymore.
3. Now it's not windy anymore.
4. Now it's not snowing anymore.
5. Now it's not raining anymore.
6. Now it's not foggy anymore.
7. My friend does not like the hot weather anymore (now).
8. His father does not like the cold weather anymore (now).

28·3
1. 今天晚上北京不会下雪。*Jīntiān wǎnshang Běijīng bú huì xiàxuě.* It won't snow in Beijing tonight.
2. 明天上午伦敦不可能下雾。*Míngtiān shàngwǔ Lúndūn bù kěnéng xiàwù.* It probably won't be foggy in London tomorrow morning.
3. 今天下午洛杉矶不会下雨。*Jīntiān xiàwǔ Luòshānjī bú huì xiàyǔ.* It won't rain in Los Angeles this afternoon.
4. 下个星期纽约不可能刮大风。*Xià ge xīngqī Niǔyuē bù kěnéng guā dà fēng.* It probably won't be very windy in New York next week.
5. 天气还没有热呢，他们现在还不用买短裤。*Tiānqì hái méiyǒu rè ne, tāmen xiànzài hái bú yòng mǎi duǎnkù.* It's not (getting) hot yet. They needn't buy any shorts yet.
6. 天气还没有冷呢，你们现在还不用买毛衣。*Tiānqì hái méiyǒu lěng ne, nǐmen xiànzài hái bú yòng mǎi máoyī.* It's not (getting) cold yet. You guys don't have to buy any sweaters now.
7. 天气还没有凉快呢，我们现在还不用穿T-恤衫。*Tiānqì hái méiyǒu liángkuai ne, wǒmen xiànzài hái bú yòng chuān T-xùshān.* It's not (getting) nice and cool yet. We needn't wear any T-shirts now.
8. 现在天阴了，工人们还不应该休息。*Xiànzài tiān yīn le, gōngrénmen hái bù yīnggāi xiūxi.* Now it's cloudy. The workers shouldn't rest yet.
9. 现在天晴了，职员们还不用去公司上班。*Xiànzài tiān qíng le, zhíyuánmen hái bú yòng qù gōngsī shàngbān.* Now it's clearing up. The clerks needn't go to the company to work yet.
10. 现在雨停了，那些运动员还不用去体育场运动。*Xiànzài yǔ tíng le, nàxiē yùndòngyuán hái bú yòng qù tǐyùchǎng yùndòng.* Now the rain has stopped. The athletes don't have to go to the stadium to exercise yet.

28·4
1. 现在天气凉快了吗？—天气还没有凉快呢。*Xiànzài tiānqì liángkuai le ma? Tiān hái méiyǒu liángkuai ne.*
2. 他妈妈现在喜欢热天气了。*Tā māma xiànzài xǐhuan rè tiānqì le.*
3. 天气现在暖和了，姑娘们不用穿毛衣了。*Tiānqì xiànzài nuǎnhuo le, gūniangmen bú yòng chuān máoyī le.*
4. 现在天气不冷了，不会下雪了。*Xiànzài tiānqì bù lěng le, bú huì xiàxuě le.*
5. 下个星期学生们应该买温度计了。*Xià ge xīngqī xuéshengmen yīnggāi mǎi wēndùjì le.*
6. 今天下午洛杉矶可能下雪吗？—不可能下雪。*Jīntiān xiàwǔ Luòshānjī kěnéng xiàxuě ma?—Bù kěnéng xiàxuě.*
7. 明天上午，伦敦会下雾，巴黎会下雨。*Míngtiān shàngwǔ, Lúndūn huì xiàwù, Bālí huì xiàyǔ.*
8. 后天纽约会不会是阴天？*Hòutiān Niǔyuē huì bu huì shì yīntiān?*
9. 天气冷了，他们现在得穿大衣了吗？--现在他们还不用穿大衣。*Tiānqì lěng le, tāmen xiànzài děi chuān dàyī le ma?— Xiànzài tāmen hái bú yòng chuān dàyī.*
10. 天气暖和了，我们现在要买短裤了吗？--现在你们还不用买短裤。*Tiānqì nuǎnhuo le, wǒmen xiànzài yào mǎi duǎnkù le ma?— Xiànzài nǐmen hái bú yòng mǎi duǎnkù.*

29·1 1. 你比我小。*Nǐ bǐ wǒ xiǎo.*
2. 奶奶比爷爷瘦。*Nǎinai bǐ yéye shòu.*
3. 妈妈比爸爸慢。*Māma bǐ bàba màn.*
4. 我的扑克比她的旧。*Wǒ de pūkè bǐ tā de jiù.*
5. 小黄的腿比小白的短。*Xiǎo Huáng de tuǐ bǐ Xiǎo Bái de duǎn.*
6. 我的朋友比你的少。*Wǒ de péngyou bǐ nǐ de shǎo.*
7. 洛杉矶的房子比北京的便宜。*Luòshānjī de fángzi bǐ Běijīng de piányi.*
8. 纽约的春天比上海的冷。*Niǔyuē de chūntiān bǐ Shànghǎi de lěng.*

29·2 1. 对 *duì* 2. 错 *cuò* 3. 错 *cuò* 4. 对 *duì* 5. 对 *duì* 6. 错 *cuò* 7. 对 *duì* 8. 错 *cuò*
9. 对 *duì* 10. 错 *cuò*

29·3 1. 一点儿 *yìdiǎnr* 2. 得多/多了/很多 *de duō/duō le/hěn duō* 3. 三公分 *sān gōngfēn* 4. 一英寸
yì yīngcùn 5. 十公里 *shí gōnglǐ* 6. 一英尺 *yì yīngchǐ* 7. 一百五十英里 *yì bǎi wǔshí yīnglǐ*
8. 得多/多了/很多 *de duō/duō le/hěn duō*

29·4 The following are sample answers.

1. 我比我的好朋友大一岁。
Wǒ bǐ wǒ de hǎo péngyou dà yí suì.
2. 我比我的好朋友高三公分。
Wǒ bǐ wǒ de hǎo péngyou gāo sān gōngfēn.
3. 我比我的好朋友胖一公斤。
Wǒ bǐ wǒ de hǎo péngyou pàng yì gōngjīn.
4. 我的腿比我好朋友的长两公分。
Wǒ de tuǐ bǐ wǒ hǎo péngyou de cháng liǎng gōngfēn.
5. 我的肩膀比我好朋友的宽一公分。
Wǒ de jiānbǎng bǐ wǒ hǎo péngyou de kuān yì gōngfēn.
6. 我的腰比我好朋友的粗一公分。
Wǒ de yāo bǐ wǒ hǎo péngyou de cū yì gōngfēn.
7. 我住的房子比我好朋友住的新得多。
Wǒ zhù de fángzi bǐ wǒ hǎo péngyou zhù de xīn de duō.
8. 我住的房子比我好朋友住的干净很多。
Wǒ zhù de fángzi bǐ wǒ hǎo péngyou zhù de gānjìng hěn duō.

29·5 1. 这件衬衫跟那件一样红。*Zhè jiàn chènshān gēn nà jiàn yíyàng hóng.*
2. 桔子比柚子甜吗? *Júzi bǐ yòuzi tián ma?*
3. 我哥哥比我矮两公分。*Wǒ gēge bǐ wǒ ǎi liǎng gōngfēn.*
4. 咖啡比茶苦一点儿。*Kāfēi bǐ chá kǔ yìdiǎnr.*
5. 剧场没有电影院这么新。*Jùchǎng méiyǒu diànyǐngyuàn zhème xīn.*
6. 饺子比米饭贵得多吗? *Jiǎozi bǐ mǐfàn guì de duō ma?*
7. 他爷爷比他奶奶瘦多了。*Tā yéye bǐ tā nǎinai shòu duō le.*
8. 这条路比那条路长50英里。*Zhè tiáo lù bǐ nà tiáo lù cháng 50 yīnglǐ.*

30·1 1. 学生们在参观北京博物馆(呢)。*Xuéshēngmen zài cānguān Běijīng Bówùguǎn (ne).*
2. 那个作家在访问白教授(呢)。*Nà ge zuòjiā zài fǎngwèn Bái jiàoshòu (ne).*
3. 医院在欢迎新护士(呢)。*Yīyuàn zài huānyíng xīn hùshi (ne).*
4. 他妹妹正在弹钢琴(呢)。*Tā mèimei zhèngzài tán gāngqín (ne).*
5. 黄律师正在跟她谈话(呢)。*Huáng lǜshī zhèngzài gēn tā tánhuà (ne).*
6. 这个工程师正在画画儿(呢)。*Zhè ge gōngchéngshī zhèngzài huàhuàr (ne).*
7. 我哥哥正打工(呢)。*Wǒ gēge zhèng dǎgōng (ne).*
8. 那些职员正修理旧家具(呢)。*Nàxiē zhíyuán zhèng xiūlǐ jiù jiājiù(ne) .*
9. 这些演员正搬家(呢)。*Zhèxiē yǎnyuán zhèng bānjiā (ne).*
10. 我爸爸种树呢。*Wǒ bàba zhòng shù ne.*
11. 那个军人割草呢。*Nà ge jūnrén gē cǎo ne.*
12. 工人们刷房子呢。*Gōngrénmen shuā fángzi ne.*

30·2 1. 农民们没在/没(有)砍树。*Nóngmínmen méi zài /méi(yǒu) kǎn shù.*
2. 她们的经理没在/没(有)割草。*Tāmen de jīnglǐ méi zài /méi(yǒu)gē cǎo.*
3. 护士们没在/没(有)刷房子。*Hùshimen méi zài /méi(yǒu) shuā fángzi.*
4. 这个商人没在/没(有)搬家。*Zhè ge shāngrén méi zài /méi(yǒu) bānjiā.*
5. 我姐姐没在/没(有)弹钢琴。*Wǒ jiějie méi zài /méi(yǒu) tán gāngqín.*
6. 这些学生没在/没(有)参观访问工厂。*Zhèxiē xuésheng méi zài /méi(yǒu) cānguān fǎngwèn gōngchǎng.*
7. 他朋友没在/没(有)修理旧椅子。*Tā péngyou méi zài /méi(yǒu) xiūlǐ jiù yǐzi.*

8. 我弟弟没在/没(有)打工。*Wǒ dìdi méi zài /méi(yǒu) dǎgōng.*
9. 他们没在/没(有)欢迎那些警察。*Tāmen méi zài /méi(yǒu) huānyíng nàxiē jǐngchá.*
10. 这个音乐家没在/没(有)画画儿。*Zhè ge yīnyuèjiā méi zài /méi(yǒu) huà huàr.*

30·3
1. 运动员们在参观体育馆吗？*Yùndòngyuánmen zài cānguān tǐyùguǎn ma?*
   运动员们没在/没(有)参观体育馆。*Yùndòngyuánmen méi zài /méi(yǒu) cānguān tǐyùguǎn.*
2. 经理们正在访问白教授吗？*Jīnglǐmen zhèngzài fǎngwèn Bái jiàoshòu ma?*
   经理们没在/没(有)访问白教授。*Jīnglǐmen méi zài /méi(yǒu) fǎngwèn Bái jiàoshòu.*
3. 那个女演员正在弹钢琴吗？*Nà ge nǚ yǎnyuán zhèngzài tán gāngqín ma?*
   那个女演员没在/没(有)弹钢琴。*Nà ge nǚ yǎnyuán méi zài /méi(yǒu) tán gāngqín.*
4. 他在跟那些工程师谈话吗？*Tā zài gēn nàxiē gōngchéngshī tánhuà ma?*
   他没在/没(有)跟那些工程师谈话。*Tā méi zài /méi(yǒu) gēn nàxiē gōngchéngshī tánhuà.*
5. 爸爸在修理旧桌子吗？*Bàba zài xiūlǐ jiù zhuōzi ma?*
   爸爸没在/没(有)修理旧桌子。*Bàba méi zài /méi(yǒu) xiūlǐ jiù zhuōzi.*
6. 那个作家正在画画儿吗？*Nà ge zuòjiā zhèngzài huà huàr ma?*
   那个作家没在/没(有)画画儿。*Nà ge zuòjiā méi zài /méi(yǒu) huà huàr.*
7. 这些服务员在搬家吗？*Zhèxiē fúwùyuán zài bānjiā ma?*
   这些服务员没在/没(有)搬家。*Zhèxiē fúwùyuán méi zài /méi(yǒu) bānjiā.*
8. 他弟弟在打工吗？*Tā dìdi zài dǎgōng ma?*
   他弟弟没在/没(有)打工。*Tā dìdi méi zài /méi(yǒu) dǎgōng.*
9. 我正在刷房子吗？*Wǒ zhèngzài shuā fángzi ma?*
   我没在/没(有)刷房子。*Wǒ méi zài /méi(yǒu) shuā fángzi.*
10. 那些护士在休息吗？*Nàxiē hùshi zài xiūxi ma?*
    那些护士没在/没(有)休息。*Nàxiē hùshi méi zài /méi(yǒu) xiūxi.*

30·4
1. 工人们在刷房子。*Gōngrénmen zài shuā fángzi.*
2. 那些军人种树呢。*Nàxiē jūnrén zhòng shù ne.*
3. 这个工程师正搬家吗？*Zhè ge gōngchéngshī zhèng bānjiā ma?*
4. 我们正在欢迎新学生呢。*Wǒmen zhèngzài huānyíng xīn xuéshēng ne.*
5. 黄教授现在正在跟她谈话呢。*Huáng jiàoshòu xiànzài zhèngzài gēn tā tánhuà ne.*
6. 你妹妹现在正在打工吗？*Nǐ mèimei xiànzài zhèngzài dǎgōng ma?*
7. 这些作家正画画儿呢。*Zhèxiē zuòjiā zhèng huà huàr ne.*
8. 那个律师在访问白教授吗？*Nà ge lǜshī zài fǎngwèn Bái jiàoshòu ma?*

R6·1
1. 妈妈昨天没(有)去商店买东西。*Māma zuótiān méi(yǒu) qù shāngdiàn mǎi dōngxi.*
2. 那个顾客刚才没(有)付钱。*Nà ge gùkè gāngcái méi(yǒu) fù qián.*
3. 黄老师昨天下午没(有)买法文杂志。*Huáng lǎoshī zuótiān xiàwǔ méi(yǒu) mǎi Fǎwén zázhì.*
4. 他们今天下午没(有)去逛街。*Tāmen jīntiān xiàwǔ méi(yǒu) qù guàng jiē.*
5. 这个星期那些体育用品都没(有)减价。*Zhè ge xīngqī nàxiē tǐyù yòngpǐn dōu méi(yǒu) jiǎnjià.*
6. 上个星期天白老师没(有)买新电器。*Shàng ge Xīngqītiān Bái lǎoshī méi(yǒu) mǎi xīn diànqì.*
7. 她晚上没(有)去文具店买纸和铅笔。*Tā wǎnshang méi(yǒu) qù wénjùdiàn mǎi zhǐ hé qiānbǐ.*
8. 上个周末那些意大利家具没(有)降价。*Shàng ge zhōumò nàxiē Yìdàlì jiājù méi(yǒu) jiàng jià.*

R6·2
1. 白小姐认识了一些德国律师。*Bái xiǎojie rènshi le yìxiē Déguó lǜshī.*
   白小姐没(有)认识德国律师。*Bái xiǎojie méi(yǒu) rènshi Déguó lǜshī.*
2. 黄教授上午借了五本中文杂志。*Huáng jiàoshòu shàngwǔ jiè le wǔ běn Zhōngwén zázhì.*
   黄教授上午没(有)借中文杂志。*Huáng jiàoshòu shàngwǔ méi(yǒu) jiè Zhōngwén zázhì.*
3. 那个经理喝了四杯法国葡萄酒。*Nà ge jīnglǐ hē le sì bēi Fǎguó pútao jiǔ.*
   那个经理没(有)喝法国葡萄酒。*Nà ge jīnglǐ méi(yǒu) hē Fǎguó pútao jiǔ.*
4. 他今天给我介绍了一个朋友。*Tā jīntiān gěi wǒ jièshào le yí ge péngyou.*
   他今天没(有)给我介绍朋友。*Tā jīntiān méi(yǒu) gěi wǒ jièshào péngyou.*
5. 他们中午去看了一场美国电影。*Tāmen zhōngwǔ qù kàn le yì chǎng Měiguó diànyǐng.*
   他们中午没(有)去看美国电影。*Tāmen zhōngwǔ méi(yǒu) qù kàn Měiguó diànyǐng.*
6. 那个音乐家唱了几首中国歌。*Nà ge yīnyuèjiā chàng le jǐ shǒu Zhōngguó gē.*
   那个音乐家没(有)唱中国歌。*Nà ge yīnyuèjiā méi(yǒu) chàng Zhōngguó gē.*
7. 这个星期服务员们扫了十间屋子。*Zhè ge xīngqī fúwùyuánmen sǎo le shí jiān wūzi.*
   这个星期服务员们没(有)扫屋子。*Zhè ge xīngqī fúwùyuánmen méi(yǒu) sǎo wūzi.*
8. 他弟弟下午上了三节汉语课。*Tā dìdi xiàwǔ shàng le sān jié Hànyǔ kè.*
   他弟弟下午没(有)上汉语课。*Tā dìdi xiàwǔ méi(yǒu) shàng Hànyǔ kè.*
9. 这个老农民早上吃了两碗米粉。*Zhè ge lǎo nóngmín zǎoshang chī le liǎng wǎn mǐfěn.*
   这个老农民早上没(有)吃米粉。*Zhè ge lǎo nóngmín zǎoshang méi(yǒu) chī mǐfěn.*
10. 那些工人租了一栋房子。*Nàxiē gōngrén zū le yí dòng fángzi.*
    那些工人没(有)租房子。*Nàxiē gōngrén méi(yǒu) zū fángzi.*

R6·3
1. 这个星期天气(还)没有凉快(呢)。 *Zhè ge xīngqī tiānqì (hái) méiyǒu liángkuai (ne).*
2. 她妈妈(还)没有喜欢热天气(呢)。 *Tā māma (hái) méiyǒu xǐhuan rè tiānqì (ne).*
3. 现在纽约(还)没有下雪(呢)。 *Xiànzài Niǔyuē (hái) méiyǒu xià xuě (ne).*
4. 现在伦敦(还)没有下雾(呢)。 *Xiànzài Lúndūn (hái) méiyǒu xià wù (ne).*
5. 明天不会是晴天。 *Míngtiān bú huì shì qíngtiān.*
6. 下个星期一巴黎不可能刮大风。 *Xià ge Xīngqīyī Bālí bù kěnéng guā dà fēng.*
7. 学生们下个月不用买温度计。 *Xuéshengmen xià ge yuè bú yòng mǎi wēndùjì.*
8. 那些工人(还)不应该去上班。 *Nàxiē gōngrén (hái) bù yīnggāi qù shàngbān.*
9. 这些姑娘现在(还)不用去买毛衣。 *Zhèxiē gūniang xiànzài (hái) bú yòng qù mǎi máoyī.*
10. 运动员现在(还)不用去体育场跑步。 *Yùndòngyuán xiànzài (hái) bú yòng qù tǐyùchǎng pǎobù.*

R6·4
1. China's area is a bit larger than the USA's.
2. These doctors are more conscientious than those doctors.
3. My friend is thinner than I am, but I am taller than he is.
4. His younger brother is two centimeters shorter than his older brother.
5. This week Mom is much more tired than Dad.
6. This river is fifteen kilometers longer than that river.
7. Grandma is much fatter than Grandpa.
8. The physics building is as beautiful as the biology building.
9. The clothes that I wear are as new as those that he wears.
10. This room is as wide as that one.
11. The houses in Los Angeles are not as expensive as those in New York City.
12. Apples are not as sweet as bananas.
13. The autumn is not as hot as the summer.
14. My older sister is not taller than my younger sister.

R6·5
1. 黄经理在刷房子吗? *Huáng jīnglǐ zài shuā fángzi ma?*
   黄经理没在刷房子。 *Huáng jīnglǐ méi zài shuā fángzi.*
2. 农民们正种草吗? *Nóngmínmen zhèng zhòng cǎo ma?*
   农民们没在种草。 *Nóngmínmen méi zài zhòng cǎo.*
3. 他爷爷正在种树吗? *Tā yéye zhèngzài zhòng shù ma?*
   他爷爷没在种树。 *Tā yéye méi zài zhòng shù.*
4. 他朋友在搬家吗? *Tā péngyou zài bān jiā ma?* (Note: the word "在 *zài*" should be added here.)
   他朋友没在搬家。 *Tā péngyou méi zài bān jiā.*
5. 这些工人在修理汽车吗? *Zhèxiē gōngren zài xiūlǐ qìchē ma?*
   这些工人没在修理汽车。 *Zhèxiē gōngren méi zài xiūlǐ qìchē.*
6. 他妹妹正打工吗? *Tā mèimei zhèng dǎgōng ma?*
   他妹妹没在打工。 *Tā mèimei méi zài dǎgōng.*
7. 那个作家正在画画儿吗? *Nà ge zuòjiā zhèngzài huàhuàr ma?*
   那个作家没在画画儿。 *Nà ge zuòjiā méi zài huàhuàr.*
8. 律师在跟她谈话吗? *Lǜshī zài gēn tā tánhuà ma?*
   律师没在跟她谈话。 *Lǜshī méi zài gēn tā tánhuà.*
9. 那个演员正弹钢琴吗? *Nà ge yǎnyuán zhèng tán gāngqín ma?*
   那个演员没在弹钢琴。 *Nà ge yǎnyuán mei zài tán gāngqín.*
10. 学生们正在欢迎新老师吗? *Xuéshengmen zhèngzài huānyíng xīn lǎoshī ma?*
    学生们没在欢迎新老师。 *Xuéshengmen méi zài huānyíng xīn lǎoshī.*
11. 这些警察在喝啤酒吗? *Zhèxiē jǐngchá zài hē píjiǔ ma?*
    这些警察没在喝啤酒。 *Zhèxiē jǐngchá méi zài hē píjiǔ.*
12. 工程师们正参观博物馆吗? *Gōngchéngshīmen zhèng cānguān bówùguǎn ma?*
    工程师们没在参观博物馆。 *Gōngchéngshīmen méi zài cānguān bówùguǎn.*

R6·6
1. F 2. T 3. T 4. F 5. T 6. F 7. F 8. T 9. T 10. F 11. T 12. F
13. F 14. F 15. T

Translations of 你知道吗?
Nǐ zhīdao ma?
Do you know?

Part I - L1

Gary Locke is American, not Chinese.
Yao Ming is Chinese, not American.
Joe Tanaka is not Japanese; he is American.

Part I - L2

Barack Obama's mother is American, but his father, paternal grandfather, and grandmother are not American.
Steve Jobs had a younger sister but no older sister, older brother, or younger brother.
George W. Bush has a wife and daughters but no sons.
Julia Roberts has a husband, sons, and a daughter.
Brad Pitt has a younger brother and a younger sister but no older brothers or older sisters.

Part I - L3

Americans like to eat bananas, apples, oranges, grapes, and strawberries. Each year, on average, each American eats 33 pounds of bananas, 18 pounds of apples, 12.3 pounds of oranges, 7.5 pounds of grapes, and 3.4 pounds of strawberries.

Part I - L4

Americans like to eat bread and cheese; they also like to eat sandwiches, pizza, and hamburgers. Each year, on average, each American eats 53 pounds of bread, 31 pounds of cheese, 23 pounds of pizza, 193 sandwiches, and 150 hamburgers.

Part I - L5

Chinese people like to eat. They invented dumplings, steamed buns with fillings, steamed buns without fillings, noodles, rice noodles, and tofu.
Europeans also like to eat. The British invented sandwiches, the Germans invented hamburgers, and the Italians invented pizza.

Part II - L6

Americans like beverages such as coffee, soda, milk, beer, and orange juice. Each year, on average, each American drinks 1,000 cups of coffee, 600 cans of soda, 25 gallons of milk, 20 gallons of beer, and 5 gallons of orange juice.

Part II - L7

In 2011, China had a population of 1.3 billion, India had a population of 1.1 billion, the United States had a population of 310 million, Russia had a population of 140 million, and Japan had a population of 130 million.

Part II - L8

Mark Zuckerberg was born in 1984. How old is he now?

Yao Ming was born in 1980. How old is he now?

How old was she? When Tatum O'Neal, the youngest Oscar winner, won the Oscar for *Paper Moon*, she was only 10.

How old was he? According to legend, when Laozi was born, he was already 81 years old.

Part II - L9

George Washington was born February 22, 1732.

Sun Yat-sen was born November 12, 1866.

William Shakespeare was born April 23, 1564.

Princess Diana was born July 1, 1961.

Mark Twain was born January 30, 1835.

Part II - L10

Mary Quant invented the mini skirt.

Jacob Davis and Levi Strauss invented blue jeans.

Sun Yat-sen invented the Mao suit.

The Chinese invented the Tang-style jacket.

The Chinese also invented the cheongsam.

Part III - L11

Deng Xiaoping was short. Napoleon was also short.

Yaog Ming is tall, but Jeremy Lin is not very tall.

Audrey Hepburn was attractive. James Dean was also attractive.

Thirty years ago, housing in China was inexpensive, but it is expensive now.

Manuel Uribe Garza (who once weighed 1,320 lbs) was not overweight before he was 20, but later he became very heavy.

Part III - L12

Northerners like to eat salty food.

Southerners like to eat sweet food.

People in Sichuan and people in Hunan like to eat spicy food.

People in Shanxi like to eat sour food.

Part III - L13

There are lots of teachers in China. In 2006, China already had 13,018,600 teachers.

In the United States, only 1% of the population are farmers.

There are too many lawyers in the United States. In 2006, there were already 1,116,967 lawyers.

There are lots of students in China. In 1997 there were a total of 217,920,000 students.

The number of nurses in the United States is not very high. In 2010, there were only 2,655,020 nurses.

Part III - L14

There are many good universities in China. The best universities in China are Peking University, Tsinghua University, Nanking University, Fudan University, and Zhejiang University.

Part III - L15

We all know the rainbow is beautiful, but do you know how many colors there are in a rainbow? There are 7 colors. The sequence of the colors is: red, orange, yellow, green, blue, indigo, and purple.

Part IV - L16

In the Gregorian calendar, there are 365 days, 5 hours, 48 minutes, and 46 seconds in a year.
In the Chinese lunar calendar, there are 354 or 355 days in a year.
In the Chinese lunar calendar, there are 29 days in a leap month.
In the Chinese lunar calendar, there are only 28 days in February.

Part IV - L17

Tian'anmen Square is right in front of the Forbidden City.
The Forbidden City is in the city of Beijing, but the Great Wall is outside of the city.
The Louvre is by the Seine.
There is water on Mars.
In the solar system, Earth is between Venus and Mars.

Part IV - L18

The Chinese statesman Deng Xiaoping liked to swim, play bridge, and what not when he took a break.
The Chinese athlete Yao Ming likes to play games on the Internet, listen to music, etc., when he has some free time.
When at home, the Chinese actress Gong Li sometimes likes to cook, read, etc.
The American actor Brad Pitt often likes to exercise or ride a motorcycle.
The American actress Julia Roberts likes to sew or play the piano when she has the time.

Part IV - L19

American children between ages 2 and 17 watch too much TV. Each week they watch 20 hours of TV on average.
Americans do not exercise enough. They exercise an average of two hours per week.
Americans eat too much meat these days. Each year they eat an average of 200 pounds of meat.
American college students do not get enough sleep. They sleep an average of only six hours per night.

Part IV - L20

Mao Zedong was kind of tall, but Deng Xiaoping was kind of short.
Pinocchio is skinny and small, but his nose is kind of long.
The American actress Audrey Hepburn had largish eyes and shortish hair. She was very pretty.

Part V - L21

Perhaps you want to ask me a question. Who invented mahjong? Let me tell you. It was the Chinese who invented mahjong.
Perhaps you wanted to ask me another question. Who invented Go? Let me tell you. It was also the Chinese who invented Go.
Now let me ask you a question. Who gave you life? It was your parents.
Let me ask you another question. Who gave students knowledge? It was their teachers.

Part V - L22

These days, 30% of American young people live with their parents.
From 2009 to 2010, there were a total of 158,000 Chinese students studying at U.S. universities, which constitutes 22% of foreign students in the United States.
From 1999 to 2000, there were only 3,000 American students studying in China, but from 2009 to 2010, there were 14,000 American students studying in China.
In the United States, about 80% of the population lives in cities now.

Part V - L23

In big cities in the United States almost nobody takes a boat to work. There are also not many people who take an airplane to go to work. But lots of people drive or take a bus to work. Some people also ride a bike or a motorcycle or walk to work. From 2005 to 2009, in Los Angeles County, about 72% of people drove to work alone, 10.8% of people carpooled, 7.2% of people took a bus,

2.9% of people walked, 0.9% of people rode a bike, 1.0% of people rode a motorcycle, and 5% of people worked at home.

Part V - L24

Lots of Chinese people know how to play mahjong. It is said that 90% of the Chinese people know it. Some foreigners also know how to play. Do you?

Lots of Chinese people know how to play Chinese chess. It is said that 50% of Chinese people know it. Many Vietnamese people also know the game. It is said that 30% of Vietnamese people know how to play Chinese chess.

Lots of Chinese people know how to play Go, and they also like to play it. Lots of Japanese and Korean people also know how to play Go and play it well.

In China, very few people know how to play ice hockey or tennis, but everyone knows how to play ping-pong. And they are all good at it.

Part V - L25

It is estimated that in 2040 the population of India will be 1.52 billion, surpassing the Chinese population of 1.45 billion at that time.

In 50 years it is possible that all households will have robots.

In the future mankind may land on Mars one day.

Part VI - L26

Many famous British and American poets died young.

The British poet Percy Bysshe Shelley died when he was only 29.

The British poet George Gordon Byron died at 36.

The British poet John Keats died at 25.

The American poet Edgar Allan Poe died at 40.

The American poet Sylvia Plath died at 30.

But they all left behind poems that will last forever.

Part VI - L27

There are four inventions that were made in ancient China.

In the Han dynasty, the Chinese invented the compass.

In the second century, Cai Lun invented the technology for paper making.

In the ninth century, the Chinese invented gunpowder.

In the eleventh century, Bi Sheng invented the technology for movable type printing.

Part VI - L28

Because of global warming, the weather these days is getting hotter and hotter.

Also because of global warming, the iceberg on the North Pole could melt.

In Los Angeles, the winter is warm, but sometimes it may snow.

Part VI - L29

Now the Chinese people live much longer than before. In 2011, the average life expectancy of women was 76.94, and the life expectancy of men was 72.68.

The Yangtze River of China is not as long as the Nile, but the Yangtze River is 25 kilometers longer than the Mississippi River in the United States.

The surface area of Beijing is bigger than that of Shanghai, but the population of Beijing is smaller than that of Shanghai.

Women are as smart as men.

In many countries, there are more men than women. In Mongolia and Somalia, there are about an equal number of men and women; but in China, India, and Saudi Arabia, there are more men than women.

Part VI - L30

The petroleum in the world is decreasing rapidly. It is estimated that in 50–60 years it will be used up.

Because the amount of oil in the world is decreasing so fast, scientists are looking for new fuel, such as flammable ice.

In recent years, the number of Chinese students studying at the United States is increasing rapidly. In 2012, it had already reached 160,000.

In recent years, the number of American students studying in China is also gradually increasing. In 2012, it had reached more than 20,000.